DAVID MCKIE was deputy editor of the *Guardian* from 1975 to 1984, and wrote both its 'Smallweed' and 'Elsewhere' columns. His books include *Jabez* – shortlisted for the Whitbread Biography Award and the Saga Award for wit – *McKie's Gazetteer* and *Bright Particular Stars*.

'A treasury of half-forgotten characters and neglected histories... a laudatory exploration of the vernacular, a gentle reminder that contemporary Britain can be beautiful and not a little bit strange, and for that a copy deserves to be placed in every bus station in the land.' Travis Elborough, *Guardian*

'Excursive, digressive and diverting beyond measure... A joyous book.' Tom Fort, *Sunday Telegraph*

'Digressions and diversions are McKie's speciality, punctuated by enjoyable pedantry... In the most mundane places, on the most mundane journeys, McKie finds gold.' Bob Stanley, *The Times*

'Fascinating... At its heart the book is a paean to the Victorian visionaries who shaped our cities and institutions.' Nigel Richardson, *Daily Telegraph*

'Accessibly erudite, funny with a serious thread, heir to the classic essayists... This book lights up places and their notables.' Edward Pearce, *Glasgow Herald*

'On his way by bus from hither to thither, McKie asks questions that have never occurred to anyone else. Oops – you're so engrossed in reading the answers that you've just missed your stop.' Iain Finlayson, *Saga*

'McKie's style is careful and gentle... He keeps you reading by some effortless, invisible means.' Andrew Martin, *New Statesman*

GREAT BRITISH BUS JOURNEYS

Travels Through Unfamous Places

DAVID MCKIE

Atlantic Books
London

First published in Great Britain in hardback in 2006 by
Atlantic Books, an imprint of Atlantic Books Ltd.

First published in Great Britain in 2007 by Atlantic Books.
This paperback edition published in 2011 by Atlantic Books.

9 8 7 6 5 4 3

A CIP catalogue record for this book is
available from the British Library.

ISBN 978 0 5789 376 5

Text design by Lindsay Nash

Printed in Great Britain by Clays Ltd, St Ives plc

Atlantic Books
An imprint of Atlantic Books Ltd
Ormond House
26–27 Boswell Street
London
WC1N 3JZ

www.atlantic-books.co.uk

CONTENTS

PREFACE

This is a book of excursions, punctuated by digressions and diversions. 'I should say', Alexander Herzen writes at the outset of his first great book of autobiography, *Childhood, Youth and Exile*, 'that I do not in general mean to avoid digressions and disquisitions; every conversation is full of them, and so is life itself.' My feelings entirely. This is the record of twenty-four digressive and divertive journeys around Britain, mainly in the summer of 2004, travelled in every case but one – the day when my postbus failed to appear in the tiny remote village of Altnaharra in northern Scotland – by service bus: itself a digressive creature, especially out of town, rarely travelling straight from A to B if it sees the chance of diverting into some minor village down some narrow, bumpy lane where overhanging trees beat on the bus roof. Not even cities are immune from this kind of behaviour. There used to be a London bus, number 45, which ran from King's Cross to South Kensington by way of Brixton: enthusiasts from the North who had come to visit the Victoria and Albert Museum found after leaping aboard that they got a more comprehensive view of the capital than they expected.

Such digressions, infuriating when you are in a hurry, can be a delight if you are not. They mean that you come across places – gracious Kilconquhar or eerie eccentric Cellardyke in Fife, or Raithby in Lincolnshire – that you would never have dreamed of seeking out, and which rarely, if ever, get written about. The bus from Clitheroe through the forest of Bowland to Slaidburn – one of the two or three most enjoyable trips I made – takes forty-three minutes. The last bus back from Slaidburn to Clitheroe does it direct in twenty-three, but that deprives you of miles of blissful country through Whitewell and Dunsop Bridge. I chose my routes not for their beauty, though some were beautiful, nor for their squalor or ugliness, though some of the places to which my buses took me *were* squalid and ugly. Their attraction in every case was what I might come across on the way, in terms of histories, oddities, and the kind of accidental commentary on life that comes from casual, largely improvised, travel. This was the method adopted by Gerald of Wales, historian and man of letters, whom we shall meet in Pembrokeshire, when, in the late twelfth century, he was required to travel through Wales in the company of a saintly but infuriating English archbishop. The purpose of their journey frequently fades from view as Gerald contemplates all the opportunities the journey offers for digressions and diversions. In that, I am Gerald's disciple.

This is not a state-of-the-nation book; it does not attempt to assess the mood or condition of Britain, though it did suggest some conclusions about that mood and condition. The most successful communities I came across on these journeys seemed to be those that balanced continuity and change. Those that do not change, atrophy; but those that abandon or crush their past seem uneasy, unsettled places. Nor did I set out to write an in-the-footsteps-of type of book, replicating earlier journeys by William Cobbett or George Borrow or George Orwell or J. B. Priestley. As far as I could, I shunned famous places already liberally written about. Cambridge, here, is simply a place to change at on the way from barely fashionable Huntingdon to wholly unfashionable Royston. Because I kept getting off buses to prowl around towns and villages, and especially to seek out their histories in local libraries, some of my journeys took me two days to complete. One, through the territories of the hated first Duke of Sutherland, whose statue continues to gaze out across Dornoch Firth (despite campaigns to remove him), needed three. Inevitably my accounts of these towns and villages are mere postcards; there is bound to be much that I missed on such fleeting acquaintance. I wish that it were otherwise, but I fear it is the nature of such excursions: visitors arrive, wander about for no more than an hour or two, and then have to move on, often missing what local people most savour.

Not all of my journeys were made in the order they are reported. Some of my original plans came unstuck, which is why my visit to Eden Camp and Langdale End was made in October – several weeks after the ride through the Forest of Bowland, on an equally beautiful day in September, which appears in this book several chapters after it. Some people shun service buses: they don't like having strangers jammed up against them. The normally gregarious Conservative politician Steven Norris once declared his distaste for using the bus because of the kind of people he found himself sitting next to. For others, the common service bus is a kind of ambulance of failures. That champion of the great car economy, Margaret Thatcher, is often quoted as saying that any man over twenty-six travelling by bus must have lost out in life. (I have spent many hours trying to establish when and where she said it, but without success.) One can't help feeling, though, that it might have done Margaret Thatcher good to travel just now and then, in heavy disguise of course, on a humble service bus alongside the people over whom she presided. Had she so demeaned herself at the height of her power, to catch the bus from Grantham to Sleaford, for instance, she might have heard conversations cautioning her against the fatal poll tax or her apparent assumption that people work best when they feel insecure.

It can't be said that every journey I took was a feast of such wise and illuminating discussion. That wasn't even the case when

Hazlitt decreed that the talk on a coach from London to Oxford was richer and more rewarding than that at Oxford's high tables. But for all the inconvenience and frustration that bus travel so often involves, all the anxious waits at lonely stops for buses that come late and sometimes don't turn up at all, all the occasions when you're left kicking your heels in some dreary bus station for an hour because your onward service has been scheduled to leave three minutes before you arrive – in spite of all that, you will certainly hear and learn a lot more on the buses of Britain about the country you live in than you ever could if you travelled only by speedy train or convenient car.

My thanks are due to Alan Rusbridger, editor of the *Guardian*, who has allowed me to draw on material first published in my Elsewhere column in the newspaper – though in every case I went back to the places involved before writing this book. Also to my friends at Atlantic Books, especially Toby Mundy, who first suggested this adventure, and Clara Farmer and Alice Hunt, twin essences of diligence, patience and kindness as my account of these wanderings took shape. I did several more journeys besides the ones recorded here – in London, Essex, Wiltshire, mid-Wales, Shropshire, across the Humber Bridge and in Cumbria – which have not got into the book, sometimes because the journeys didn't work out as I'd expected, but mainly because, had they all been put in, the weight of the book you now have in your hand might have broken your wrist. Alice in particular was full of creative solutions for cutting it down to size. Jane Robertson handled the final text with keen-eyed speed and efficiency. My wife Beryl provided much perceptive advice and has furnished the index. Other benefactors have included Glyn Jones, who lent me the history of the Crosville bus operation, which provides the theme for that chapter; John

Graham, 'Araucaria' of the *Guardian*, one of whose incomparable crosswords introduced me to the Agapemone sect that features in my Somerset journey; David Harvey, who first acquainted me with the hagiographer Nicholas Roscarrock; Robert Waller, whose mention of the snubbing of Sir Giles Gilbert Scott at Ollerton led me to his book, much quoted in that chapter; Audrey Gillan, who incited me to travel on a night bus in Glasgow; the *Guardian* reader, whose name I'm afraid I no longer have, who put me on to the story of the US film director, Charles Weston, who might with better luck have established a British Hollywood in the bootmaking village of Irthlingborough, Northants; Bryan McAllister, who came up with a wealth of information about buses, some of it culled from sources of pleasing obscurity; and my agents at Curtis Brown, Michael Shaw and then Jonathan Pegg. The hospitality of Mary and Pat Renshaw in Sheffield, Pat and Tim Cook in Cumbria, Geraldine and Julian Marshall and Jean Walker in Wales, Anne and Malachi Fearon in Liverpool, and Monica and Owen Edwards and Carol Craig and Alf Young in Scotland made a welcome change from my usual B & Bs, though most of those were excellent.

But above all, I want to acknowledge what I owe to too many local libraries and librarians to be listed here, and to all the local historians, living and dead, whose work I found in these places. The lot of the local historian is in many ways unrewarding. Because they are dealing with limited local communities, their book sales tend to be thin, which means that advances are small (or in some cases non-existent), and even the most assiduous, reliable and instructive writers may have little reputation outside their own territory. Despite all of which, they toil nobly and faithfully away, charting areas of our history and heritage whose record would have gone unpreserved without them. The millennium helped. For a tiny fraction of the cost of the Dome, millennium money made it possible for histories of places previously uncharted to be compiled and published. It is now a routine event to come by chance in a local library, as I did in Hemsworth, on a history of a place put together from written texts and recorded interviews, unlocking the memories of people who have lived there all their lives and whose testimony might otherwise have been buried with them. It's impressive too how often local historians have been given a boost by the furnishing of a preface by some great practitioner. The late W. G. Hoskins of Exeter was one such hero; another, perhaps the most generous of all, is Professor Asa Briggs, now Lord Briggs, whose book *Victorian Cities* helped to fire my taste for the kind of exploration which makes up this book. To them, and to all who keep the history of unfamous places alive, the book is dedicated.

1
LEEDS

George Orwell, returning from Spain, has his spirits restored by
red buses – Leeds buses are painted green – the might of W. Vane
Morland and the controversial hegemony of Alderman Rafferty –
ostentation in Kippax – deregulation opens the way for
predation – from emblems of municipal pride to emblems of
the triumph of Mammon.

Bradford's were blue. Sheffield's were cream and blue. Halifax's
were green and orange, as if they had somehow escaped from
Glasgow. In Leeds, ours were green; a slightly dour, urban green.
Southdown's, on the south coast, were a more meadow-like shade
of green; Bournemouth's, or so it was declared by those who had
holidayed there, were an exotic buttercup yellow. And London's, as
everyone knew, were red. Returning, wounded, from the Spanish
Civil War, George Orwell reflected in *Homage to Catalonia* on the
changeless nature of Britain, on the 'huge peaceful wilderness of
outer London', and finally, on the heart of the great city: 'the familiar streets, the posters telling of cricket matches and royal
weddings, the men in bowler hats, the pigeons in Trafalgar Square,
the red buses, the blue policemen…'

Those red buses, whether navigating the drab streets of Stepney
and Whitechapel, picking travellers up and putting them down in
salubrious suburbs from Harrow to Totteridge and Beckenham to
Richmond-upon-Thames, or surging majestically up Whitehall to

circle Trafalgar Square, told you at once where you were, bringing a sense of unity to London's vast disparity. In Leeds, the corporation buses were green by order of the municipality after the war. In wartime – not in order to confuse the Germans, as people sometimes supposed, but because the old paints were no longer available – both buses and trams had turned a dingy khaki. With peace, the trams re-emerged as red and the buses as green. The Conservatives, turned out by Labour in the council elections of 1945, protested that this was political manipulation. If the trams were to be dressed in socialist red, then the buses, they insisted, must be painted Conservative blue. But the chairman of the transport committee, Alderman Rafferty, said this was stuff and nonsense. The choice of red for the trams was purely pragmatic. Leeds was buying up London trams as London dispensed with them, and London's trams were red. 'Dozens of people have written in praise of the colour of the red tram in Leeds,' the alderman robustly claimed.

In a sense, the trams were more of an issue in Leeds than the buses. Clanging their way through the city from the Odeon on the corner of the Headrow, down Briggate, past the arcades and the dummy mannequins in Mathias Robinson's windows, along Boar Lane, past Holy Trinity Church and the beggar whose legs were turned almost back to front by rickets, and into City Square with its statue of the Black Prince and the juicy bare-breasted nymphs I tried not to let my mother catch me looking at, the trams were loved, where buses were merely respected. The trams had mysterious notices on the upper deck: 'Do not put your head out of the window', 'Please do not spit'. (Why, I wondered as a child, were warnings to that rough lot, the spitters, prefaced by 'please', while the other notice was not?) Once, on a tram, the conductor let me wind the handle which changed the destination from Roundhay to

Lawnswood: a thrill never to be forgotten. On buses, only the driver could do that. The top route numbers all belonged to the trams; the buses had to start where the trams left off, which when we lived in Leeds was route 29, the Domestic Road circular: Swinegate, Meadow Lane, Elland Road for the football ground, Domestic Street, City Square and neatly back to Swinegate. Nor was there ever much doubt that that the trams were the particular pride of W. Vane Morland, high priest of Leeds municipal transport, whose name was inscribed on the side of every tram and bus in the town, along with the Leeds coat of arms. This showed some rather unlikely birds and a sheep suspended in a sort of truss, at the very least couchant, more probably dead, with the legend *Pro Rege et Lege* ('For King and Law').

On the eastern edge of the city centre, beyond Kirkgate market, in the shadow of Quarry Hill flats – sometimes claimed in Leeds to have been the biggest such complex in Europe, erected by a pioneering housing department in days of huge municipal pride and endeavour – stood the city bus station. The services ran as far as the city boundary, but were not permitted to cross into alien territory where goodness knows what perils might lie in wait for them. The exception was the number 72. By a special dispensation, negotiated in person, one had to assume, between W. Vane Morland and his mighty Bradfordian counterpart, our green number 72s ran into their city and their blue ones ran into ours. Other, commercial companies, whose remits were more cosmopolitan, despatched their fleets to such destinations as Huddersfield, Harrogate, Hull and Halifax. The West Yorkshire Road Car Company, based in York, had its own bus station behind the Ritz cinema, from where its bright red buses headed out for the north and east. Here too, if you were fortunate, you might encounter one of the elegant light-blue buses of Hull and East Riding with their strange tapered tops designed to get them through the North Bar at Beverley. Samuel Ledgard and Son, a company still commemorated in Leeds in the annual meetings of the Samuel Ledgard Appreciation Society, despatched its services to Otley and Ilkley from a modest side-street lodgement near the Central Station. In a similar street, the buses of the Yorkshire Woollen District rested awhile before returning to Batley and Dewsbury. Yet even the central bus station made provision for the odd interloper bus. On the very far side there were platforms to which Leeds corporation had graciously deigned to admit the bright green fleet which served places east and south of the city such as Wakefield and Selby. And on the outermost stand were the most exotic buses of all: the red, orange and yellow conveyances of Kippax, Garforth and Ledston Luck, an amalgamation of several small companies serving mining villages, some of which, even then, no longer had working pits. It always seemed odd, yet somehow exhilarating, that these gay, even garish creatures should come from a territory otherwise free of all ostentation. How drab the streets of Kippax, Garforth and Ledston Luck must have seemed when the company went out of business.

Quarry Hill Flats, judged cramped and archaic and no longer worth the cost of repair, as well as, by latter-day standards, suspiciously Stalinesque, were demolished in 1978. We had almost lived there. As refugees from Hitler's V bombs in London, one of which killed my father in June 1944, we had lived with an aunt in Whitkirk until my uncle returned from the war and wanted us out. My mother, brother and I were rescued by the Leeds housing department. They offered us a flat in the Quarry Hill complex but, desperate though our predicament was, my mother rejected it as too dark and claustrophobic under its lowly ceilings. Instead they found us a house that belonged to a man who had been imprisoned in Singapore. It was on the hill up from Chapel Allerton into

Moortown, quite an expensive territory. You got off the number 2 Circular tram at the Kingsway cinema, which later became a synagogue, known to us lads as the cinemagogue. Even now I cannot look at it without recalling the matchless exhilaration of the night when the wartime ban on neon lights was at last rescinded and the name of the Kingsway glowed in the evening sky and throughout the city the streets were full of people gazing in rapture at a lightscape, now taken for granted.

It took a long while for the old Leeds to die and the new super-Leeds – that transformation of the heart of the city from grim and intensely Yorkshire to glittering celebration of big European money – to replace it. One part of this new enrichment, occupying one end of the old Quarry Hill site, is the hugely successful West Yorkshire Playhouse. At the great plate-glass windows of its café-restaurant you can sit with your cappuccino or Americano (products quite unknown in my childhood) and watch today's buses wheeling in and out of the bus station, carrying passengers to destinations not even dreamed of in Alderman Rafferty's time. There is one that serves both Odsal Top and Stanningley Bottom. In summer, you can even catch a bus that runs directly to Blubberhouses. In territory once dedicated almost exclusively to serving the city suburbs, there are buses – some sporting colours which make the old Kippax, Garforth and Ledston Luck seem positively pusillanimous – to places all over the county and well beyond. Here are multicoloured Black Prince buses, each one it seems a different concoction of shades from the Black Prince before it, a blue and white Keighley and District with a big red 'K' making it look like an advert for breakfast cereal, and a red and cream Harrogate and District still decorated with the legend 'Bus Operator of the Year 2002'. There's a Pink Line and an Indigo Line (though sadly their buses are not painted pink or indigo) and

Coastliners to Whitby and Scarborough and Flamingoland. Some of these buses carry ads on their sides, offering, for no more than it costs to get you to London or Edinburgh, trips to destinations that many in Leeds would never even have heard of in Alderman Rafferty's heyday: Venice, £21; Malaga, £23.

Meanwhile, the suburban buses mostly run from the city centre, sparing shoppers the trail though Kirkgate market (now only half the size that it used to be, since a disastrous fire). The services have been 'rationalized' since the first wild days of deregulation in 1986, which means in effect that the big operators – Arriva and First – have eliminated or gobbled up smaller ones. Even plucky Black Prince, the last Leeds independent operator of commercial services, was breathing its last in the spring of 2005 as the mighty maw of First opened a little further to swallow it. That is the general pattern. Outside London, where bus regulation continued, the pattern of bus provision became essentially a free-for-all. But where in the early stages a thousand operators were offered a chance to bloom – and began to compete with each other with an avidity and sometimes a ruthlessness which recalled the bus wars of the 1920s – in practice the big companies progressively outmanoeuvred, and often extinguished, most of their smaller rivals, leaving the Big Five – Arriva, National Express, First, Go-Ahead and Stagecoach – operating some 80 per cent of the services in the densely populated areas covered by the seven UK passenger transport executives. And although bus travel has risen sharply – up by around one third – in regulated London, it has fallen – by roughly a third – in the rest of the land. Some of this reflects the cost of getting around by bus. The umbrella organization for the seven passenger transport executives, PTEG, estimated in 2005 that the cost of bus travel over the past twenty years was up by nearly a third while, despite the ceaseless complaints of drivers, the cost of private motoring was almost unchanged. Local government, mean-while, shorn of its old predominance in municipal transport, is required to prove the subsidies to save unremunerative routes from extinction. Sometimes the money runs out, and villages are left less accessible than at any time in the twentieth century.

There's one benefit, however, in having fewer operating comp-anies. In Alderman Rafferty's day you could go to the bus station office and ask for a timetable. For 3d or so they would sell you a book which covered every route that the corporation operated. After deregulation you were left to work your way through racks of com-peting timetables, leaving you to compute which of five different buses you should use to get to Crossgates. The only disappointment in my old corporation timetables was the flatness of the advertise-ments, so unadventurous compared with the pun-filled ads in the programmes at Elland Road, where one outfitter promised Saturday after Saturday to make your Outside Right (the name of the position occupied then by the man in the number 7 shirt). Deprived of such ingenuities, Alderman Rafferty's customers were invited to ponder the woes of the human condition, and their vul-nerability to conditions such as indigestion, biliousness, dyspepsia, heartburn, palpitations and gastric catarrh.

The tables of routes were much more alluring, especially those that covered swathes of the city to which you had never been. For some reason, the circular routes were the best: they tended to go to places with evocative names like Accommodation Street and Easy Road. Such places at the end of the Second World War still seemed to me to be the essence of Leeds, along with the uniform streets run up by late-nineteenth-century builders who frequently chose a random name and applied it to a thicket of narrow streets, giving, in one characteristic sequence in the old Harehills, Conway Road, Conway Drive, Conway Street, Conway Avenue, Conway

Terrace, Conway Mount, Conway View, Conway Grove and Conway Place.

Most of these houses were torn down long ago, their inhabitants often decanted to newly created estates on the edge of the city, such as Seacroft, which when we first lived in Leeds was largely farms and fields through which my household would walk at my mother's insistence at that drabbest time of the week, Sunday afternoon, to some country village like Scholes or Stanks. Even formerly middle-class Moortown, which used to mean a cluster of genteel shops around the end of the tram route, where queues would form in the shopping street on a Saturday morning for a gateau for the weekend, now chiefly consists of a huge estate on what used to be the open moorland through which the number 35 bus made its way towards the fabled, golf-playing affluence of Alwoodley. Monotonous though such post-war expansions are, they are not the worst of the city. Pre-war estates like the Gipton look as drab and troubled, and sometimes as alarming, today as they ever were. Believers in the so-called trickledown theory, which holds that the benefits that accrue to the rich will benignly feed through in time to the poorest, can never have taken the bus from the new, rich cosmopolitan Leeds to deprived and neglected outposts like these.

There is no disputing that nationally the Thatcher bus revolution brought a zest and variety, and a readiness, saving tired old legs, to travel down roads close to home which no bus before would have aspired to penetrate, which purely municipal services were rarely likely to match. But what has been lost is the sense of one's home town as a proud and distinctive entity. On trains back from London, even before the long curve of the railway around the Elland Road football ground, and the sight of the young Cuthbert Brodrick's iconic town hall, it was always the first glimpse of some loyal green bus dipping in to the stops on the southern estates of the city like a bee at the work of pollination that gave me the warm and comforting sense of having come home. There it all was: the familiar streets, the posters telling of John Charles, hero of Leeds United and Wales, and Len Hutton, hero of Yorkshire and England, the men in caps, the kindly shop assistants who called everyone 'love', the Yorkshire Symphony Orchestra playing in the town hall under the baton of Maurice Miles (not one of the world's great conductors perhaps but loved by women for the rhythmic flap of his hair), the woman in the basement record department under Hopkinson's piano shop who could tell you from memory the number of any record you asked her for – but above all the reassuring business of red trams and green buses exclusively dedicated to the service of Leeds pouring out to Armley and Rawdon, Halton and Osmondthorpe, Sheepscar, Potternewton, and the coveted avenues of Alwoodley. Their corporate presence spoke of continuity, civic pride and a sense of place, where the liveries of their successors speak simply of money.

2

Woodlesford — Wakefield — Fitzwilliam
Hemsworth — Grimethorpe

BARNSLEY

*On the trail of local heroes and favourite sons – Hunslet
transformed – through the homeland of British rhubarb – a
fine novelist's low opinion of Wakefield, and its low opinion of
him – a great batsman undervalued, though not by himself –
probing the multicultural nature of Hemsworth – grim times in
Grimethorpe – how to tell Dickie Bird from Arthur Scargill.*

For most of those who are waiting on the edge of the city bus station
(you could hardly call it a queue: queues are replaced these days
by gaggles of hoverers ready to make the dash to be first aboard),
the 446 Arriva bus means an opportunity to carry one's city centre
shopping back to Hunslet, Thwaite Gate, Stourton, Woodlesford
and beyond. For me, it's a chance to pay homage to a writer I venerate, of whom Orwell wrote: 'I am ready to maintain that England
has produced very few better novelists.' Poor, gifted, thwarted and
doomed George Gissing was born and grew up in Wakefield, nine
miles to the south of Leeds.

There are various routes to get you from Leeds to Wakefield. The
one I take goes out through Hunslet. I knew this road out of Leeds
fifty years ago, and travelling it now is like finding myself suddenly
and inexplicably transported to a foreign country. There seems to
be little left of the Hunslet where Richard Hoggart grew up, absorb-
ing and beginning to analyse the dying working-class culture he
later commemorated in *The Uses of Literacy*; or when the Parkside

ground was home to the Hunslet XIII, one of the most celebrated teams in the rugby league, good enough in its day to hold its own even with mighty Leeds. On my number 446 an elderly couple are trying to recall the buildings that stood on this roadside when they were young – all gone as if they had never been. And this pattern persists. Rothwell colliery, further south, is now no more than a brightly painted wheel on a neat roundabout.

Just beyond, largely untransformed, is rhubarb-rich Woodlesford. Whenever I have travelled this road I have peered through the windows in the hope of seeing rhubarb-harvesters at work. I picture brawny-armed, broad-beamed Yorkshire women, plucking this strange and beautiful vegetable from the earth while singing the ancient songs of their region, as yet uncollected by any great musicologist. But even in spring I have never seen any, nor have I observed any other signs of the rhubarb crop which has made this triangle south-east of Leeds so famous.

We are not far out of Wakefield now, and as the bus comes down the hill past the Pinderfields hospital I begin to look out for celebrations of Gissing. My first job when I started a life in newspapers was in Keighley, part of a tract of West Yorkshire where you can't get away from the Brontës. The obsession starts in a quiet way at Thornton, now a suburb of Bradford, where the sisters were born, and reaches its climax at Haworth, just outside Keighley, where they wrote and suffered. In those days the Brontë industry was limited and restrained. The attraction of Haworth held out to me when I joined the reporters' room of the *Keighley News and Bingley Chronicle* was the cinema, where on a Saturday night, it was said, you stood a very good chance of seeing not just the advertised film but a 'reet good punch-up'. You can get some idea of the Brontëfication of this area now from the Bradford phone book, where you will find, for instance, a Brontë Balti house, a Brontë caravan park, a Brontë estate agent, a Brontë Park nursing home, a Brontë Precision Engineering Company, Brontë Taxis, and Brontë Whirlpools Ltd (whirlpool bath manufacturers). The same disease affects Coventry, a city that seems from its phone book to be obsessed with Lady Godiva.

Yet where, as we run into Wakefield, are they: the Gissing Arms, the Gissing Kebab House, Gissing Computers, the Grub Street food mall – all named in honour of the man who left us *New Grub Street*, *By the Ionian Sea*, and *The Private Papers of Henry Ryecroft*? There is only the Gissing centre, which consists of two rooms in the house behind George Gissing's father's pharmacy where the boy grew up. Here laid out for inspection are his books and family pictures and other touching mementoes. But with minimal resources, the exhibition is far from lavish. It is open only on Saturday afternoons in summer, and in winter not at all.

But if Wakefield shows no enthusiasm for George, that's perhaps because George never showed much for Wakefield. The Brontës had difficult times at Haworth, but they never denounced it, while Godiva, if we believe Roger of Wendover (which perhaps we shouldn't), earned her acclaim by giving her all, or at least displaying it, to save the people of Coventry from the vicious taxes her husband Earl Leofric planned to impose upon them. Although he felt compelled to return there from time to time to visit his family – his mother and unmarried sisters; his father had died in 1870 when George had just turned thirteen – Gissing found the place oppressive and complained that he could not write there. 'I am in the wrong world'; 'The atmosphere of Wakefield would soon make a dullard of me'; 'No sleep at night. No work today. Misery,' he wrote in his diary during visits to Wakefield.

Wakefield finds its way into some of his novels, but it only takes centre-stage in a book called *A Life's Morning* which he finished in

1885. He was twenty-seven. His feelings about his home town are reflected in the name with which he feebly disguises it: Dunfield (dun means greyish-brown, mouse-coloured, dingy). The story, like so many of Gissing's, is all about class and privilege and struggle and poverty. Dunfield and its environs are mostly described with disgust. There are local beauty spots, affording relief and refresh-ment, like Pendal Castle (Gissing's name for Sandal Castle, just outside Wakefield), but even here the ugliness of industrialism can't be escaped. From the relative beauty spot of the Heath, the lovers Wilfrid, a son of green and privileged Surrey, and Emily, who grew up in the dreary backstreets of Dunfield, look down on the town: 'The view from this point was extensive,' writes Gissing, 'and would have been interesting but for the existence of the town itself.' The contrast between Wilfrid's Surrey home, to which Emily comes as a governess, with her own in Wakefield, enrages him. To compare them, he says, 'was to understand the inestimable advan-tage of those born into the material refinement which wealth can command, of those who breathe from childhood the atmosphere of liberal enjoyment, who walk from the first on clean ways, with minds disengaged from anxiety of casual soilure, who know not even by domestic story the trammels of sordid preoccupation.'

Most of Gissing's novels are grim but his life, in a sense, was his grimmest work. *The Private Papers of Henry Ryecroft*, one of his greatest successes, is not so much a disguised autobiography as a dream of his life as he wished it had been. Indeed, as it might have been, had he, like Ryecroft, come into money, or had he made the kind of marriage with a woman of education, taste and breeding which, being always poor, he imagined to be beyond him. All his life, he was trapped 'in the wrong world'. The plots of his books often describe the sad fates of good people, and he seemed in his own life almost to contrive situations which were bound to end in despair. His talent as a writer was overwhelmed by his talent for self-destruction. Expulsion and imprisonment for a theft while at college, two utterly – and predictably – disastrous marriages, books which attracted warm notices but failed to sell – all were part of an inescapable pattern. As early as 1890, when he was thirty-three, he had begun to suffer from congestion of the lungs, the condition that had killed his father. In a final, hopeless attempt to restore his health, he moved to France with a woman called Gabrielle Fleury, with whom he lived in what, since he had not divorced his wife, was a bigamous marriage. Here, in a village at the foot of the Pyrenees, he died in 1903. He was forty-six. His dreadful last hours are harshly described in the autobiography of his friend H.G. Wells, whom he had summoned to France. Gissing had long been obsessed with the glories of Greece and Rome, and now in his final hours he seemed to believe he was there. 'He had passed altogether into that fantastic pseudo-Roman world of which Wakefield Grammar School had laid the foundations,' Wells wrote. 'He babbled in Latin, he chanted fragments of Gregorian music...' He may have owed little to Wakefield, but at least his schooling there gave him a passion for the classical world which became in the end the core of his life.

The death of George Gissing left the *Wakefield Express* in some difficulty. While eager to claim him for Wakefield – 'Death of Mr George Gissing' its headline said, 'Great Novelist a Wakefield Man' – it unhappily knew very little about him. 'The number of Wakefield people who retain a vivid recollection of the unfortunate litera-teur's early career', it observed with a touch of melancholy, 'is dwindling to microscopic proportions, and it will be sufficient at present to say that he received his early education at Mr Harrison's once famous academy.' In his life thereafter in London, 'he experienced the bitter lot common to many men who have no influence beyond their own genius to enable them to keep body and soul together, to say nothing of any hopes they may nurse of securing a niche in the Temple of Fame'.

With that sadly accurate epitaph, it is time to push on into a mining country whose condition today, now that the pits have gone, might have filled Gissing with as much rage and despair as the condition of Wakefield more than a century earlier.

Wakefield bus station, to which I return to resume my journey, is new, big, brash, busy and friendly. The driver of our bus to South Elmsall is relating to the driver next door an incident with another bus which tried to steal a space he was heading into. He lost. 'But *he*,' he says, as if in mitigation, 'were an Olympian'. An Olympian? Zeus, in Wakefield bus station? But an Olympian, I've discovered, having bought a magazine called *Buses* from the station bookstall, is a kind of large and superior bus. To your true bus devotee, and as anyone who has been to their rallies will know, they are many, the buses that swirl around Leeds bus station are not just Arrivas or Firsts but Leylands, AECs, Guys and Dennises, Titans and Olympians, Atlanteans and Lodekkas. The route 496 Arriva to South Elmsall is sadly not an Olympian, but a modest single-decker which sets out on the Doncaster Road past the house where Gissing's family lived, now part of the Stoneleigh Hotel, and Heath Common, where his characters walked, and on past Nostell Priory, an eighteenth-century mansion built for Sir Rowland Winn, Bt, and now a National Trust attraction. After this glimpse of the world of the aristocracy, it diverts down a lesser road, to Fitzwilliam.

Fitzwilliam is a powerful concept around here. It's one of the names of the family who lived at the great mansion of Wentworth Woodhouse. They owned much of the land in these parts, as well as some of the collieries, and did this village the honour of bestowing their name upon it. Fitzwilliam is not at the best of times especially prepossessing and it's certainly not looking its best on an April afternoon of cold wind and spitting rain. The bus puts me down at a stop called Fitzwilliam Hotel. There's a bilious yellow pub called the Rover's Return, and just beyond, in front of the cricket ground, a sign advertising John Smith's Tadcaster Ales. But no hotel – only the sign and an empty site. Nor could I find any indication that one of England's greatest cricketers was born in this village. Another distinguished son, left unrecognized. Geoffrey Boycott should have been born at Ackworth, just down the road, but the nursing services thought the house was unsuitable, so the birth was relocated to his grandmother's home in Earl Street, Fitzwilliam. When Geoffrey was three, the family moved to a neighbouring street in Fitzwilliam, Milton Terrace. There is no plaque at Milton Terrace and none at Earl Street, but then there aren't any houses either. They have all been torn down for redevelopment.

Fitzwilliam, in any case, may have ambivalent feelings about its famous product. Though Ackworth has a Boycott Drive, and South Elmsall a Boycott Way, no street in Fitzwilliam commemorates the master. Few would deny that by sheer determination and application he made himself one of the world's great batsmen. In 193 test match innings he made 8,114 runs, including 22 hundreds, leaving him with a final average of 47.73. He was always especially good at not getting out. As one admirer exclaimed after England wickets had tumbled in the summer of 2001: 'What England would not give for a Barrington or a Boycott who would bat all day!' (Geoffrey Boycott, *Daily Telegraph*, 6 August 2001). Yet even many devoted Yorkshire supporters were never able to warm to him because he seemed to play so much for himself. Perhaps a new pub will arise on the site of the one that has vanished, though the tendency in old mining villages is for old pubs to close rather than for new ones to open: too little money about, no mighty pit-induced thirsts to be slaked of an evening. How just it would be, even so, if some enlightened brewer were to create a new pub on this spot close by the Hemsworth miners' cricket ground with a picture of Geoffrey Boycott as its pub sign. They could call it the Master Batsman.

The bus on from neglectful Fitzwilliam is a rattly single-decker run by a small independent operator called B and L, and is full of schoolchildren voraciously texting. The centre of Hemsworth, a village once ringed around with pits, is small and compact, with three pubs and the church of St Helen's raised above the road on a mound, a chippy called Fryer Tuck's Delight, and an old town hall that hints at former glories. This was the heart of a parliamentary seat which time and again put up record Labour majorities. In the library there's a book of local reminiscences called *We're All Immigrants Around Here*, which recalls those solidly socialist days when the chance of sending a man from the local pits to Parliament never failed to bring voters out in their thousands. 'The reds always won in our village,' one woman remembers, 'and it has never changed.' Children sang:

Vote, vote, vote for Mr Guest
He is sure to win the war
For we will get a salmon tin
And we will put the other man in
And he won't come voting any more.

Mr Guest was John Guest, miner, local alderman and magistrate, who represented Hemsworth from 1918 to 1931. The Tories never had a chance in the seat, even when they fielded candidates who sought to claim some connection with mining. In 1929 the lamb who came to the slaughter was Lieutenent Commander Broughton, who had served at Jutland. He had worked, his party assured the voters of Hemsworth, as a miner in a local colliery in order to gain practical knowledge of mining conditions. The voters of Hemsworth weren't fooled. Labour's majority was only just short of 60 per cent. Guest was succeeded in 1931 by Gabriel Price, checkweighman at Frickley Colliery, also alderman and JP. This time the Unionists picked a man called Garthwaite. He had worked, his party claimed, 'at different manual trades in Canada', which failed to conceal the hard truth that he was now a Lloyds underwriter. Even in a catastrophic election for Labour, the party held on by more than 13,000 votes.

A further procession of miners followed, through to George Buckley, a miner at South Kirby colliery, in 1987. That was after the miners' strike, an event of great turmoil and misery, but one, according to the book in the library, which pulled a previously disparate place together. 'There has always been this thing about them and us in Hemsworth,' one woman remembers. 'First it was West End being better than Common End. I was always told as a child "don't go mixing with that lot down Common End. They're not like us". Then when all the Scottish miners and their families moved in to the new estate that was being built, it was "Don't go up there. Keep away."' It is easily forgotten that those in the rugged ranks of Yorkshire miners were quite often Scottish miners or Durham miners, not always fully assimilated. But the strike unified them at last: 'When you face that kind of intimidation,' one woman said, 'you never question whether the miner standing next to you is Scottish or Yorkshire. We were all the same. We certainly got to know who our real friends were during the strike. It was a bad time, but it healed a lot of long-standing bitterness.' Yet even this old mining bastion could not remain impervious to the loss of its staple industry and the wider ramifications of late twentieth-century change. When Buckley stood down in 1992, Hemsworth picked not another miner but a former teacher of classics, who was now an adviser on Third World issues in Brussels and a holder of the Order of Merit of Guinea Bissau.

For the next stage of this journey I take a double-decker of Yorkshire Traction, route 244, which runs up the hill out of Hemsworth, past the Chinese restaurant and the Ebenezer Gospel Hall, past great tracts of demolition and into a land of smart private developments designed to lure the middle class and introduce them beyond the village limits into an unspoiled world of green undulation, pitted with distant spires glimmering in splashes of sun interspersed with the rain clouds. For a moment or two it is easy to envisage how green this land must have been before the arrival of industry. Then we are into Brierley, an ancient settlement to which now much more famous Grimethorpe was once a minor addendum. We pass a derelict house which was once (not that there's much competition) Grimethorpe's one distinguished building, Grimethorpe Hall.

And who are the favourite sons and daughters of Grimethorpe? The most famous are probably Ewan McGregor and Tara Fitzgerald, who starred in the British movie success *Brassed Off*, along with the Grimethorpe Colliery Band. Sadly the stars had little to do with the village, and neither in fact did the band, since that long ago ceased to be a contingent of mining lads skilled at the cornet, horn and euphonium and is nowadays staffed by professional players who never worked down the pit. The film portrayed the Grimethorpe of the early 1990s, lightly disguised as Grimley, as a tough and depressing place where life was a struggle and Thatcherism a disaster – an exercise in slow, relentless strangulation. Yet the Grimethorpe you saw on the screen, though rough, was romanticized. The name of the fish and chip shop, In Cod We Trust, suggested a pawky Yorkshire wit, triumphing over adversity. But both the shop and its name were the film-makers' invention.

Grimethorpe is all too clearly a place that had had its purpose cut out from it. It used to consist of three parts. Up the hill to the south a concrete estate, the White City; on the Brierley Road, a brick estate known as Red City; and northwards down the hill from the main street an area known as the Seaside, because most of its streets were named after holiday towns in the south of England. An erratic main street linked the three segments loosely together. When I first visited Grimethorpe, drawn there by having seen *Brassed Off* and curious to discover how the image squared with reality, the Seaside was much the saddest. The once neat, proud houses of Margate Street, Brighton Street, Eastbourne Street – names that evoked comfortable middle-class couples in deckchairs on the prom sharing the *Daily Mail* – were for the most part filthy and vandalized, many abandoned and boarded up with large imperious notices warning that those who intruded risked death.

'Grimey', by now, was far worse than merely grimy. At least when it was grimy there were jobs, with two working pits, a coking plant, a power station, and the Barnsley area headquarters of the National Coal Board. Not that Grimethorpe felt secure even then. There were constant rumours that Houghton Main and Grimethorpe pits would join the long procession of Yorkshire mines already struck out by the Coal Board. The Coal Board denied it, but Arthur Scargill said it was true. If they didn't fight, he told them at the start of the coal strike, they were doomed. There were doubts about him in Grimethorpe. At the start of the dispute, although it had been counted as a militant pit, the response was cautious. But events left little doubt that Arthur's claims had been justified. Houghton Main shut down in 1993; Grimethorpe, the following month. The place had lost almost everything. Its social problems had predated the strike and the closure, but now they grew worse. Where glue-sniffing had once been the problem, now it was heroin. Crime, and especially vandalism and arson, increasingly haunted the streets. Even middle-class lives were threatened: as soon as you quoted the Grimethorpe post code, deliveries were refused and credit denied. Sociologists call this 'postcode blight'. It serves as a kind of informal index of shattered communities.

Ministers pledged that whatever the cost Grimethorpe and places like it were going to be rescued. Lavish plans were laid, and lavish sums of money allotted. Soon there were diggers, tractors and bulldozers everywhere, shunting, scooping, swivelling and disgorging to create a new industrial site where the pits had once been, and a spanking new road to the south, to ease the isolation of a village which until then had been on the way to nowhere. All around there were signs of prodigious planting of trees and the eradication and transformation of slag heaps: valleys were being exalted, mountains and hills made low, the crooked made straight, and rough places plain. As most of the Seaside estate was swept away, so a new millennium green was established, opened in December 2000 by Pete Postlethwaite, who had played the Grimethorpe bandmaster in *Brassed Off*. It was all designed not just to cleanse and brighten the place but to change its internal psychology, and with luck to prove to the outside world that Grimethorpe was on its way up.

That was never going be done in ten minutes, but now on a cold drab April evening, Grimethorpe looks far from recovery. On the Seaside estate, just three houses survive in New Street, while all around them is bricked and boarded or gone. Though it's not yet five, much of the high street is shuttered, either for security or because the business is bust. The Grimethorpe Hotel – where in

Brassed Off Tara Fitzgerald invites Ewan McGregor in for a cup of coffee, and he says he doesn't drink coffee, and she says she doesn't have any coffee – is gone: just a gaping hole, like the hotel site at Fitzwilliam. In Cod We Trust still flaunts its spurious name, but the building is all bricked up. To the plaque on the millennium green (deserted this afternoon), Jodie and Milly have added their names, as has Ashley Gillespie. Emma loves David, while less romantically it's asserted that someone whose name is fortunately illegible has sex every day. The Anglican church of St Luke's, opened in 1904, not the kind of building to gladden the heart of Nikolaus Pevsner, has launched, its noticeboard says, a centenary appeal. 'To save the building from demolition, to create a beautiful restored parish church, and give the community of Grimethorpe a quality village hall, we need to raise £1.5 million. With God, we can do it together for Grimethorpe.' Newspapers tell us a million is not what it was, but it's still a lot of money in Grimethorpe. The last word on Grimethorpe belongs with Gissing. 'Indigence', he says somewhere in *A Life's Morning*, 'is the death of the soul.' That is sometimes true of places as well as people.

The 244 Yorkshire Traction bus out of Grimey terminates at Barnsley, which is reached by way of a route punctuated by dead pubs and dead filling stations. The bus bowls into Barnsley past the ground of the local football team, whose old heroes – Danny Blanchflower, tricky winger Johnny Kelly, resolute take-no-prisoners defender 'Skinner' Normanton – were made famous by a journalist son of Barnsley, Michael Parkinson. Boycott is sometimes assigned to Barnsley, which is right only in the sense that he used to bat down the order for a town cricket team in which the innings was opened by Parkinson and the man who would become the world's most famous umpire, Dickie Bird. Bird's only serious rival today for the right to think of himself as Barnsley's most famous son is Arthur Scargill. Although they come from comparable backgrounds, they have finished up at opposite ends of the political and psychological spectrum. In his autobiography, which made him a great deal of money, Bird recalls a visit to Buckingham Palace, where he turned up four hours early rather than risk being late, and the Queen called him Dickie and offered him grapes. I doubt if you'd ever catch Arthur Scargill confessing to something like that.

3

SLEAFORD

An aristocratic sprig disappears without finishing breakfast –
a productive Italian ménage à trois – though provoked, the Pope
decides to turn a blind eye – Margaret Thatcher loses her head –
she is failed by the civic leaders of Grantham – the Victorian
heyday of Sleaford – the fiancée of an aristocrat disappears in
Marshall & Snelgrove on the eve of their wedding – her victim
takes a belated revenge on the racetrack.

And so south and east into Lincolnshire, where my journey has to
do with two dramatic disappearances, one of an aristocratic young
man from his kitchen, the other of an aristocratic young woman
from a West End shop. There is also the disappearance of Margaret
Thatcher's head from her body, though that was only momentary.
My journey begins at a village called Harmston, on the main road
south out of Lincoln, on a route pursued by the spick and efficient
number 1 Lincolnshire Roadcar. Leaving South Common, one of
the spots where visitors congregate to admire the distant view of
the city of Lincoln with its cathedral perched on the peak of a hill
as if it were floating above it, my bus has begun to run on a road
with a broad valley to the west, perhaps fifteen to twenty miles of
it. We are now on the side of a hill known hereabouts as the Cliff.
The road, like so many in Lincolnshire, is straight, and narrow
enough to make overtaking a hazardous exercise, as attested by
signs displaying daunting accident rates. The more fortunate

villages – Harmston is one – are off the A607. They cling to the side of the hill.

At the heart of the village is the church of All Saints: at the heart of the church there are Thorolds. This is one of the great Lincolnshire families with branches established in various parts of the county. These are the Grantham lot. Sir George Thorold, the first baronet, sometime Lord Mayor of London, entirely rebuilt this church in 1717. His monument seems bleak, its tribute dealing mainly with his genealogy. Sir George married Eliza Rushout, daughter of Sir James Rushout, Baronet of Worcestershire; they had a daughter (unnamed) who died young. A weeping cherub is in attendance. But it was another Thorold who brought me to Harmston: Henry, cleric, peripatetic preacher, teacher, raconteur and topographer, joint author of the *Shell Guide to Lincolnshire* and sole author of several other books in the series. He died in 2000. In 1996, this cheerful eccentric published a Pimlico Guide to his native county in which he tells a curious story about an early eighteenth-century Thorold. Nathaniel had never expected to inherit Harmston, and when he did, seemed unable to cope with it. Soon he was deeply in debt and harassed by creditors. So he fled – so suddenly that when people came to the house to look for him, they found his uncompleted breakfast still on the table, with chairs overturned on the floor. For many years no one knew where he had gone. In fact, he had taken ship for Italy, where he began a new life, first in Leghorn and then in Naples. With the help of a Neapolitan friend, he invented a method of salting cod which made him a fortune. Also, as a history of the family by the Venerable Edward Trollope, a former Lincolnshire rector who was then archdeacon of Stow, decorously records, he 'met a lovely girl of Capri, and was hence attracted to visit her native island, where he lived with her in a house he built of such character as to be termed a "palazzo", adorned externally with his armorial bearings, and became a collector of Greek and Roman antiquities'. What the Archdeacon failed to add was that he 'collected' the beautiful girl of Capri as well, although she was already married to a Signor Antonio Canale. Canale raised no objection to his wife's new passion, and allowed the baronet's children to take his own name as they all lived together in a happy *ménage à trois*. The Bishop of Capri was less complaisant and complained to the Pope. Scandal was being caused, he protested, 'by the cohabitation for many years of a certain married woman with an heretical English nobleman'. But the Pope, for whatever reason, remained unmoved.

When Nathaniel died in 1764, his son Samuel came to Harmston to claim his inheritance. Before long he was known as Thorold, not as Canale. At twenty-one, he married the daughter of a Yorkshire parson (also a baronet) and at twenty-five was installed as High Sheriff of Lincolnshire. 'Not bad going,' wrote Henry Thorold 'for an illegitimate half-Italian.'

It is now a benign April morning and the village has an air of honeyed tranquillity. On the road down to the pub (which of course is the Thorold Arms) I meet a man with a child in a pushchair. It's a really lovely place to live, he says, but so are they all, these villages along the Cliff. The number 1 bus, which runs hourly, subscribes to the image of local perfection by arriving exactly on time, and soon we are bowling along the A607 towards Grantham. The first village we encounter is Boothby Graffoe. A hundred years from now, wiseacres will no doubt say it was named after a late twentieth-century/early twenty-first-century comedian, but the consensus at present is that Boothby Graffoe has been Boothby Graffoe for hundreds of years and the comedian (real name, James Rogers) saw it on a sign while he was driving through and cheekily nicked it. As the man with the pushchair said, the villages on this road are almost uniformly endearing. Navenby is on the main road; so are Wellingore and Welbourn with its curious spire and Leadenham with its handsome one. But Fulbeck is sensibly tucked away, leaving the Hare and Hounds pub to represent it on the main road. And so on through Carlton Scroop and Honington, where we meet that characteristic Lincolnshire device, the level crossing, and Belton, where National Trust notices try to lure you to see the great house – most beautiful of all late seventeenth-century English houses, according to Henry Thorold. Manthorpe's rows of pretty, uniform nineteenth-century cottages indicate that this was a model village. And Manthorpe elides into Grantham. We are entering Thatcherland.

What ought one to do with a two-ton, eight-foot-high statue of Baroness Thatcher which has no home to go to? That question convulsed much of Britain in the winter of 2001-2 when the House of Commons, having commissioned the statue, found it could not install it on a vacant plinth in the Members' lobby because of a rule which banned representations of former premiers until five years after their death. The obvious solution seemed to be to lodge it in Grantham, her birthplace. The chairman of South Kesteven council was in favour in principle – 'she shouldn't go anywhere else', he said, 'especially in London' – but wasn't quite sure where to put it. When eventually it was offered a billet at the Guildhall of the City of London, somebody cut off its head. And yet there certainly seemed at the time several suitable slots available to accommodate Grantham's eight-foot Iron Lady. One possibility, an address sublimely attuned to her economic philosophies, was the market place, but the best spot there is occupied by the market cross.

Or what about the birthplace itself? It stands at the point where the Barrowby road meets the old A1 to Newark and Great Gonerby, and is marked by a plaque which says: 'Birthplace of the Rt Hon. Margaret Thatcher, MP, first woman prime minister of Great Britain and Northern Ireland'. The old grocer's shop where she learned so much at her father's knee, which somebody later tried and failed to run as a café-cum-shrine, subsequently became a holistic and chiropractic centre, with silver stars in its windows labelled peace, unwind, rebalance, pamper and so on. Not very Alderman Roberts, I'd say. My own preference at the time was for the statue to be suspended above the A1 as Grantham's answer to the Angel of the North at Gateshead: a sort of Angel of the East Midlands. But some drivers might have stopped to venerate her and others to curse her, so sadly, on safety grounds alone, that was out.

Another possibility was St Peter's Green, at the heart of the town, a place with a real sense of occasion, in front of the pleasantly bulbous Guildhall, with the fine spire of the parish church of St Wulfram beyond it. The central spot on the green is occupied today by Sir Isaac Newton (not born in Grantham, but schooled there). He broods on his pedestal with a look of mild displeasure, perhaps because he's directly opposite a shopping mall named after him, and if he doesn't much like what he sees he won't be alone in that. But the most appropriate spot of all for a Thatcher statue, even though it's at present occupied by one of the town's longest serving MPs, would be at the southern end of the green, looking down towards London and fame and fortune – and just across the road, I notice, from the Nag's Head.

Yet coming to Grantham by bus I see there's another entirely suitable site which I missed before: the bus station. Grantham bus station, when my Roadcar deposited me there, was a disgrace. There was no comprehensive noticeboard to tell you which buses would depart from which platforms. There was nowhere to ask advice from officials: what was once the bus office was abandoned and empty. 'They're all upstairs,' said a woman when I asked how to get to Sleaford. 'They go in that door there, but you have to know their code to get in.' Were a statue of Margaret Thatcher to be erected here, it would surely shame them into making more of an effort. Slovenliness could not survive under her withering eye.

From Roadcar service 1 to Roadcar service 609, Grantham to Sleaford. Can there really be more than 600 routes operated by Lincolnshire Roadcar? The numbering of bus routes is sometimes very mysterious. Somewhere in one of those books of miscellaneous facts which sell so abundantly nowadays there is probably a claim for the highest route number on any regular service. You might think the lowest on record was number 1, but that isn't the case: there was one that ran briefly in Sheffield that called itself route 000. Route 609 goes out of Grantham where route 1 came in, through Manthorpe and Belton and Barkston, until it reaches Honington where it strikes off north-east. This is not an eventful journey: there are parts where the illusion, dispersed by route 1 during the morning, that Lincolnshire is uniformly flat and boring, begins to feel like the truth. A road sign announcing that we are entering Ancaster seems promising: this is a Roman town, and has given its name to the grey Ancaster stone you meet across the county. But the 609 doesn't seem to like the look of poor Ancaster. It has hardly entered the town (nowadays more a village) before it sheers off down a side street as if anxious to escape it as soon as it possibly can. Almost as if the atmosphere there might be somehow morally deleterious: it is, after all, a place which used to host Roman orgies.

There are twenty minutes to go before we get into Sleaford, featuring Wilsford (which is where, rather than Ancaster, you find the Ancaster quarries) and South Rauceby, where the church has its devotees, but the journey is soporific, and the outer reaches of Sleaford, the usual standard twentieth-century houses which might be anywhere, drawn up in the usual featureless rows, don't make you look forward to seeing the town. Sleaford is the sort of community that attracts researchers studying the decline of the English market town. You can tell from the market place what a self-contained, self-confident and, this being Victorian England, self-satisfied place it must have been; smaller, but no less important or valuable, to those who lived there and ran the place, than your puffed-up Granthams or Bostons. Even now, the square, with the parish church presiding benignly over it, has a style and swagger about it. It must have been at its best around the middle years of the nineteenth century, around the time that it opened its new corn exchange, and the local historian Edward Trollope declared that he could not find a better regulated, cleaner or more rapidly improving town in the whole of Lincolnshire. It was also then that a statue of Henry Handley, Liberal MP for the town from 1832 to 1841, was erected in Southgate. It seems odd that Handley was given such favoured such treatment, when this area was represented for nearly forty years by a much more eminent figure, Henry Chaplin, at his peak a member of Salisbury's Cabinet.

Chaplin was famously rich. He owned a celebrated house down the road at Blankney, built by another Thorold, Sir Anthony, but strenuously remodelled, as well as large estates elsewhere in the county and in Nottinghamshire and Yorkshire. He was a racehorse owner who won the Derby, founded the Blankney Hunt, and was constantly talked about in London and Lincolnshire, though less perhaps for his political status than for his extravagant ways and above all for the story of what ought to have been his first marriage. There were several exotic versions of this in circulation, but even the authorized one, contained in a memoir of Chaplin by his daughter, the marchioness of Londonderry, would be toothsome enough for most tastes.

Chaplin was an adventurer. At Christ Church he got into trouble with the dean, Dr Liddell, father of Lewis Carroll's Alice, for various offences, including the wearing of hunting kit under his surplice. 'You seem to regard Christ Church as a hunting box,' the dean wrote to him. 'You are hardly ever in college, and I must request you, unless you change your habits, to vacate your rooms and make way for someone who will benefit from his studies during his residence at the university.' Chaplin survived, but did not take his degree, informing the dean he was off to the Rocky Mountains. In 1864, at twenty-three, he fell in love with a famous beauty called Lady Florence Paget. He proposed; she accepted. A few days before the marriage, she drove in her father's brougham to the doors of the fine London store of Marshall and Snelgrove, which she entered from Vere Street, telling the coachman she would make some purchases and return. In fact, she walked straight through the store to the Oxford Street entrance, where the marquis of Hastings was waiting for her. They were later seen by a friend, in a cab, heading for Euston. Chaplin's daughter prints the letter that Florence then wrote him. 'To you whom I have injured more deeply than anyone,' she said, 'I hardly know how to address myself. Believe me, the task is most painful and one I shrink from. Would to God that I had had moral courage to open my heart to you sooner, but I could not bring myself to do so. However, now the truth must be told...There is not a man in the world I have a greater regard and respect for than yourself, but I do not <u>love</u> you in the way a woman ought to love her husband, and I am perfectly certain that if I had married you, I should have rendered not only <u>my</u> life miserable, but your own also. And now we are eternally separated, for by the time you receive this I shall be the wife of Lord Hastings...'

Society soon knew all about it. 'It must have added to Mr Chaplin's mortification,' his daughter wrote, 'to know that the woman he was in love with had thrown in her lot with a man who was quite unfitted to make her happy. Lord Hastings might have been the model for a sensational hero for the fiction of that period.' And indeed he was generally held to be a bit of a waster. Though Master of the Quorn, he was said to be languid and ignorant in the hunting field. (Chaplin's skills as a huntsman were hugely admired.) He bet heavily and, more often than not, he lost. After he married Florence he went, according to Lady Londonderry, rapidly downhill.

Chaplin, however, recovered his spirits and in time met and married another Florence. In the end he got a peculiarly satisfying revenge. He owned a horse called the Hermit, which was down to run in the Derby, but it was given little chance, especially when shortly before the race it suffered an injury and it seemed would have to be scratched. But to everyone's surprise the horse recovered well enough to take part; and to everyone's still greater surprise, it won. No sweeter triumph could have gladdened the heart of Chaplin while few greater humiliations could have befallen Hastings: he had bet heavily against the Hermit, and lost a great deal of money. And a horse called Lord Hastings, Lady Londonderry does not omit to report, finished fourth.

I leave Lincolnshire with reluctance. A company called Brylaine Travel (its founders were a Bryan and an Elaine) advertises flexible interconnecting services which would take me to Ashby-by-Partney, Belchford, Claxford St Andrew, Dalderby, Fulletby, Mareham-on-the-Hill, Miningsby, Scremby, Skendleby Psalter, Tumby and Tumby Woodside, Ulceby and Wickenby. It was the music of place names which first lured me, late in life, into neglected Lincolnshire: Claxby Pluckacre, Sloothby, Hagworthingham, Yaddlethorpe, Wrangle...So much enticing interconnection...but not now. It is time for me to resolve pressing questions on the other side of the Wash about the missing years of Attila the Hun.

4

Hunstanton — Fakenham — Attlebridge
Norwich (Hungate) — Attleborough — Bury
St Edmunds — Haverhill — Saffron Walden

UTTLESFORD

*The missing years of Attila – did he invade Hunstanton? – a
wealth of produce in Fakenham market, little of it home-grown –
a hypothetical fifth-century outrage at Attlebridge – leisure
delights of a well-fed parson – Attila reaches Norwich and
Attleborough, possibly – I fall in love with Bury St Edmunds,
but less so with Haverhill – decorum at Saffron Walden –
Attila's engagement at Uttlesford, and what may or may not
have ensued.*

What I want, says Mr Gradgrind in *Hard Times* by Dickens, is Facts.
Facts alone are wanted in life. For generations, most academic historians meekly subscribed to that teaching. Never stray too far, they told themselves, from established fact. The moralities of the discipline demanded it. In recent times, however, a more daring breed of historians and biographers has tried to escape from that tyranny. There ought, they assert, to be room for the kind of intelligent speculation that comes from empathy with your subject and the play of imagination. 'Conjectural historiography', as one might call it, enables a richer, more colourful picture to emerge than your timid, dry-as-dust practitioners could ever hope to provide – as well as attracting lucrative newspaper serializations.

In 1997, Australian writer Kimberley Cornish published a book called *The Jew of Linz*, from which the *Sunday Times* ran extracts, which broke new ground for this genre. His theme was the life of

the great philosopher Ludwig Wittgenstein. As Hitler explains in
Mein Kampf, his hatred of Jews began with a bad relationship in
his schooldays. But who was this hated schoolmate, 'this boy', as
Cornish puts it, 'who turned Hitler into a killer of six million Jews?'
Although he concedes there is not much to go on in Hitler's book,
it is possible, he says, to make a 'fair bet' that this mysterious figure
was none other than Wittgenstein – a boy just a few days younger
than Hitler, who joined him at the Real Schule in Linz in 1904.
Though there were other Jewish boys at the school, Wittgenstein
fits the bill perfectly. They even had shared interests. Both admired
Wagner; both were good at whistling. 'We face, I think,' Cornish
wrote, 'the astounding possibility that the course of twentieth
century history was radically influenced by a quarrel between two
schoolboys.'

What Hitler went on to do is clear enough. Some of what
Wittgenstein did is more shadowy. As he deploys the forensic tools
of conjectural historiography – 'it is surely possible that...'; 'is it not
striking that?'; 'unavoidably there comes a startling suspicion
that...' and even 'if one lets one's mind drift speculatively...' –
Cornish's mind drifts speculatively to the conclusion that his hatred
of Hitler led Wittgenstein to develop a secret life. Wittgenstein, he
says, was in Cambridge in 1929 at the very same time as Philby,
Burgess and Blunt. Donald Maclean was nearby. All, we now know,
spied for the Russians. 'Of course,' Cornish accepts, 'the mere fact
of their attending Trinity at the same time proves nothing.' Yet
Wittgenstein must have known them through his work, his homo-
sexuality and his membership of the Apostles. 'I do not wish to
labour the point,' Cornish goes on, 'but one has to consider a question that has never been satisfactorily resolved: who was the Soviet
recruiter who created the spy ring?' One hypothesis is that this man
was none other than Ludwig.

The dedicated application of such techniques – the readiness to rely on what another biographer who employs them classes as 'informed likelihoods' – makes it possible to unravel mysteries that have baffled conventional historians for centuries. One of these concerns Attila the Hun. Though much of his life is satisfactorily documented, there's a period between 435 and 439 which remains entirely obscure. Where was he, what was he doing? It seems a fair bet that he was doing what he usually did: moving in with his force of Huns on to other people's territory, killing many and terrorizing the rest, and conducting campaigns of rape, looting and pillage. But where? I do not wish to labour the point, but the answer, my bus journeys through East Anglia will suggest, has been staring us in the face for centuries. Attila the Hun was here, in England. What is even more curious is that this assertion has been made before, but until now the narrow approach of conventional historiography has led it to be largely ignored. The historian Priscius of Parium says that after the Treaty of Margus, Attila went on to rule 'the islands of the ocean'. What islands were these? Most historians now assume they were somewhere in the Baltic. Yet as reputable an authority as the Nobel prizewinner Theodor Mommsen (1817–1903) believed that the evidence pointed to Britain, and specifically, that *this was what Priscius intended to tell us.* (A little burst of italics always helps get the message across, don't you find?) As Kimberley Cornish might say, we face the real possibility that the great and terrible Hun invaded these very islands on a mission that might have changed the entire course of world history – had he not been so valiantly repelled.

My attempt to plot the trail of Attila begins in the decorous Victorian holiday town of Hunstanton – known to locals, significantly you may think, simply as Hunston. It stands on the edge of the Wash just north of King's Lynn and the Queen's most favoured residence,

Sandringham. Like so many resort towns this one developed when the railways came. The dominant local family, the L'Estranges (they later altered the name to Le Strange) commissioned the architect William Butterfield to lay it out in the 1860s, and he did his work well, creating a pattern of greens running down to the sea and shady squares and gardens and pleasant spaces. The Golden Lion hotel and what used to be the town hall superintend the main green. The road running north along the clifftop towards Old Hunstanton comes to a lighthouse, close to which there's a ruined wall with a plaque which explains its origins. It was at this point, it says, that St Edmund, King of East Anglia, landed when he came from Germany to claim the crown bequeathed to him by King Offa.

This is surely, as we conjectural historiographers say, suggestive. What made St Edmund land at this point? Could it be that he knew this sheltered spot had been used for such landings before? Attila, whatever his less desirable tendencies, was a master strategist. Had he set out from Germany to conquer Britain he would never have taken the obvious course of landing on the east coast of Norfolk; he would rather have gone for surprise, as well as for calmer waters, by rounding the headland and landing on the county's west coast. That, it seems fair to deduce, is why this spot was later known as the town of the Hun. And once this truth is accepted, it is easy enough, especially if you can lay your hands on one of those children's books which has terrifying artist's impressions of militant Huns setting out for a morning's rapine and pillage, to imagine Attila's hordes storming up this shore, past the Golden Lion hotel and the old town hall and out of town into the forests of Norfolk.

And where was his destination? Could it have been to the west – Emneth Hungate, near Wisbech? Or directly east – Hunworth, just south of Holt? Arguably, yes: even more arguably, Attila may have been heading for a spot whose name irresistibly seems to suggest that once the great Hun was there – Attlebridge, on the road from Fakenham to Norwich. So now I take the Hunstanton to Fakenham bus, operated by Norfolk Green, which runs one day a week, on Fakenham market day, which is Thursday. It sets off first north into Old Hunstanton, a pleasant cluster of cottages with a pub called the Neptune Inn. The favoured building material round here is a local flintstone which incorporates flashes of orange. The coast turns the corner just out of Old Hunstanton and now my bus runs eastwards, through a string of enticing villages all with the sea behind them. Thornham puts on a parade of particularly glowing cottages and the King's Head pub and some splendid Georgian houses. Then come Titchwell and Brancaster, which was once the Roman Brandonum. The bus is filling up now, and it's clear from the level of chatter that the Fakenham market bus is a mobile social occasion as much as a means of getting to market. It may be the sunshine, but everyone on this bus seems astonishingly cheerful, most of all the driver, who greets even the most tottering ancients with 'hello, young lady'. 'Hello, cheerful,' he says to a scowling middle-aged man, who immediately smiles.

The villages get better and better. Burnham Market – a wide street with greens, one or two splendid houses, a bookshop, a gallery – looks especially browsable. And so through North Creake and South Creake and Sculthorpe and past a huge green with attendant houses to the car park of Fakenham Superbowl, which is where Norfolk Green says goodbye to us, with the driver thanking the passengers even before – according to the pretty custom that has developed since one-man buses came in – we thank him.

You can hear the buzz of Fakenham market long before you arrive there. Above the joyful hubbub there rises the sound of a violin playing traditional English folk tunes, so poignantly that, turning the corner, I almost expect a scene out of Hardy, perhaps with some rapscallion trying to sell his wife. At moments like this it seems as though the England that used to be is with us still. The market has long outgrown the old market place, and here in a yard on the hillside, a traditional English greengrocer is entertaining his clientele with traditional English banter while he wraps them bags full of Belgian strawberries, Spanish lemons, Turkish star ruby grapefruit, Brazilian limes, Italian kiwi fruit, Moroccan tangerines, Israeli dates, Spanish celery, Dutch celeriac, washed Fen mushrooms and Devon swedes. But Fakenham is merely a staging post (as it has always been, though now only one of the coaching inns in the market place is still a hotel). The road towards Attlebridge aligns itself with the river Wensum and stays with it for most of the way. At Foulsham, it noses down a narrow lane with very few passing places into the village – big long church, several desirable houses, and a fish shop which promises frying on Friday. Lenwade is full of signs proclaiming the proximity of the Norfolk turkey king, Bernard Matthews. Beyond, the house and gardens of Weston Park have become a dinosaur centre.

I get off just outside Attlebridge. Even today's intrepid bus drivers are not called upon to take their vehicles down its narrow and twisty streets. There's not a lot now to Attlebridge: a flinty church which looks somehow under-nourished, as if waiting for Bernard Matthews to feed it up, and a road which bounds over the little hills towards Felthorpe. Yet once, it is easy to think, especially if you have your Ladybird book clasped tight in your hot hand, this tranquil scene would have rung with the howls of the invaders and the shrieks of their victims as Attila threw down his improvised bridge over the Wensum, and his Huns stormed across it.

The buses on this road run two hourly, and two hours is a good hour and a half more than you need to drink in the ambience of Attlebridge, so now is the time to forget the Hun for a moment and take the minor road south to the village of Weston Longville, where James Woodforde, later famous for his *Diary of a Country Parson*, lived and wrote from 1776 to 1803. You could not exactly say that his living was easy: there are too many burials, often of quite young parishioners, recorded in the diary, and too many appeals from the destitute. But there seemed to be limitless scope for gargantuan feasting. On 11 December 1787, for instance: 'We had for dinner today a boiled leg of mutton with capers, a couple of Chickens rosted and a Tongue, a Norfolk plain batter pudding, Tripe, Tarts, and some blamange with 4 sorts of cheese. For supper some oysters, a wild Duck rosted, Potatoes rosted, and some cold chicken &c.' His church is still there, with a tribute to him; also the graves of some of the people whom he met on his daily rounds and enjoyed gargantuan feasts with; though the house he lived in has gone, as has the home of the Custances, squires of the village. There's a pub in the village named after him, with a riproaring menu offering such attractions as rabbit, venison, beef, duck, lamb and chicken. The parson might well have ordered the lot.

And what, you may ask, has Parson Woodforde to do with Attila the Hun? Quite a lot, and more than he knew. It is surely suggestive enough to constitute an informed likelihood that the lane which brings you here from the main road at Attlebridge goes on to somewhere called Honingham, which could well, as students of Norfolk dialect would confirm, have transmuted from Hun-ingham. And the parson's diaries make frequent references to friends who lived near enough to his parsonage to call on him at the end of their evening walks. We have here to confront the astonishing fact that the place these people lived in, now gone from the map, was called *Hungate*.

That Attila and his followers had been marching in this direction irresistibly suggests that their target must have been Norwich. The Romans made their headquarters at Caistor, just south of the present city, but that site was abandoned when the last garrison left. The Romans who remained and merged with the British found Norwich – which simply means a situation to the north – a more appropriate spot for settlement than Caistor, which is how the city began. And sure enough, there's a church in the centre of Norwich called St Peter *Hun*gate. Only after leaving his mark at Hungate, one is moved to conclude, would Attila have turned south-west on to a road which led to the greatest city of all.

The First X56 bus is hardly out of Attlebridge before it becomes immersed in the suburbs of Norwich. None of the names here seems suggestive, although some younger and more impetuous conjectural historians might argue that suburb of Hellesdon refers to the hell that Attila created there. The bus from Norwich to Attleborough is given to deviations, venturing into the outskirts of Wymondham but sadly never penetrating the heart of this delicious small town. Like most of the bigger towns on this route, Attleborough is no longer on the route of the A11, though you would hardly think so when trying to cross its roads. This used to be a place famous for turkeys and cider, but today it's another reduced kind of place, no longer the hub of the district that it must have been in its heyday. Its two chief attractions seem to be its church and its Sainsbury's. The Norman tower of the church makes a commanding sight as the traffic gyrates around it, and inside it is light and airy. Here, too, there's persua-sive evidence – well, all right then, the odd hint – that St Edmund, King of East Anglia, must have been well aware that Attila had dom-inated Norfolk before him: on becoming king, Edmund took a year's sabbatical to study at Attleborough, a place no doubt then still full of folk memories of the Huns' reign of terror.

It is early evening now and it takes rather more of an effort than it did back at Attlebridge to imagine the Huns fighting their way through this territory, perhaps cutting down the innocent towns-people in their hundreds in somewhere like Surrogate Street. Yet perhaps there is also an echo of these battles in the name of a minor road, not much more than an alleyway, close to the church: Defiant Precinct. Attila, one may conjecture, would learn the meaning of native defiance soon.

Our next destination now lies in Essex, just outside Saffron Walden. The logical route would be straight on through Thetford and Newmarket and down the A11; an easy choice for Attila but one infuriatingly unprovided for by twenty-first-century bus compa-nies. This route, having treated us to only a tiny taste of richly historic Thetford, the native town of Tom Paine, abandons the A11 and, like it or not, we have to proceed through Bury St Edmunds. Yet this enforced deviation is welcome: it will furnish even more evidence that Attila was here. It's a dim and dismal evening. The driver on route X31 has Radio One playing discreetly, its music interrupted by road reports of ghastly jams on the motorways. The M1, M6 and M42 are all in big trouble, and soon we are warned that Terry and Dave have rung in to say they've been stuck for an hour on the M45. There is something deeply satisfying in bowling along on an almost unimpeded A134 while motorists able to travel on reputedly faster highways are trapped at their wheels in fuming impotence. The effect is so soothing that one almost forgives the X31 for not turning down the lane that would have taken us to the gates of RAF *Hon*ington.

We are on our way now to Bury St Edmunds, named after the saint who, as we now know, copied Attila when he landed in Norfolk, and who gives his name to the town and to the abbey, of which not much apart from the gatehouse remains. For those who love towns, this one is a foretaste of heaven. Outside the Abbey gates is the Abbey square, with the Athenaeum Club and the Angel Hotel and the county offices and elegant town houses ranged around it. For much of the day this space is full of parked cars: you need to be here early or late if they're not to distract from the buildings around them. Along with its grandiose statuary and symbols of fructification, the Corn Exchange in the centre of town parades the inscription: 'The earth is the Lord's and the fullness thereof', and there's plenty of fullness in Bury St Edmunds, from ceremonial buildings such as Robert Adam's town hall to a dozen gorgeous streets. Guildhall Street, in particular. No one designed it, yet here is a perfect harmony. The street has two or three buildings of some distinction, including the old Guildhall, but even the duller ones somehow contribute to the charm of the whole. Walking down from the civic buildings to the foot of the hill and the sadly clumping Catholic church is a treat; walking back up the hill even better. Again, if you're not on the trail of Attila, you'd be mad not to linger here longer. But if you miss the bus that leaves for Haverhill at 9.30, you will have to wait for most of the day before there's another that goes by way of Hundon.

Unlike so many bus stations on this journey, the one at Bury isn't dominated by the big bold ravenous beasts that are First, Arriva and Stagecoach. Local independents still have a lot of the business: Chambers, Neals, Burtons and Symonds of Botesdsale. Ours is a Burton which has the curious habit of uttering what John Aubrey, describing the disappearance of an apparition, called 'a most elodious twang'. It twangs past some rather grand houses: Horringer Manor, Ickworth Hall (now a hotel). There are only three passengers as we twang our way down the A143: no wonder such buses have to be so heavily subsidized. Through Chedburgh it twangs, past an unexpected industrial estate, and then off the main road to Wickhambrook, though unhappily not to a village a little beyond it named Attleton Green, suggestively close to Hundon. There may or may not have been a gory battle at Hundon; on the whole I think not. This is just the sort of spot, with its billowy terrain and huge green views in every direction, where battle-exhausted Huns might have resolved to desert and put down their roots. There is mist on the distant hills, which makes it all the more romantic.

We are picking up passengers now as we close in on Haverhill. The conversation is about flowers, the state of one's busy lizzie compared with the woman next door's, and the imperfections of grown-up children. This features two kinds of indictment. One: why do I never see my son and his children? They never come anywhere near me. Two: why do my son and his children never let me alone? It's always, can you take Rory and Jessica next weekend while Angelique and I jet off to Rome? Refreshing to note that in this age of 'I was like...' that the hallowed introductory expression, 'I said to her, I said...' is still very much alive in west Suffolk.

Haverhill announces itself with decent Victorian terraces, but don't be misled by that. This is a Suffolk town, not much more than a village, that was picked out for London overspill, but was either transformed too much or not quite enough. The High Street, as I hear a man in a coffee shop complaining, has lost its old local flavour; but it hardly sports the range of attractions that Londoners would have been used to. It is one of a class of places that I came, on these journeys, to think of as Peacock towns, which is to say that they're too small for a Debenhams, and the nearest thing they have to a department store is the successful if rarely celebrated discount operator Peacocks. A church in the high street has been transmogrified into an arts centre where films are shown intermittently and Pam Ayres, I see, is due this coming Saturday. There's also an open market, but with none of the buzz of Fakenham and certainly no violins. As for Queen Square, let's hope the Queen never sees it.

And so to the final stage of my bus-powered pursuit of Attila the Hun. The number 59 Hedingham service for Audley End via Saffron Walden begins with a sweep around the edge of the town which does little to flatter Haverhill: great grey blocks are scattered about the place, looking distinctly unSuffolky. Across the county border, in Essex, is Helions Bumpstead: Hell lions' Bumpstead perhaps? This is another collegiate bus, full of people who seem to know each other well. A debate has begun about a house which may or may not be for sale in Stable End and who used to own it. No consensus emerges. And one or two participants clearly don't like their views being challenged. It is not exactly a structured debate, and the driver's duties preclude him playing the much-needed role of Speaker. Now we are into villages the names of which carry more than a hint of military activity: Castle Camps, Shudy Camps. Down one narrow lane we get stuck behind a stationary horse box. Tooting ensues, and slowly, reluctantly, the horse box begins to move, only to find itself balked by a parked car. There is further dissension aboard the bus as to whether the horse box has any chance of passing the car without serious damage to both. Some people seem rather to hope for at least a scrape. The driver, whose judgement is probably better than anyone's, remains stolidly neutral. By easing into the hedge, the horse box vindicates the optimists, and our bus being rather thinner, we know we are safe. The Haverhill crowd have now mostly departed and a Saffron Walden contingent is joining. 'Your bus is late,' an elderly woman complains to the driver. 'I've never seen so much traffic through

Helions Bumpstead,' he tells her. We go over a sizeable pothole. 'Tell Leslie he'd better watch out round here,' someone says to a friend on her mobile. 'It could take out his front suspension.' In just these tones, ploughmen once warned in the pub that several weeks of high winds, frost, sleet and hail, thunder and even perhaps a murrain of frogs might well be on the way.

We come into Saffron Walden past a large green where people are sitting out in the sun, but this being Saffron Walden there are no bikinis, no sun-tops even, and mercifully no gross men in inadequate shorts. You will need to go elsewhere in Essex for those. We see something of Saffron Walden's elegant swooping high street, though too little of the fine square and the entertaining side streets beyond. The shoppers depart, replaced by people heading for Audley End station – some of them, a rare sight on my buses these past two days, possibly not yet twenty. There is quite a long queue to get on, and an elderly man perches on the edge of the step of the bus while a woman in front delves in her purse for her fare. His face is a picture of agony: just look, he seems to be saying, at the pain I am having to suffer because of this female dithering. 'Back giving trouble again?' the driver inquires. 'It's my knees playing up,' says the sufferer. The way he says 'knees' resembles a horn call in Mahler. The bus climbs out of the high street and past the headquarters of Uttlesford district council. The man with the knees has exhausted that topic and is now addressing himself to the iniquities of the law on leasehold. He addresses his complaints to a *soignée* middle-aged woman sitting in front of him, who smiles at him sympathetically but is canny enough to say nothing. The road dips down and crosses the river just short of the A11 near a pub called the Fighting Cocks. Fighting cocks: this is where I recall Attila and have to get off.

This is Uttlesford. There isn't strictly speaking a location called Uttlesford now, but when the present local authority was created they chose the name of an ancient hundred rather than making the surrounding territory accept the apparent suzerainty of Saffron Walden. People often assume that a place name ending in 'ford' relates to the river it crosses. Sometimes it does: Sleaford is on the Slea. But often it doesn't: Oxford is not on the Ox, nor Stafford upon the Staff. Nor does Uttlesford derive from crossing the Uttle. Though I do not wish to labour the point, what we face here is the very real possibility that Uttlesford means the ford of Attila. We shall need our children's book picture of Huns again to create the necessary sense of the numinous here, for the river you have to cross is really more of a stream, easily wadeable by anyone more than 1 ft 6 inches high. Perhaps it rages rather more in the winter. The trees dip deep into the rippling water, festooned here and there with old plastic bags bearing the names of supermarkets. Nearby there's a Second World War pillbox, instigating the thought that these tranquil reaches might once again have taken on high strategic significance had Hitler come to Essex as Attila once did.

And where did the conquering Hun go next? Could it be that having wiped the floor with the opposition at Uttlesford, he marched his forces on to Bishop's Stortford, skirmished with local resistance at a place suggestively called Hunsdon on the road between there and Hoddesdon, where they turned south towards London on the old Roman road; that this brought them to Cheshunt, where a battle then took place in which Attila's hitherto invincible forces, weakened by the desertion of troops who had dropped off to settle and till the land in bucolic places like Hundon, were violently repulsed (Cheshunt, after all, sounds suggestively like Chase-hun-t, wouldn't you say?); that this taste of defeat, an experience to which he was so unaccustomed, made him resolve to quit what Priscius called the islands of the ocean as soon as might conveniently be arranged; and that he subsequently ordered that all record of this humiliation should be destroyed, thus ensuring that this period in his era of conquest became a mystery, as it remained for 1,600 years, until I embarked on these bus journeys?

But all that, of course, is mere speculation.

5

South Woodham Ferrers
Burnham-on-Crouch

BRADWELL-ON-SEA

My plan to divide the county of Essex, and its critics – how the plotlanders were banished from South Woodham Ferrers – my Thursdays-only bus fails to run, although it's a Thursday – snoozy delights of the Burnham waterside – an idyllic ride up the Dengie peninsula amidst evidence of local delinquency – I meet a prince among bus drivers – a seventh-century church outlives a twentieth-century power station – my plan for the division of Essex, revised.

My brief immersion in Saffron Walden and the dishy villages around it brought me back to an existential question that has troubled me for two decades. There is still only one county of Essex although it has long been plain that there ought to be two: the Essex of genteel country towns and thatch and Thaxted and windmills and clapboard and sleepy villages clustered around gorgeous greens; and the Essex of arterial roads and roadhouses and spectacular hairdos and vertiginous cleavages and Basildon and Southend. The more decorous northern county could perhaps be named after one of the early Essex kings, Sigebehrt, who converted it back to Christianity after a pagan lapse. Sigebehrtshire has a very distinguished ring to it. Its capital would be Colchester, one of oldest towns in the land, and once considered greater than London. The other county, along the Thames estuary, could take its name from its modern Boudicca, the combative HRT-powered, more Thatcherite-than-Thatcher-herself former Tory MP for Billericay, Teresa Gorman. I would call it Gormandy.

You could draw a convenient boundary along the line of the ancient road from London to Colchester, which is roughly the dividing line between the very different geologies of these disparate entities: boulder clay in the north-west, London clay for the rest. Since the A12 ring road runs south of it, that would put the present rather disappointing county town, Chelmsford, into Sigebehrtshire. In discussing this proposition from time to time with Essex inhabitants, I have always advanced my case in a spirit of compromise. Wivenhoe, on the university side of Colchester, for instance, which I understand to be a nest of artists and intellectuals, would need to be accommodated in Sigebehrtshire. Even so, my scheme has been met with less than general acclaim. Some people say they would feel trapped in the wrong sort of body. There are people in my proposed Gormandy who would feel more spiritually drawn to my Sigebehrtshire; then there are those who would find Sigebehrtshire discomfitingly snooty and would feel more at home in Gormandy. The famously snooty resort Frinton-on-Sea, for instance, would find itself unpleasingly lodged in Gormandy, which it might resent, though some uncharitable observers have argued that putting Frinton in Gormandy would serve it jolly well right. But one ought on the whole to respect the fears of troubled minorities, so it might be just to redraw the dividing line, taking the line of the A414 rather than the A12 out of Chelmsford and making the boundary line run south of Maldon, a pleasant town on a hilltop whose churches, moot hall and quirky side streets, with the river below, mark it out as Sigebehrtian.

Yet problems persist. What should be done with the Dengie peninsula? What about South Woodham Ferrers, whose present-day townspeople, living in territory once the preserve of plotlanders, tend to inhabit decorous middle-class houses in roads with fey middle-class names like Gandalf's Walk? What about yacht-rich Burnham-on-Crouch? And what, above all, about Bradwell-on-Sea; or as some Sigebehrtians who live there still like to call it, Bradwell-juxta-Mare? How would these places fare if thrust into Gormandy?

South Woodham Ferrers was the scene of a battle in which plot-landers – people living in simple houses, even sometimes in shacks, which quite often they had built themselves – took on the forces of improvement, the enemies of the untidy, and lost. The plotland development started at the end of the nineteenth century when landowners with disappointing returns from their agriculture chopped their estates into slices and sold them in portions: £10 for a patch 200 feet by 20 feet on which you could put your home, shed or hut; £20 for a smallholding. Some landowners specified when they sold that huts, caravans, tents or homes on wheels would not be permitted. That did not prevent them appearing.

Over the years, local authorities tried to regulate these places and tidy them up. The plotlanders fought tenaciously to save both their properties and their way of life. But in 1968, new planning legislation, part of it specifically designed to deal with the problem of plotlands, made it easier for local and central govern-ment to get such places knocked down and replaced by estates that most people thought more proper and decorous. Planners who came to the area to explain what the county council proposed left feeling fortunate to be still alive. 'This is the type of thing Hitler did,' one objector told a hall of 200 angry people, 'it's Nazism.' Turning on the planner, he added: 'If you knock my house down, I'll knock yours down, and the county planning office will come down too. If you come on my land, every blade of grass will be turned red.' The county council promised that no one would suffer and all would be compensated for genuine loss. But that wasn't going to keep them in Woodham Ferrers. The proposed new utopia was going to be rather above their price range. As Dennis Hardy and Colin Ward say in a history of these communities, *Arcadia for All: The Legacy of a Makeshift Landscape*: 'As always the private visions of the relatively poor were sacrificed for those of the relatively affluent.'

A melancholy list of properties scheduled for compulsory purchase duly appeared in the local press. Waters Edge was to go, and The Chalet, Fen Creek, Log Reach, Cosy Corner, Rookery Nook and Creekway, each a home and a garden, which, whatever the world might think of them, was lovingly cherished and could not be replaced by something conventional. In November 1973 a public inquiry was called. It lasted for eighteen days. Passions were high: one of the leading objectors died one morning on his way to attend the inquiry. The dispossessed were told they would learn their fate in three months. In practice they were kept in suspense far longer. But the verdict, as they expected, went in the council's favour.

The plotlanders left, for the most part, quietly. No planner was killed; no blood was spilled on the green grass of South Woodham Ferrers. In place of Cosy Corner and Rookery Nook the county council built what it called a new riverside town. Not a new town in the sense of Basildon or Harlow – vast encampments for families decanted from the East End – but much smaller and more select: a model for such relocations, the county believed. Its style was, in essence, pastiche: mostly pastiche of the buildings of Essex, but some of it pastiche of Dutch domestic architecture, reflecting, its creators maintained, the ancient links between the estuarine county and the other side of the North Sea. The result is a place of one hundred per cent contrivance, nil evolution. There are walk-

ways and squares and little alleys to echo the charm of older towns.
One principal square is flanked by a mysterious wall of vaguely
religious appearance. No clue is allowed as to what happens
behind it. You have to go round to the front to find out. It's the back
of Asda.

Almost everything here has been integrated with almost everything else. The public library is part of the school, and my studies
in South Woodham Ferrers history are repeatedly interrupted by
messages summoning pupils back to their classrooms. It is just a
few days before A-level exams and a cheerful group of students is
engaged in a casual discussion of the nature of transubstantiation.
This takes the form of asking Ashley to tell them about transubstantiation and, while he is at it, about almost everything else.
'Come on, Ashley,' one girl pleads, 'just tell me all the things I ought
to have learned in the past year.' But at this point Ashley is summoned back into the school. Perhaps one of his teachers has come
across some point he did not understand. Will Ashley, one day quite
soon, be named Britain's youngest bishop? Probably not. Given his
fluency, it's more likely he will turn up on television, appearing in
one of those series in which the presenter ponders the world's
great mysteries while wandering through an endless procession of
cloisters and brooding in ominous gateways.

Many sentient architects, I reflect as I make for the bus stop,
would flee South Woodham Ferrers with strangled cries of
'Poundbury'. But I like it, and the people who live there and shop
there look as though they enjoy it too, though the sound of the young
crying 'boring!' can no doubt be heard on occasion. The illusion of
continuity which comes from this kind of pastiche offsets the bleak
feeling you get in so many new towns that these places have no real
roots and no history and therefore, in a deep sense, no real
meaning. In any case, I cleave in these matters to the teaching of

G.K.Chesterton. 'One sun,' he wrote, 'is splendid; six would be only vulgar.' A proliferation of South Woodham Ferrerses would suggest that the nation had taken leave of its senses. But one is entirely acceptable: even pleasing.

The Fords of Althorn bus to Bradwell-on-Sea is due to leave from a lay-by near Asda. My Essex County timetable says it runs on Thursdays only at 2.15. I present myself at the bus stop with fifteen minutes to spare. Sometimes, I have discovered, buses leave early. By 2.45 there's still no sign of it. By 3, I am losing hope. I ring Fords of Althorn. 'Where is your bus to Bradwell-on-Sea?' I enquire. 'It isn't running today,' a courteous woman tells me. 'But it says in my Essex County timetable that it runs on Thursdays,' I whine. 'Ah yes,' she replies sagaciously, 'but it doesn't say it runs every Thursday, does it. It ran last week, and it will run again next week, but it isn't running today. It's alternate weeks only.'And sure enough, there's a line at the bottom of the timetable that I'd somehow missed. *Fortnightly*, it rebukes me.

This is a blow. It seems I shall have to come back next week. But my situation is not after all beyond rescue. If I can get to Burnham-on-Crouch I can pick up a bus for Bradwell; and fortunately that is possible today. Fords of Althorn also run, on those Thursdays when they don't run the Woodham Ferrers to Bradwell route, a Burnham–Southend service. Joining the groups on the upper deck makes one feel a bit of an interloper. This is a regular shopping crowd. These are nearly all elderly people (as I am) and they're overwhelmingly cheerful, vigorously offering rival nominations as to where best to have your tea in Southend, and whether the place that makes the best pot of tea is also the best for a buttered scone; from which a debate develops on the fattening effects of bread pudding. It reminds me of the judgement of Hazlitt. 'You will hear more good things on the outside of a stagecoach from London to Oxford than if you were to pass a twelvemonth with the undergraduates, or heads of colleges, of that famous university.'

Southend accompanies us: all along the route you can see it across the flat meadowlands down to the estuary. Beyond there's a tower which must be across the water in Kent. One man whose verdict I seek is sure it is Sheppey, though a moment later he's equally sure it's the Isle of Grain. The roads are narrow and winding. We deviate through Southminster, the last station on the railway line out of Liverpool Street that also serves South Woodham Ferrers and Burnham. And soon we are entering Burnham, past the church, which is curiously divorced from the town, and the cinema, which has yet to go over to bingo or bike repairs, and into the long main street, where the last of the revellers home from Southend say their fond goodbyes and go their separate ways until Thursday week.

Burnham is all about boats. Edward Heath used to sail there in the days when advisers told him to take up yachting to burnish, or perhaps it was varnish, his image. Political reporters, one of whom I was in those days, used to be assiduously briefed about his various expeditions, with a hint here and there that a rather gorgeous girl would be crewing for him. The words 'he never married' might not after all, it was finely implied, occur in the final line of his obituaries. (But of course, when he died in the summer of 2005, they did.) Whatever drove him to take up this pastime, his enthusiasm was genuine, and from time to time he used to confide his warm affection for Burnham to reporters of the *Maldon Standard*.

Burnham today, as Fords of Althorn deposits me at the clock tower, is awash with a wonderful idleness; as if one could stay here an hour, a day, a week and nothing at all disturbing would happen. There's a long main street with an Adnam's pub where you can sit outside, and a curious clock tower which Norman Scarfe's *Shell Guide to Essex* unkindly but memorably calls 'dumpily reminiscent of the Queen whose jubilee it marks'. There are several openings from this street through to the waterside where you can sit outside any one of several inviting pubs and watch a hundred yachts rocking and lolling gently as they wait for the arrival of their weekend commanders. Here is a life of days on the water, nights at the pubs or still better perhaps the clubs – the Royal Burnham Yacht Club, the Royal Corinthian Yacht Club – for Burnham was once the resort of crowned or at least coroneted heads, a social cut above mere prime ministers. But my too brief sojourn in Burnham-on-Crouch is already over. The Village Link B Arriva bus has parked beside the dumpy memorial, and is ready to take us up the peninsula.

This too is one of those companionable local buses where almost everyone knows almost everyone else and all (except me) are well known to the driver. The bus tacks out through the usual gleaming new speculative estates as if following some intricate knitting pattern. Beyond Southminster, we are in pure country, with meadows away to the west, and out to the east the marshlands of the Dengie peninsula. The sun shines benignly, cattle graze; now and then there's a fleeting village. Inside the bus the talk is of local delinquents. A teenage boy mourns the fate of Greg's cat. It was twenty-six, he says, 'one of the oldest cats in this part of the county', and now it is gone, and in ugly circumstances. And he knows who did it. He thinks it was Lemmy. Lemmy has recently been acting strangely. And not for the first time, either; he used in earlier life to boast of having coated his hamster in oil and fried it. A horse looks over a fence beneath great grave trees. 'I had thought of beating him up,' the boy tells his fellow passengers, 'but I decided instead no longer to talk to him socially.' A kindly woman a seat or two back says he couldn't beat him up now anyway, since Lemmy was arrested last night for breaking and entering. The lad says Vaughan is no better. He and his mate went to the shop at Tillingham, bought a bottle of sherry, drank it, filled the empty bottle with water, returned it saying they didn't want it, and made off with the refund. But the boy is confident that Vaughan and his mate are going to get caught: 'There are not that many people who buy sherry in Tillingham.' Ah, what infamy lurks among these pleasant and peaceable acres! As Sherlock Holmes told his faithful companion: 'It is my belief, Watson, founded upon my experience, that the lowest and vilest alleys of London do not present a more dreadful record of sin than does the smiling and beautiful countryside.'

Although I have never been to Bradwell before I know a few things about it. I know that Tom Driberg, Labour MP, plotter and shameless roué, lived in the former rectory here, which he bought in 1938 when a gossip writer for the *Daily Express*. Though he was better paid in the service of Lord Beaverbrook than he would be later on as an MP, he rarely enjoyed the kind of income he needed to meet his towering aspirations, and could not have bought the house he coveted had he not been involved in an accident and been compensated for a broken nose and a broken knee. This was – still is – a distinguished house with a handsome belvedere, refurbished by Robert Adam for a former rector. In time, this louche figure was joined here by his wife, having made a marriage which astonished a world which knew him as a predatory homosexual. Seeing a picture of Driberg coming away from the marriage ceremony with his not especially prepossessing new spouse on his arm, Winston Churchill is said to have commented, well, buggers can't be choosers. Driberg, of whom there is a wonderfully entertaining biography by Francis Wheen, was by now MP for the local constituency, Maldon, and a figure of some local consequence, especially to himself. He would never countenance the use of the name Bradwell-on-Sea rather than juxta-Mare. At one point he complained to the Assistant Postmaster General, a man called Gammans, that the slot in his nearest pillar box was too small for the envelopes he liked to use for his important communications. The dutiful Gammans arranged that the local postman would stand in the garden of Bradwell Lodge each Sunday and whistle to signal his readiness to collect such outsize envelopes as Driberg might deign to entrust to the post.

There were other attractions, though, to bring me to Bradwell. One is its nuclear power station, built on the site of a wartime airfield, which opened after five years in construction in 1962. It looms up, huge and severe, on the coastline at the northernmost point of the Dengie. But the most inviting prospect of all is the church on the eastern shore, St Peter on the Wall. It was built on the former wall of the old Roman fort Othona, which Rome vacated around the year 410, by King Sigebehrt no less, and presented in 654 to the Bishop St Cedd, one of four brothers all of whom became bishops. (The others were Cynebil, Celin and Chad. We shall meet Chad later on, at Lichfield.) Too small for a growing community, it became a chapel of ease to the church of St Thomas, in the centre of the present village, across the road from Driberg's fine house. For three centuries afterwards it was used as a barn, until the farmer who owned it suggested to the diocese that a building of such importance deserved a better fate. Reconsecrated as a place of worship in 1920, it is still very much in use; some evening services are transferred there from St Thomas's and every July it's a centre of pilgrimage, attracting, it's said, as many as 2,000 people.

By the time we reach Bradwell Square at just gone five I am Arriva's only passenger. 'Which road do I take for the seventh-

century church?' I ask the driver. 'It's down there,' he says, pointing past Driberg's house. 'But' (doubtfully) 'it's a very long
way...Tell you what, though' (restarting his engine) 'I can give you
a lift part of the way.' And he does, until the road becomes too
narrow to take us further. I thank him profusely and ask when the
bus is due to go back down the peninsula. 'Just after six,' he says.
'But you'll never make it.'

The church is still somewhere between a mile and a mile and a
half away. There is time for only a cursory inspection of the site
and the church's exterior. Even to one in a tearing hurry, it seems
a place of healing calmness, with hardly a sound to be heard but
the cry of seabirds. Beyond the church, just as in the days of St Cedd,
there is marshland running down to a huge and empty sea. There
is no one else about except a woman with two young children and
two bounding affectionate labradors. It is just before six when,
panting and gasping, I regain the square in Bradwell village. In a
moment or two, well before time, the bus reappears. 'You made it!'
the driver says disbelievingly. 'Told you I would,' I boast. 'I was just
coming down the lane to look for you,' he tells me. 'This is really
beyond the call of duty,' I say. 'We on the Dengie,' the driver replies,
'like to give satisfaction.'

Even so, I feel cheated. Had Fords of Althorn run their bus weekly
rather than fortnightly, I would have had three hours in Bradwell,
and plenty of time to look at the church with the respect it deserves.
So next day I go back. It's a curious scene: the church, now little
more than its nave, and beside it a sad and nondescript hut whose
shape seems feebly to echo that of the church, as if it were a stunted
grandchild. The interior is simple and modest, with a modern altar
made up of three stones – from Iona, from Lindisfarne, where Cedd
had his education, and Lastingham in North Yorkshire, which was

founded by Cedd, and where, in 664, having retired from St Peter's, he would die of the plague. It is said that when they heard he would never visit them again, a party of thirty people from Bradwell made the arduous journey to Lastingham to pay their respects, where all but one of them emulated the example of Cedd by dying of the plague as well.

The peace and purity of this place are astonishing. The huge distant bulk of the power station follows me all down the lane. Surprisingly, it is not the visual outrage that its bulk seems to threaten. There is something mysterious about it, though belonging to a department of mystery far removed from the mysteries of God and St Cedd. It might be some towering monolith erected for pagan worship. But mercifully – since the timelessness of this place is its essence – St Peter's itself is shielded from it.

This is a glorious morning, and while official notices forbid you to walk straight down to the beach – it's a nature reserve, and a marsh – there's a coastal path along the old sea wall. As I walk northwards towards the turn of the coast a sailing barge appears, one of the old Thames barges, with a huge brown main sail and lesser sails fore and aft, issuing out of the estuary, serenely broaching the sea. Once you've started this walk you cannot stop. The nuclear power station becomes a little clearer with every step; you can now distinguish its separate twin blocks and even begin to count the identical gullies that run down their frontages. Across the water to the north there are clusters of houses and boats. The power station buildings, which I reach in perhaps forty minutes, are silent and seem deserted. The gates are open, but the tourist centre is closed. A woman security guard explains it's no longer in service now that Bradwell is being decommissioned. The station was built for forty years' service; now that term has been served and there is no reprieve.

This walk of perhaps two miles between these two mysterious centres of power has spanned fourteen centuries. And the irony is that it is St Cedd who is still open for business and nuclear power that is shutting its doors. The religion practised here on the Essex coast has survived for all these years and may survive for ever, unless or until some emanation of nuclear power blows us all to bits. Modern technology yields to yet more modern technology while, as the old hymn says, the voice of prayer is never silent, nor dies the sound of praise away, here in the land of St Cedd.

This is a territory which my original plans – my naive and insensitive original plans – for the division of Essex would have awarded to Gormandy. Standing here on this quiet coastland I see that would be an outrage. The church of St Peter, especially since it would not have been here at all but for Sigebehrt's reconversion of Essex, the old sea wall, the Thames barge with its fine brown sail heading out to the sea on a perfect morning, the memorials in the church of St Thomas, the tree-lined quiet of the Bradwell square between the church and the pub – all of these clamour for justice. Gormandy shall not have them. They belong to the blessed patrimony of the saintly King Sigebehrt. That is the resolution I carry with me as I haul on my backpack again, and set off for the coast of Kent.

6

Folkestone — Hythe
Romney Marsh — Rye

WINCHELSEA

Fear of the French in Folkestone – a railway tycoon dreams of
tunnels, even ones that the French might march through –
similar qualms at Hythe – I fail to engage with the numinous on
a bus across Romney Marsh – Rye: its literary distinction, its
vulgar blandishments – the mysterious calm of Winchelsea, now
that the French have stopped knocking it down.

Ensconced in his fourteenth-century castle at Saltwood, a little
inland from Hythe, Alan Clark, Conservative politician, serious military historian, besotted admirer of women at large, and Margaret
Thatcher especially, used to brood on the threat of invasion. The
Channel Tunnel, he believed, was a dangerous piece of folly, a gift
to any intruder set on taking away our national independence. But
the fear of invasion has always haunted this coast. That was why
between 1805 and 1810, on orders from William Pitt, no fewer than
seventy-four defensive towers – Martello towers, they were called,
a name derived from a tower in Corsica which had given the British
problems – were built on the shores of Kent and East Sussex to keep
Napoleon out: the first ones at Folkestone, the largest collection at
Hythe, and the final ones away to the west at Seaford. Today this
coast is patrolled by the number 711 Stagecoach bus from Dover
through Folkestone and Hythe to Rye and Winchelsea, two more
towns that have often lived in fear of the French, and so through to
battered, disconsolate Hastings and its hilltop suburb Silverhill.

Folkestone and Hythe are among those seaboard towns which are frequently talked of in pairs, like Brighton and Hove, Portsmouth and Southsea, Hastings and St Leonards-on-Sea, and Blackpool and Lytham St Anne's. Although in a sense they are married, they often dislike each other. Hove was created to be a class above Brighton (one lives in Brighton, it used to be said; one *resides* in Hove). Folkestone and Hythe, separated by Sandgate – which insists on not being part of either – have for political purposes long been shackled together. And for more than twenty years from 1874, they combined to send to the Commons, sometimes without opposition, one of the most remarkable men ever to sit there; and one, even more remarkably, who, just as he could not contemplate the map of his country without wanting to build railways all over it, could not look at a stretch of water without longing to build a tunnel beneath it. And that, despite Folkestone and Hythe's traditional fear of the French, included the English Channel.

Despite being born in Salford, Edward Watkin, later Sir Edward, was considered a Manchester man. He followed his father into the cotton trade, but his dream was always the railway. He began with the Trent Valley Railway, tried his hand in the US and Canada, then returned as general manager of the Manchester, Sheffield and Lincolnshire. Canada lured him away again as president of its Great Trunk Railway, but the offer of the chairmanship of the MS&L brought him back to England. He added to that the chairmanship of the South Eastern Railway and then the London Metropolitan, in which role he conducted tough, sometimes vicious, and largely counterproductive battles with the chiefs of the District line. A long and thorough biography of him by David Hodgkins is called *The Second Railway King*, putting him next in line to the equally ingenious, flamboyant and ruthless, but markedly less honest, George Hudson of York. It was always Watkin's dream, though it took him most of his life to achieve it, that the MS&L should be linked to London, making it truly national.

Men of lesser imagination challenged him. Bills to authorize the extension were thrown out in Parliament. There was outrage when his projected line into Marylebone was seen as threatening Lord's cricket ground. Even this enterprise, the Great Central, was in Watkin's scheme of things a mere preliminary. One day, he believed, a man would be able to board a Watkin train in Manchester and travel direct to Paris. That this would mean constructing a Channel tunnel made the notion even more succulent. At various times he also dreamed of a tunnel under the Humber, linking his MS&L with Hull and North Yorkshire; of a tunnel linking Scotland with Ireland – likely to help, he claimed, in settling the Irish question; also of a canal through the centre of Ireland to speed up travel by boat to America. But the Channel tunnel was Watkin's most compelling ambition. He became so determined to make a start that he ordered excavations at the spot close to Folkestone he had picked out as the most appropriate – but which, as officials were quick to point out, belonged to the Queen. Watkin was unimpressed with such objections. Attempts to obstruct him were orchestrated, he declared, by his rivals, the Channel Tunnel Company. In the end the Board of Trade was forced to take out an injunction to halt his operations until a Commons committee had considered the matter. But the majority of the committee came out against it, moved, it was thought, by the stalwart objections of the day's most celebrated general, Sir Garnet Wolseley, that once the tunnel was built, enemy troops might soon come thundering gleefully through it.

Sir Edward was, ostensibly, a Liberal, but his parliamentary ambitions had far more to do with promoting his railway and tunnelling interests than with the doctrines of Gladstone. Here was a man, the party whips used to complain, who would vote for anyone or for anything if he thought it would boost the chances of building his tunnel. Having served for four years as Liberal Member for Stockport before being unseated, he offered himself in 1874 to the Liberal Party of Hythe and Folkestone, where he was already well known through his connection with the South Eastern Railway, declaring that though he was liberal in his opinions he was no party man and would vote for anything that in his view conduced to the public good.

Watkin had a close and affectionate relationship with Gladstone, and sometimes took him on trips to agreeable places. One of these was Paris, where they gazed together at the Eiffel Tower, a sight that inspired the great entrepreneur to contemplate building a tower for London much like Eiffel's – only, of course, rather bigger. Eiffel refused his invitation to act as consultant, but Watkin went ahead anyway, at a site at Wembley in Middlesex. His tower was to be 1,159 feet high, with theatres and dance halls and Turkish baths and exhibition halls and restaurants and a big sports complex around it. The French, he firmly intended, were going to be quite insanely envious. But here he miscalculated. Londoners would not make the trek to Wembley, revenues fell well short of expectations, and the project was never completed. In 1907, six years after his death, what had been built of the Watkin tower was pulled down. Yet the site did indeed eventually attract the fame he had hoped for; Wembley stadium was built on the spot where his doomed tower had been.

True to his promise of open-mindedness, the Liberal Member for Hythe and Folkestone so often voted against his own party that some local loyalists sought to remove him, but a rival Liberal who stood against him in 1885 was crushed. The seat, said the *Folkestone Chronicle*, was his as long as he wanted it. Nobody stood against him in 1886 or in 1892. But by then he was well past seventy and his health had begun to decline. Though his lust for exciting new transport adventures persisted, he gave up his railway chairmanships and stood down at the general election of 1895. His second wife Ann died the following year. They had married four years earlier. The bridegroom, whose son and daughter had tried to prevent the marriage, was then seventy-two; the bride, whose five daughters all warmly approved, was seventy-nine. But Watkin was there, in a bath chair, for the opening in 1899 of his long-dreamed-of Great Central line,when the first through train ran from Manchester into Marylebone. His other great dream, the tunnel under the Channel, would not be completed for ninety-five years.

Watkin would be part delighted, part dismayed, with the condition of Folkestone today. The Watkin years were boom years for the resort, not least because his railway made the town accessible to the holiday public – although the visitors it hoped to attract were the better-heeled holiday public, since Folkestone was determined not to be Margate. Some of Watkin's plans to enrich and expand the town were blocked in the interests of resisting tripper invasion by the Earls of Radnor, who owned a great part of it. (The Radnors too, in an age with no ASBOs, employed a policeman to patrol the sea front, carrying a stick with which to beat naughty boys.) But many of the attractions which brought Folkestone prosperity dated from Watkin's day: the lift that still carries you from the Undercliff to the Leas, the pleasure gardens, the Victoria pier. The residential streets at the top of the town retain the elegance the Radnors hoped to preserve. It's a sadder story, though, when you walk down through the old town to the harbour, from where the ferry lines sailed for France until the Chunnel destroyed the service. Watkin's cherished project has not been good for the town. It is Ashford, where it surfaces, not poor marginalized Folkestone, which has prospered from its creation. And yet, in the first decade of the new century, a sense was developing of a town that had taken a turn for the better, helped by the money that Saga, now much its biggest employer, has brought to the town. Further along the sea front once elegant terraces fallen upon bad days are awaiting refurbishment. Marine Crescent was a desperate sight when I was there, but work had begun to make it once more the dignified seaside address that it was in Sir Edward's day.

The number 711 for Hythe runs first through Sandgate, which boasts Saga's flagship pavilion, and quite a distinctive shopping street which includes a Little Theatre and a pub which calls itself, I'm sorry to say, the Providence Inne. H.G. Wells once lived in Sandgate, one of a cluster of late nineteenth-century artists and writers settled along these shores. The sea, having ducked for a while behind the Sandgate shops, reappears to reveal to passengers on the 711 on this sunny morning plump mums and gaily bikinied daughters disporting themselves on the shingle while clusters of seabirds whirl around them.

There are hills ahead, closing in on the sea, and very soon, squeezed between them, is Hythe, a place that as one of the original Cinque Ports (in the days when there really were only five of them) is eager to boast a rather longer history than Folkestone can claim. St Leonard's church, set on the hill, presides benignly over the town. Hythe's main street, punctuated by pubs, some of their windows proclaiming in original lettering their noted ales and fine stouts, is busy and cheerful; there's a quirky 1794 town hall, and enough of the shops have local names, rather than those of familiar chains, to make you feel that this town has escaped the dull homogenization which blights so many in England. Beyond the main street is the military canal, another device to repel Napoleon, constructed in 1805, rudely mocked by Cobbett a few years later: 'Here is a canal made for a length of 30 miles to keep out the French: for those armies who had so often crossed the Rhine and the Danube, were to be kept back by a canal, thirty feet wide at the most.' The Martello towers didn't impress him either: 'I think I have counted upwards of thirty of these ridiculous things, which I dare say cost five, perhaps ten, thousand pounds each, and one of which was, I am told, sold on the coast of Sussex the other day, for two hundred pounds! There is, they say, a chain of these things all the way to Hastings! I dare say they cost millions.' Peaceable rowing boats now occupy the canal, some elegantly propelled, some less so, but on a day as benevolent as this, expertise hardly matters. Beyond, down tranquil terraced streets, is the sea front, once, before the sea receded, a tract that the waters covered: West Parade and Marine Parade, all very warm and still, until you turn back into town up St Leonard's Street, past even more pubs. Yet Hythe has not lost its old fighting spirit. In 1999 a motion was moved at a town meeting that local celebrations of the new millennium should be postponed for a year. The Victorians, the proposer argued, had rightly determined that the twentieth century would not begin until the nineteenth was over, which in their view would not occur until New Year's Eve 1900. Therefore Hythe should refrain from hailing the third millennium until 1 January 2001. Though warned by the mayor that this would leave the town out of step with the rest of the nation (as indeed with the rest of the world) the meeting carried the motion by eleven votes to four.

It is time to rejoin the 711 on its journey across the great marsh. Like some of the streets in town (Barrack Hill, Battery Road, Rampart Road), this next phase of the route has a military presence about it, as the bus traverses the Hythe Ranges, which used to house no fewer than nine of the towers that were meant to defy Napoleon. Then we are back to the sea, with the Romney Hythe and Dymchurch light railway line an intermittent accompaniment. Some gaze, this hot afternoon, out of the windows; others prefer their newspapers. 'Shock at Villager's Beating' (*Kentish Express*). 'Big Cat Sighting – Latest' (*Hythe Herald*). The marsh is an empty place – empty at least in the context of this corner of England where so much is crammed together; a tract of land reclaimed from the sea and made fertile, though a place that was long seen as dangerous, not just because of the threat from France but because of the threat of disease. Those few (says the *Shell Guide*) who lived on the marsh got fever and died. The clergy who watched over the spiritual welfare of the people of the marsh usually lived somewhere healthier. On the main road, houses and bungalows offering B & B proudly proclaim 'No Vacancies', though even in high summer those with rooms to spare seem to outnumber them.

Beyond these sporadic settlements, as the bus turns west after that notorious rotten borough, New Romney, with its pleasant, battered town hall, there are flat and limitless marshes stretching down to places where the number 711 does not venture, presumably because too few potential passengers live there. One is Dungeness, with its nuclear power stations, whose plump towers you see in the distance, and Prospect Cottage where, after being diagnosed HIV-positive, the film-maker Derek Jarman created his now-famous garden. Lydd – one of the two Cinque Ports invited to join the original five (the other was Rye) – has a pleasing high street with a town hall that hints at an importance it no longer enjoys. Thereafter, the 711 enters a ravaged and scrubby landscape with only occasional houses, sometimes a few in a terrace. Swans sail on a stretch of water within an old quarry. There's an oddness about this whole landscape that is better perceived on foot: no place observed from the 711 bus could be described, as the marsh sometimes is, as 'numinous'. 'The world, according to the best geographers,' wrote the Reverend R. H. Barham, rector of Snargate and author of *The Ingoldsby Legends*, 'is divided into Europe, Asia, Africa, America and Romney Marsh.'

The 711 crosses out of Kent into Sussex; and into the heart of the British summer holiday. As the road returns to the sea there's a huge un-numinous car park; the sun on the roofs is so dazzling that one has to avert one's eyes, away to the glistening sea where the surf-boarders are weaving and whirling. Row upon row of caravans signal the imminence of Camber Sands. There are donkey rides, a golf course, and a wonderfully derelict houseboat in its final resting place in somebody's garden. And there, ahead, on its hill, is the ancient, eventful and artistically and intellectually fecund East Sussex town of Rye.

I'm afraid I think Rye is a bit of a tart. That's not to say it isn't an unusually blessed kind of town, with a generous collection of pleasures from the moment you cross the narrow bridge over the brown River Rother at the end of the harbour. There's a web of tightly clustered streets, some of them cobbled. Mermaid Street, the most famous and most photographed, leading up past the Mermaid Tavern, is a wild profusion of flowers in baskets, outrageously picturesque. That's where doubts set in. Is there a street in Britain which runs to more copious floral displays than this one? Doesn't it seem to be trilling: 'Just look at me! Am I not irresistible?' Well, the town is packed with visitors who presumably do not mind, though some of them shake their heads over the price of lunch at the better hotels. One group, I notice, complains about them in French.

Rye's fear of the French is a regular undertone in histories of the town. The French menaced and raided the coast, seized Rye's boats both in peace and war and came close to destroying its fishing. There were constant rumours and fears of invasion. It was famous too as a hotbed of crime, smuggling especially. The notorious Hawkhurst gang was said to have 600 members. 'I found people willing to hear the good word at Rye,' John Wesley recorded in 1773, 'but they would not part with the accursed smuggling.'

But that still left them scope for other crimes too. Down by the station a plaque records a famous murder. In 1742, a butcher called John Breads killed a prominent local man called Alan Grebell. Grebell was the brother-in-law of the mayor. It seemed to be a case of mistaken identity: the mayor himself, James Lamb, who had fined John Breads for giving short weight, was the intended target. The confusion occurred because Grebell, deputizing for Lamb at a town occasion, had borrowed the mayor's cloak. The job of trying Breads fell to the mayor, who ordered his execution. It is part of the charm and comforting continuity of Rye that the town hall notice board when I was there in the summer of 2004 showed that four of the current ten councillors shared the surname Breeds, which is hauntingly close to Breads.

Henry James lived in Rye for eighteen years, until 1916, in a fine house called Lamb House, built by the mayor who tried Breads, and open, some days, to the public. Later the ownership passed to E. F. Benson, always known as Fred, novelist, biographer, archae-ologist, torrential anecdotalist and wry observer of life. Fred was one of the wildly dysfunctional family of Edward Benson, Archbishop of Canterbury. The archbishop's wife, who was also his cousin, to whom he first proposed when she was twelve and married when she was eighteen, was a lesbian. This was nothing like a marriage of equals. 'She was afraid of papa,' her son Arthur wrote later, 'and it must have been terrible to be so near him and his constant displeasure.' I remember reading somewhere that the Bensons kept a parrot. One morning, a visitor calling on Mrs Benson was treated by the parrot to a long and abusive tirade. 'I gather his grace was in good voice this morning,' the visitor exclaimed. Like most of his household, the archbishop suffered severely from depression. The oldest and perhaps most balanced son, Martin, died while a schoolboy at Winchester, of meningitis. The second child, Nellie, died early too, of diphtheria leading to heart failure. But depression, probably manic depression, severely blighted the life of the next in line, Arthur, an academic best known today for writing the words of 'Land of Hope and Glory'. His diaries ran to 180 volumes, even though four years are blank because he was too depressed to write. The next child, Maggie, fell into mental derangement, was removed from the household, and was cared for the rest of her life by kindly people in Wimbledon. The youngest son, Hugh, became an Anglican priest but converted to Catholicism as soon as his father died. An obsessive worker, like his father, but also an obsessive smoker, he died in his early forties.

Rye was Fred's refuge from life. He wrote light social novels, many based on the town. The very popular books which feature Lucia and Mapp are what is usually called a 'thinly disguised' pastiche of life in the borough, which is to say that there's hardly any attempt at concealment. There were also volumes of biography and reminiscence, of which *As We Were* is a very great treat. It is packed with astonishing anecdotes, some vastly embroidered and some possibly invented. 'Inaccuracy,' says a biographer, 'was a Benson failing. Fred was by far the worst, and would shamelessly improvise upon any circumstance or occasion he was relating for the sake of a good story.' He never, as they say, married and his writing suggests a degree of hostility towards women, though less so to boyish ones.

Rye at the top of the hill is very much the town that Henry James and Fred Benson knew. The church of St Mary the Virgin is decorously surrounded by low, sweet upmarket houses. Nearby, next to Simon the Pieman ('the oldest tearoom in Rye'), there is Fletcher's House and Tearooms, named after the Elizabethan dramatist John Fletcher, who was born here, and beyond that, the house where the painter Paul Nash once lived. But other parts of this town are not what they were when James and Benson shopped here. Aladdin's Cave (new stock just arrived) would not have been there; nor Around A Pound; and possibly not even JD's tattoo studios.

Though they're not joined on to each other, Rye and Winchelsea go together. Winchelsea is little more than a mile away on another hill, but this is a different world. Where Rye is throbbing with visitors, Winchelsea is deserted. Where Rye clamours for one's attention, Winchelsea is mysterious and reserved. What goes on behind the walls of these elegant houses? Even my number 711, now two and a quarter hours out of Dover and contemplating the final stage of its journey to Silverhill, feels like a kind of intruder. The best way to look at Winchelsea, while I can still face the climb, is to get off the bus by the Bridge Inn at the foot of the hill. There's a road which runs westwards, parallel with the river. A little way up, you come to one of the old town gates, where you can rest for a while in a little hut and take in the view down towards the river and out to sea. That is where the first Winchelsea stood, until it was overwhelmed by the sea in 1287. 'Old Winchelsea, drowned' it says on the Speed maps. Later the waters retreated, cutting New Winchelsea off from the sea.

The hut is a place of pilgrimage on a summer evening. Steve and Deb were here on 29 September 1999 and carved their names, as had Dennis and Luce in April, seventeen years earlier. And so, through delicious streets of handsome tile-hung houses, with only the whirr of lawnmowers to disturb the dignified stillness, one comes to the climax of this strange, withdrawn and serious place. Where Rye just happened, Winchelsea was meticulously planned: the work of Edward I, or his agents. In the final years of the thirteenth century he laid out plans for a large new town on a grid system, on an unoccupied promontory known until then as Iham. His town was to be divided into thirty-nine squares like a kind of irregular chessboard. Only a fraction – a quarter, perhaps – was ever completed. Rent rolls of 1292 have survived which give the names of its first inhabitants. They are listed in a history of the town by its then town clerk, Malcolm Pratt: Sander de Brokeyelong, Walter Spytewymbel, Stephen Blaunchpain, Wymarch Piggesteil, William Halfhering. The church, dedicated to St Thomas the Martyr, was designed as the centrepiece, but it too is incomplete. Five times within 200 years it was burned and extensively damaged by French invaders. Eventually, Winchelsea gave up trying to restore it: perhaps half of the original stands there now. Within are several fine memorials, particularly the sumptuous commemoration of Gervase Alard, first admiral of the Cinque Ports. Above him are carved heads of Edward I and his second wife, Margaret of France. Outside the church is a tree under which John Wesley preached his last open air sermon – or rather a replacement; the original tree has gone. And nearby is the town museum – closed for lunch when I approach it, but the curator turns back, unlocks it again, courteously ushers me in, patiently postponing his lunch until I have done. Among the artefacts are memorials of Winchelsea's municipal history, for this was a borough, and a rotten borough at that, returning two MPs.

Spike Milligan lived at Udimore, just outside Winchelsea, in a house which he used to complain was horribly ugly. He is buried in St Thomas's churchyard. For some time the grave had no head-stone. Spike had often said he wanted his tombstone to carry the inscription 'I told you I was ill', and after protracted negotiations the Chichester diocese gave permission for these words to be used – but only if they were given in Gaelic. The actress Ellen Terry had a home here too. It feels like the sort of place to which one might come to escape from celebrity-worship. Winchelsea would give you a courteous nod rather than clamouring for your autograph. They don't go in for excessive public display in Winchelsea. There's no great recourse to hanging baskets of flowers. Everything feels calm and dispassionate. I imagine they've even forgiven the French.

7

WITLEY

The ghastly deaths of two Surrey entrepreneurs – the
Universal Provider, a benefactor famed for his meanness –
contentment among the elderly in the village his riches
created, except when buses run late – a delinquent hermit
and a miserly Midas along the roaring A3 – exploring the
meaning of 'Godalming' – the Croesus of Witley: his opulence,
downfall and death.

My journey though George Gissing's favourite county, and one of
mine too, is linked with the lives of two grand entrepreneurs, each
of whom built an impressive commercial empire and died a
sudden, violent death. It takes me from Whiteley village in the
ruriburbian expanses of north-west Surrey, to Witley, in its deepest
rural south-west. Whiteley village is named for William Whiteley,
creator of London's first great department store. If you walk
through the ornamental gates and up the long drive off the road that
runs south-west from Hersham, past the lake with willows fringing
the water and the cricket ground and the bowling green and the hospital and the chapel, you will come to his statue: a modest unshowy
affair, crowned by a figure representing industry. The dedication
says: 'This monument is erected in memory of William Whiteley of
Westbourne Grove Queen's Road in the county of London esquire
by whose munificent bequest this park was purchased and these
cottage homes were built for the comfort of old age and as an

encouragement for others to do likewise. Blessed the man that provideth for the sick and needy – Psalm XLI.' Understandably, given the lurid circumstances in which he died, it does not go on to quote the words that come next in this psalm: 'The Lord will deliver him in time of trouble. The Lord will preserve him and keep him alive.'

The back of the monument has a plaque which gives some account of Whiteley – an edited account, it needs to be said, for there were aspects of Whiteley's life unsuited to be displayed on memorials. He was born, it says, at Agbrigg, Yorks, in September 1831, educated at Pontefract, and apprenticed at the age of sixteen to a Wakefield draper. When he went to London in 1851 to see the Great Exhibition, the busy life of the metropolis attracted him. He spent ten years of thrift and constant study with a City firm and then started a business of his own, at 63 Westbourne Grove. Before very long, he had won for himself the name of the 'Universal Provider', and for his business, a worldwide reputation. He was the pioneer of the great London retail stores of the nineteenth and twentieth centuries. He died in London on 24 January 1907.

There are not many places in Britain named after their founders. Porthmadog on the Welsh coast was the creation of an entrepreneur and MP called William Maddock; Leverburgh in Scotland was Obbe before the Lancastrian industrialist William Lever acquired it; while Bognor came close to being called Hothamton, after Sir Richard Hotham, who after he lost his seat in the Commons, went off to the coast and created it as a resort. Whiteley did not create Whiteley: he simply made the money which furnished a big enough legacy to enable his trustees to build it, ensure that it fulfilled his requirements, and perpetuate his name.

In the years when he was painstakingly piecing together his great pioneering stores off the Bayswater Road, adding property acquisitions together and alarming and undermining his competitors by pruning his prices and perpetually broadening the range of the products he offered, his reputation was hardly that of a generous benefactor. He was far better known for what his memorial discreetly calls thrift and what others considered rank meanness. In the 1880s his shops suffered a series of fires. The first, on the night of 15 November 1882, was followed by another on Boxing Day morning. A third broke out in April 1884, a fourth in June the following year, a fifth in 1887 while he was away in Ostend, and a sixth, much the most disastrous, with people buried among the ruins, on 6 August 1887.

You didn't have to be William Whiteley to suspect this was more than coincidence, and his reputation ensured that there wasn't a shortage of suspects. Could it be the competitors, small tradesmen in and around Westbourne Grove, whom Whiteley's had blighted and even put out of business? Or could it be the work of people whom this autocrat had entrapped in the petty litigation which seemed so much to his taste? Or could it – and this was by far the most prevalent theory – be the work of some of the employees he had underpaid, ill used, sacked for apparently minor offences and quite often gone on to prosecute? 'His whole system is one of slave driving from top to bottom,' one malcontent told the *Pall Mall Gazette*. The warm and welcoming smile of 'the Universal Provider' when he stood at his door to welcome the nobility and gentry switched off once he said goodbye to his rich customers. And even they cannot have loved him as much as he thought: when he put his portrait on sale, only four copies sold.

As he moved into his sixties Whiteley's energy showed no sign of decline. His eye for an acquisition or a new line of business remained undimmed. And then on 24 January 1907, a man arrived at his headquarters at Porchester Terrace, demanding to see the boss. He claimed to have a message from Sir George Lewis, Whiteley's solicitor (and the Queen's). When Whiteley returned they were closeted together for half an hour, at which point Whiteley came out of his office, apparently very upset, and asked for the police to be called. He refused, he said, to continue the conversation. 'Then you are a dead man, Mr Whiteley,' the visitor said, and he pulled out a gun and shot him dead.

The name of his assailant was Horace Rayner. He was convinced that Whiteley was his real father. Richard Lambert, who published the first biography of Whiteley – *The Universal Provider* – in 1938, thought he might have been right. But Linda Stratmann, whose book *Whiteley's Folly – the Life and Death of a Salesman* was published in 2004, denies it, drawing on evidence Lambert could not have seen. In 1867, at the age of thirty-five, Whiteley had married one of his shopgirls, Harriet Hill, who was just twenty-two. Four children were very soon born. But his energies, prodigious as they were, were not confined to business. They took him on weekend trips to Brighton with a friend called George Rayner. On one of these predatory expeditions they picked up two sisters called Emily and Louise, a plasterer's daughters from London. Rayner took a particular fancy to Emily, and soon they were living together. A son was born, whom they called Horace. Whiteley, meanwhile, had installed Louise in a hideout in Brighton, where he lavished presents on her, tried to improve her, and even took her advice on business affairs. In time, Mrs Whiteley found out about Louise, left the family home at Finchley and settled in Folkestone. Divorce proceedings were stalled in favour of a judicial separation.

Rayner, meanwhile, had begun to have doubts about Whiteley and Emily. He came to believe that Horace was not his child, but a son with whom the 'Universal Provider' must have provided her. Horace came to share this suspicion, all the more so since he had met the man he thought was his father and admired his success and power. In 1888, Whiteley and George Rayner fell out. Whiteley felt Rayner was growing too close to Louise. Both couples split up: Horace chose to live with his father, where the Universal Provider's true nature and Horace's true provenance were no doubt discussed at length.

By 1907, when he called at Whiteley's office, Horace was in deep financial distress. A series of enterprises on which he'd embarked had failed. He was married with two young children and a third on the way, but was living apart in a hostel. On 24 January he had come in despair to Whiteley, in the hope that his always unlikely dream of salvation might be made to come true. But the man he believed was his father, he told the jury at his subsequent trial, had been cold and forbidding, not even moved when he described the plight of his wife and children. If he needed help, Whiteley told him, he should try the Salvation Army.

When the trial of Horace Rayner opened at the Old Bailey, he pleaded not guilty. The only real issue before the court was his mental state, but medical witnesses closed down that line of defence. The jury took just ten minutes to find him guilty. The judge, Lord Alverstone, sentencing him to death, entreated him 'most earnestly to spend the time which may be allowed to you in earnest communion with your maker'. A wave of public sympathy followed, which suggested that some at least were convinced that Whiteley had got his deserts. Petitions were organized. Large sums were raised for Rayner's wife and young family, and the Home Secretary, Herbert Gladstone, recommended a reprieve. The sentence was reduced to life imprisonment. Horace Rayner was sent to Parkhurst. He was let out after twelve years.

William Whiteley was given a lavish funeral and buried at Christ Church, Lancaster Gate. He left more than £1 million – about £60 million today. His trustees were told to spend as near as they could to £1 million to found, provide and maintain Whiteley Homes for the aged poor – women over sixty, men over sixty-five. The bequest was not confined, as is sometimes assumed, to his former employees. As Linda Stratmann points out, Whiteley was extremely specific about what he required. The buildings must be of good and substantial character and of plain and useful design. Those living there must be 'persons of good character and sound mind and not affected by any infectious or contagious disease, and not having been convicted of any criminal offence'. The trustees sought to vary his terms by building on several sites rather than one, but his sons objected and the case came to court, where in February 1910 Mr Justice Eve ruled in their favour. Whiteley had wanted a single site, and his wishes must be respected. 'I think it is impossible,' said the judge, 'to read the will without coming to the conclusion that the testator was a man of strong individuality, the nature of whose charitable dispositions was, in part, determined by his wish therewith to identify his personality, and thereby to perpetuate his memory.' And clearly one Whiteley village could do that – does indeed now do that – as a scatter of them could not.

Some 500 elderly people make their homes in the village now, in the pretty and various cottages designed, to ensure diversity, by several different architects. Many have heard of the place through advertisements placed in magazines such as *The Lady*. A small group of women over sixty, mostly well over sixty, who are waiting today for the Staines to Guildford shoppers' bus, Tuesdays and Fridays only, delight in the place. Theirs seems to be a state of contentment rarely found in their age group. Their thoughts about the bus service, though, are rather less charitable. Two weeks ago, they complain, the bus didn't turn up at all (a contention I could confirm, since I'd waited in vain for it too). But this week it does, to a tiny ironic cheer and some genial ribbing of the driver.

The route through Surrey takes us into a world which Whiteley's poor oppressed shop staff would only have known about through the occasional taking of orders from the kind of customer privileged enough to live here. There are one or two great estates along the roaring A3. At the roundabout where we join it are the old gates of Painshill Park, rescued from dereliction in the 1990s by the Painshill Trust and now reopened to give its visitors a taste of what an ingenious and enlightened eighteenth-century aristocrat could do with his money. As the bus speeds down towards the M25 you can just catch sight of the gothic tower which Charles Hamilton, ninth son and fourteenth child of the sixth earl of Abercorn, made the highest focal point of his pleasure ground on the eastern side of the road. Hamilton also found room for that favourite conceit of the eighteenth-century lord, a hermitage – although the hermit whom he installed for this one didn't last long; he was found three weeks or so into his service rather the worse for wear in a pub down the road.

Soon after, on the western side, the shoppers' bus passes the severe brick walls of Sutton Place, once the home of John Paul Getty, a man infected, his detractors say, by a Whiteleyesque meanness, with his lavish displays of priceless possessions and a payphone for use by his visitors. The house is now owned by a trust and can be visited, the website says, by arrangement with Mrs Tupper. At Guildford bus station, the Whiteley contingent disperses with a warning to be back in good time for the trip home. The driver, as I leave the bus, sighs heavily, as if he had taken the rebukes of the Whiteley villagers seriously. But he tells me, when I sympathize, that compared to his previous job, driving in central London, this run is really enjoyable: indeed, he is happy to commute from

Ealing to Staines, where the shoppers' bus starts, to do it. So much less tension, so much less aggravation... But he has to cut the conversation short, since he's now required to transform his bus into the number 29 service to Woking.

And so to the former kingdom of my second famous and opulent but doomed entrepreneur, Whitaker Wright, who by backing his judgement made fortunes out of the mining industry, but in the end, fatally, gambled too often. There are two routes from Guildford to Witley, the 70 to Midhurst and the 71 to Hindhead. The 71 passes close to the churchyard where Wright is buried; the 70 runs past the great tract of land he bought in which to site his magnificent palace. My number 71 runs out on the old Portsmouth road, past the College of Law at Braboeuf Manor, and the Les Caves de Pyrene wine park, through decorous suburban developments which foster the popular wrongheaded view of Surrey, offering no view to make you gasp and few even to make you admire. The villages we first come to are a mixture of both kinds of Surrey: a linear green at Peasmarsh, rather too much ribbon development at Milford. But our driver, decidely grumpy at Guildford, seems to be cheering up. The reason is his conversation with a man who has come aboard bemoaning England's test match performance against South Africa and the catch that the captain (Nasser Hussain) has unaccountably dropped. (This is the summer of 2003.) A splendid old moan about falling standards ensues. 'What a disaster!' the driver exults. 'Yes, what a disaster!' the passenger enthusiastically responds. 'Why don't they bring back Maurice Leyland?'

I am one of the few aboard this bus who would have seen Maurice Leyland, a Yorkshire and England batsman who made a century in the 1938 'timeless test' when Len Hutton assembled his then record score of 364, and was still a staple part of the Yorkshire side in the late 1940s. What is more, I happen to know that another member of the same post-war Yorkshire eleven, the batsman-wicket-keeper Paul Gibb, a good enough cricketer to have made a century in his first game for Yorkshire and another century on his debut for England, ended his days driving buses in Guildford, usually the 273 Alder Valley service to Shamley Green. He died while booking in for an early shift at the garage. It seems wiser, though, not to reveal this information. 'Tell you what,' says the jolly, rubicund passenger, 'his bat [they are talking of the South African captain Graeme Smith] seems three times wider than any of our batsmen's!' Beside me, I notice, a man in a cap is reading *El Pais*.

By now we are moving – just – through the narrow and cluttered main street of Godalming, the sort of affluent town where the foreign papers sell in abundance, and not just to au pairs. What a strange name it is, this Godalming. There are many such participles scattered around the land – Mucking, Bocking, Fobbing in Essex alone – some of them wondrous strange, suggesting all kinds of activity, some of them mildly indecent. I once rode on a train to Sheffield which had a party of Swedes on board. Mostly they sat in Scandinavian taciturnity, possibly even depression, but when we came into Kettering they became quite exuberant. 'Kettering!' they cried to each other in Swedish: I guess that what they said next must have meant: 'What is this kettering? How does one do it?' Godalming, I guess, is something you do in church, possibly involving incense.

But at length, though a little late, we are out on the open road, and soon we are into Witley. Here, by a pub called the Star, the two routes divide. The 71 goes on past George Eliot Gardens (she lived nearby, in a house called The Heights) into the heart of the village, a place that was once a lure for artists and intellectuals, gathered around the popular if not always critically acclaimed painter of sentimen-

tal English countryside scenes, Myles Birkett Foster. Tennyson had
a place down the road, just over the county boundary, in Sussex. The
street is full of pleasant and sometimes distinguished tile-hung cottages, some marked as buildings of historical interest and others not
far behind. On a gentle lane to the west stands the church of All
Saints, with a turrety tower. Everything about this place suggests
prosperity. 'Witley fair is expected to have made about £9,000,' says
a notice. 'Christine Parrott is holding some items of lost property
from the fair, including one very expensive item left in the tea tent.'
Very expensive items left in the tea tent! That sounds like the world
of Whitaker Wright.

On 30 January 1904, a day of harsh east wind and driving rain, a
melancholy procession arrived at the gates of this church. At its
head was the glass hearse which had brought the body of Whitaker
Wright down the narrow wooded lanes from his palatial home, Lea
Park, two miles away down the road which the number 70 takes, in
the hamlet of Brook. The first coach behind it carried his son and
his two teenage daughters; the fourth brought housemaids from
the estate. Villagers lined the route all the way to All Saints, where
some 500 more were waiting for the service to begin in the churchyard. The church itself could not be used, because of the
circumstances in which the famous financier had died. The facts
of Wright's life, unlike those of his death, are difficult to disentangle from the fictions, some of which were Wright's own invention.
Though people often assumed from the way he spoke that Wright
was American, he was (probably) born and grew up in Cheshire,
trained for the Methodist ministry, and crossed the Atlantic to seek
his fortune when the death of his father left the family without
resources. Beginning as an assayer, he was shrewd and daring
enough to seize on the opportunities of the mining boom, and his

speculations brought him £200,000 – around £10 million today – within ten years. He returned to England in 1889 with a beautiful American wife, and set about building a new business empire.

This time it was the Australian gold boom that looked ripe for exploitation. Wright created a network of companies whose integrity seemed to be guaranteed by the eminent men he recruited to serve on his board. With his record as an entrepreneur and such eminent figures as Lord Loch, former high commissioner to South Africa, and the Marquess of Dufferin and Ava, former governor-general of Canada and viceroy of India, on his letterheads, the success of his British and American Corporation, the Standard Exploration Company and the London and Globe Finance Corporation seemed assured.

Any doubts that might have remained about his magical touch with money were swept aside by the lavishness of his private life. A grand mansion in Park Lane, right next door to Lord Londonderry's. A racing yacht called the *Sybarita*. Wildly expensive parties, attracting the cream of London society... The impression of almost unlimited riches was further confirmed by his purchase of several separate estates close to Witley to form his new Xanadu at Lea Park, creating a tract of land so extensive it was said he could walk to Haslemere station without ever leaving his property. Bought for £250,000 (around £12 million today), it cost him at least £400,000 more to develop and refurbish. Hills were levelled and new hills created. A theatre and a glorious ballroom were built. A vast lake, complete with a boathouse commissioned from Lutyens, was designed as a centrepiece. Beneath it, reached by tunnels, was a smoking room in the form of an underwater conservatory, so that as they smoked his guests could watch fish, or sometimes even swimmers, disporting themselves overhead. A further tunnel led to an artificial island where, on summer afternoons, tea could be taken. There was statuary brought from Italy, and expensive paintings arrived to adorn the walls. There was stabling enough for fifty horses. Some of the local roads, newspapers said, had to be lowered so that massive blocks of marble needed for his creation could be carried under the bridges. The message of all this activity, public and private, was irresistible. 'For a time,' said the *Daily Telegraph*, 'everything he touched turned – or seemed to turn – to gold. The name of Whitaker Wright became a synonym for success and magnificence.'

But the economic climate grew harsher, and that, along with Wright's decision to commit substantial resources to the new underground railway from Baker Street to Waterloo – a project in which the railway titan of one of my previous journeys, Edward Watkin, was also involved – began to throw up results which would not look so good on the balance sheet. As he sought to redeem himself, Wright's speculations grew wilder and his subterfuges more dishonest. Figures were written into the books that would prove to be pure invention. In the end, even Wright's fabled ingenuity could not cope with the scale of the losses; and three days after Christmas in 1900 his empire collapsed. Optimistic and exuberant as always, he talked of a reconstruction to minimize the losses of those who had entrusted their fortunes to him. But that, like much in his life, was fantasy. Gross assets he valued at £7 million were found to be worth £1.5 million at most. Some of those who had lost huge sums in the crash pressed for a prosecution, but the government's law officers said they could find no way to proceed. Wright's unfortunate victims, though, would not accept defeat, and in March they persuaded Mr Justice Buckley to issue a warrant for his arrest.

Wright had by now left the country, first for Paris and then for New York. With his niece Florence Browne he had booked one of the best suites on the French Transatlantic company's boat *La Lorraine*. But their flight had been detected and a 'Wanted' notice issued. When the boat docked at New York, the police were waiting to welcome him. He was taken away to prison and threatened with extradition, which he vowed to resist. Then quite suddenly he agreed to go home and face trial. The case came to court in January 1904. With characteristic confidence Wright maintained he had done nothing wrong, and the crash was entirely due to the schemings of his enemies in the City. 'I am sorry we ever set eyes on England or planted our feet on English soil,' his wife told the *Daily Mail*; after which, 'with a queenly sweep of the trailing skirt of her blue silk gown, she added: "Ah, but he will clear himself. I know he will."'

So sure did Wright seem that the only outcome must be acquittal that the villagers of Witley arranged a torchlight procession with music by the Mouse Hill Band to celebrate his return. His mood in court remained buoyant until in the final stages he was subjected to a lethal cross-examination by one of the day's great advocates, Rufus Issacs. By the end of their exchanges his defence had been shot to pieces. The jury took only forty-five minutes to convict him on twenty-four counts connected with the falsification of balance sheets. 'I do not think I have any option,' Mr Justice Bigham told him, 'but to visit you with the severest punishment which the act permits, and it is that you go to penal servitude for seven years.' 'My lord,' Wright replied, 'all I have to say is that I am as innocent as any person in this court of any intention to deceive or defraud the shareholders.' But the sentence cannot have surprised him. In the closing hours of the trial, he was doodling on a note pad the letters WW, the word 'intent', and the Roman numeral VII.

He was allowed to wait in an anteroom, before his conveyance to prison, with his solicitor George Lewis, who was William Whiteley's solicitor too, and a friend called Eyre who had stood bail for him. Two court officials were present. Wright's mood appeared, the inquest was later told, to be buoyant once again. He took off his watch and chain and gave them to Eyre, saying (in a sentence that took on much greater significance later) that he wouldn't need them where he was going. He asked for a cigar, and puffed at it once or twice. Then his appearance changed and he staggered and fell. Within a matter of minutes, Wright was dead. Waiting reporters were told that he had probably suffered a fit of apoplexy, and that it was how it appeared in some newspapers next morning. The truth came out at the inquest. Wright had asked to be taken to a 'private room' – presumably the lavatory. How exactly he took the poison was not quite clear: he probably concealed it under his tongue and swallowed it back in the room with a sip of water. He had measured his dose with his usual extravagance: it was enough, the coroner was told by a medical witness, to kill several men. Every organ in the body, a pathologist testified, emitted the unmistakable smell of prussic acid. When the body was searched, a silver-plated gun with six chambers loaded was found in his pocket. Whitaker Wright never did things by halves.

On the morning of the funeral, the gates of Lea Park were opened to villagers to come and pay their respects. Reporters wrote in their national newspapers that people in Witley seemed to have nothing but good to say of their lost local hero. In the graveyard later, the vicar led the villagers in Psalm 143: 'Hear my prayer, O Lord; give ear to my supplications...and enter not into judgment with thy servant; for in thy sight shall no man living be justified.' The grave is an unexpectedly modest affair. Also buried there is his wife Anna Edith, who outlived him by twenty-seven years.

In October 1952 a fire broke out in Wright's great ballroom which swiftly destroyed the house. Lea Park is now Witley Park, a conference centre. If you take the 70 bus and walk down a lane called Lea Coach Road, you will find what are now the main gates. As I stood there, doing no more than contemplating them and musing on the fate of Whitaker Wright, a car emerged whose driver asked 'Can I help you?' in the tone in which people make that inquiry when they think you are up to no good. Even if you make an official request, they won't let you in unless you are attending one of their conferences, and you only do that if you work for an organization that is able to afford their ambitious prices. I cannot afford to pay their ambitious prices. Nor, I resolve, shall I stand at their gates begging humbly, even obsequiously, for admission. I think on the whole I would much rather go to Slough.

8

BASINGSTOKE

Towns that are commonly vilified – redeeming features of
Slough – how, though a royal town, Windsor is forced to accept
subordination to Slough – redeeming features of Staines, also
routinely vilified – I ride through affluent country to Camberley
with the boyfriend of a dancer from Billericay – Basingstoke is
also routinely vilified, but does rather deserve it.

It didn't have to be Slough. There are other names that might have
been chosen. Why didn't they get a second opinion? Bunyan's
Slough, in *A Pilgrim's Progress*, was a Slough of Despond: 'this miry
Slough', Christian is told by a man called Help, 'is such a place as
cannot be mended; it is the descent whither the scum and filth that
attends conviction for sin doth continually run, and therefore is it
called the Slough of Despond'. As you emerge from its dingy, mono-
lithic late twentieth-century bus station on to its raging A4 relief
road, with its bumper to bumper car parks, present-day Slough
feels like a place of despond too. It is one of those British towns
which people most like to sneer at – and did so long before
Betjeman prayed for German bombs to come and fall on it. And
though certainly it's no beauty spot, one can't help feeling that,
along with some other frequently vilified towns, it suffers partly
because of its name. Surbiton, always good for a knowing laugh in
a drawing-room comedy, is a case in point. There was a time when
the habit of sneering at Surbiton seemed to be fading, but then

came the BBC series *The Good Life*, and the British began to giggle at Surbiton all over again. Most of those who sneer will never have been there. They imagine a place of primped-up, dried-up, buttoned-up lace-curtained respectability. When they laugh at Surbiton, they're really mocking suburbia. What they subliminally hear is Suburbiton. Had they been there, they would know that most of it was extremely pleasant to live in, with wide avenues, shady trees, a fair profusion of pubs, and the soft summer sound of the back-and-forth pat of tennis ball over net.

But because of the name, none of this fits the image. Surbiton was once called South Barton, and if they'd had any sense they'd have kept it that way. Likewise Slough, where previously separate hamlets merged into a single entity, could have opted for Upton-cum-Chalvey or later for Upton Royal, but settled for Slough instead. Would Betjeman, however much he loathed the place, have blighted it for ever by writing: 'Come, friendly bombs and fall on Upton-cum-Chalvey'? Of course not.

The road to Slough was paved with good intentions. The road to the west enriched and expanded it first, as a coaching town. Then came the railway, Brunel's line from Paddington out to Bristol – steering through Slough because Eton College would not allow it on to its land – swelling the population and tempting in entrepreneurs like the Ellimans, makers of a world-famous embrocation that was publicly endorsed by Queen Victoria. It became the home town of Horlicks, too, an operation begun in the Wisconsin town of Racine which reached Slough in 1906.Vast areas were taken over during the First World War to accommodate military supplies. When the war was over and the country was drifting deeper into depression, Slough seemed an ideal place to house modern factories bringing jobs and hope to the unemployed, not just from the local area but in many cases from Wales – so much so that it developed a name for its male voice choirs. Forester Mars, who brought the world the Mars bar, built his first English factory here in 1932. Industrialization and immigration helped make it the biggest town in Buckinghamshire. If, as Betjeman moaned, there wasn't grass to graze a cow any longer, this was why.

It was too late now to call the place Upton Royal, as a group of concerned citizens had proposed back in 1870. The once lively and pleasant Upton-cum-Chalvey high road was now subsumed in a place which owed its name to conditions much like the ones into which Bunyan's Christian had blundered, or which Shakespeare evoked ('Run away...for so soon as I came beyond Eton, they threw me off...in a slough of mire; and set spurs and away, like three German devils, three Doctor Faustuses.' Bardolph, in *The Merry Wives of Windsor*, Act IV, scene 5). In 1900, once pre-eminent Upton ceased to be a civil parish. It's still a distinctive part of the town even so, and much the most distinguished. 'An almost perfect Norman church,' David Watkin says of St Lawrence in his *Shell Guide to Buckinghamshire*, written before Slough was detached from Bucks and thrust into Berkshire. Behind the church is Upton Court, a medieval manor house, harmoniously extended in 1988 and housing the headquarters of the *Slough and Windsor Observer*. A frieze within carries a legend, in Latin, which says: 'The man who pursues after pleasure will find grief for himself, but the huntsman urges me to pursue after truthfulness...' – a very proper inscription for a newspaper office.

The church of St Lawrence was locked when I went there, but the churchyard made up for that. It has often been claimed in Slough that Thomas Gray wrote his elegy here, rather than down the road in pushy Stoke Poges. The graveyard here, it is argued, answers better to the description than the one at Stoke: it has much the more impressive mantle of ivy. And certainly the graveyard has a haunting clutch of epitaphs and memorials. George, eldest son of Edward Purser, died on 2 July 1860:

A sudden change, he of a moment fell
No time allowed to bid his friends farewell.
Tis nothing strange. Death's summons comes to all.
Reader, prepare, tomorrow thou may'st fall.

There is said to be a stone here carrying the rebukeful message: 'praise on tombs doth but ambition feed'; and another which honours Sarah Brampton, spinster, of Eton, 'who dared to be just in the reign of George the Second'; but I could not find them.

And so to the centre of town, much ravaged by 'improvements', whole streets stopped up or supplanted with the understandable, indeed laudable, ambition of giving the place a centre which would keep shoppers there rather than having them bus off somewhere else. 'The whole of Curzon Street, most of Mackenzie Street, the Crown Inn, the Methodist Hall, and many many more locally known and loved buildings were demolished to be replaced by new shopping centres...and a rather bleak [too kind: repulsively bleak, I would say] widened Wellington Street with its roundabouts and new approaches from the west and east,' laments one local historian.

The high street is closed to traffic, but the road that replaced it is so close into the town as to be almost inescapable. The shops in the high street and particularly those in the shopping mall (this one is called Queensmere) are just the same shops you find in shopping malls everywhere, with hardly a hint that shopkeeping can be local as well as national. It's no better, no worse than most such creations, and the customers seem contented enough. The most encouraging place in the centre of Slough is the library, built in

1972: spacious and bright and airy and blessed with a local studies collection reflecting the fact that the abolition of Berkshire has allowed the old county's collection of books and papers relating to Slough to be congregated here.

But Slough never escapes for long. What *The Good Life* did to Surbiton, Ricky Gervais's *The Office* did for Slough, stirring new mockery. Nor is that kind of disdain a wholly modern development. Visitors had disparaged the place long before Betjeman got there. In a book entitled *Pen Sketches by a Vanished Hand*, the nineteenth-century writer Mortimer Collins disconsolately described it as a place 'about which there is nothing to be said. Once possibly it may have been a place with a distinctive character; now it is a mere railway junction, the home of dust, of steam whistles and coal odours.' As for Bunyan, I see from another book in the library that it was while he was passing through Slough that he caught the cold that killed him.

The next stage of this journey through sniped-at communities takes us to Staines – a mere staging post, in these terms, but another place whose name might have been reconsidered. What do advertisers do when they run campaigns with themes like 'removes unsightly stains'? Do they exercise their tact and delete this town from their plans? Shakespeare honoured Staines, in a fashion, by including a reference to it in *Henry V*: 'Prithee, honey-sweet husband, let me bring thee to Staines,' a hostess begs Pistol. Route 41, operated by First, takes us to Staines by way of Eton and Windsor: much-admired places, both, yet each in a sense has had to acknowledge from time to time the superior power of Slough. For many years until its liberation in 1983, Eton was locked in an uncomfortable electoral alliance with Slough, which meant that whatever Eton preferred, the seat usually elected Labour MPs. As for Windsor, its letters are franked as coming from Slough, since Slough has captured the postcode. When the Queen travels by royal train, she departs from Slough rather than Windsor, since Slough is on the track to places of consequence in a way that Windsor is not. In 2002 the House of Commons public accounts committee was told of a journey the Queen had made with Prince Philip from Slough to Haverfordwest, at a cost of £18,277 (return). She could, I imagine, have gone more cheaply by service bus. That way she would have met more of her subjects and gained more insight into their lives. There's an excellent organization called Xephos based in the Isle of Wight which would gladly have worked out a route for her, as it has often done for me on these journeys, though going by train was undoubtedly quicker. It was also to the bench at workaday Slough that Princess Anne had to answer when her dog Dotty was accused of biting two children. They found the case proved and fined her (the princess, that is, rather than Dotty) £500.

The bus gives a generous tour of Windsor, both the regal bits and the rest, some of which is hardly more lovely than Slough. There's a splendid view on the way in of the long low viaduct that carries the branch railway line into the town, and then of the castle, where the flags are flying to show the Queen is in residence. The talk aboard my bus has mainly to do with mortality, as so often when it's mainly the old who are travelling. 'She'd only just got her stairlift installed, and then she goes and dies,' says one woman somewhat uncharitably of the death of a friend. We pass a field of cows which may or may not belong to the Queen. In the distance, a horseman is riding at speed in the royal park. 'The trouble with Ronnie is, he just won't go into sheltered accommodation,' the critical woman complains.

The bus is ambling now; it's ahead of schedule. It gives us an encouraging view of the sunny river and the Bells of Ouzeley public house, then potters on into Englefield Green. There's a splendid green here with a cricket ground with a serious pavilion – a scene, this, straight out of the old-fashioned England that exiles dream of. A little way on we come to the grandiose buildings of the Royal Holloway College of London University, the gleaming turrets of which light up the drive down the M3. So-called not because, as I had assumed, it had decamped at some stage from Holloway in north London, but because it was founded by Thomas Holloway, a successful manufacturer of pills and ointments. His wife, Jane Driver, encouraged him to use his money to found a college for the higher education of women, and Holloway instructed his architect, William Henry Crossland, to model it on the chateau of Chambord. Sadly, both Jane and Thomas were dead by the time the Queen came to open it in 1886.

Passing signs for Runnymede, we arrive at 'historic Egham'. Soon we're approaching a town: Centric is here and Fujitsu, and Homebase, and Halfords, and Sainsburys. A sign says 'Welcome to Spelthorne', one of those names rescued from near obscurity for use by a new local authority. And now we're in Staines, whose roadside signs proclaim not its own inherent Stainesian merits but its status as the gateway to Thorpe Park.

From the bus station, I make my way to the high street through another standard shopping mall, busy but boring, with just the same flavourless flavour as you might find in Slough or Leatherhead or Burton-on-Trent. This one, the Elmsleigh, was opened, a plaque announces, by HM the Queen on 22 February 1980. Myself, I'd rather have opened a college for the higher education of women. There's another mall called the Two Rivers just beyond. The high street itself is better than Slough's only because of the market stalls down the middle which give it some lift and some localness. Against that, the street furniture, huge bowls and self-conscious trees, is woefully overdone. The sense of the nearness of London is much sharper here than in Slough. Though not part of London, Staines is part of the London penumbra. In an account of his life in the trade (*Good Moments: A Publishing Retrospect*), a bookseller called Michael Russell recalls one of his drivers who, being despatched from the west to London, returned to say he'd been unable to find it; 'he'd got to Staines,' says the forgiving Russell, 'so he was getting warm'.

Turn east from the Elmsleigh, under an iron bridge helpfully labelled 'iron bridge', towards London, and you see the worst side of Staines: mean and pinched and indeterminate. Go west, and it's not bad at all. There's a slightly misguided town hall (1880), though the worst of it is the view of the mutilated rear of the town hall, which suggests some form of harsh amputation in the days before anaesthetics. From here on, the prospects are pleasing. Turn right and you discover a lane that leads down to the church, St Mary's, which is prefaced by comely Georgian houses and a pub called The Bells, with a sign depicting a swarthy cleric with his hands to his ears, perhaps because he couldn't stand the bells or perhaps because the rasp of the planes that constantly grind above Staines is enough to damage anyone's hearing. But best of all is the river. Stand on the bridge at the end of the town (two of the three previous bridges collapsed but this one seems to be lasting) and though it's not Richmond it's a good place to be. Over the bridge is a spot called the Hythe where the only imperfection is the view across the river to the mutilated back of the town hall. When the sun shines as brightly and warmly as it is doing today, this is one bit of Staines which certainly can't be described as unsightly and which no one should wish to eradicate.

To get from Staines to my final destination, Basingstoke, I'm required to go first to Camberley, which is served by a bus which does not belong to the monsters, First or Stagecoach or Arriva, but to Dicksons, one of the small independent companies which supplement them around the shires. The bus is a number 500, which is not to say they run another 499, and it's driven by a bright young man in a baseball cap who would have an empty bus if it wasn't for me. We race off through privileged territory, back through Egham and getting a second glimpse of the fantastical roofscape of the Royal Holloway, before heading off towards Sunningdale and Virginia Water and rich homes at the end of long gated drives – some lived in by big City figures and some by famous golfers in this very golfing part of the country, and some, it has been alleged, by people who have done pretty well out of crime. There is no one at any of Dicksons' bus stops, and the driver, though making up time, is disposed to chat. We discover a common fondness for Essex: in my case for its old thatched villages, its windmills and its clapboard, and the stillness along its northern estuaries, in his for Southend-on-Sea and its vivid hinterland, a taste he's acquired since he started going out with a dancer from Billericay.

We are now in a land of heath and small well-to-do towns and the poems of Betjeman, the presumed downside for Dicksons being that most of the people who live in places like this prefer to travel by car. In the summer of 2005, a house in Windlesham was on the market at a price of £70 million. With its twenty-seven bathrooms and five heated swimming pools it would not, the newspapers warned, be cheap to run. Its forty gas-fired boilers alone, it was estimated, would set you back £250,000 a year. There are further pubs called the Jolly Farmer around here, dating no doubt from an age when farmers were rubicund chaps with straw in their hair, never happier than when passing the time of day with other convivial country folk; an image now sadly replaced by one which portrays them as perpetual whingers and whiners, always calling for someone's resignation on the BBC's *Farming Today*. When did that change take place? Do pubs in agricultural areas today call themselves the Jaded Farmer, perhaps? But now we are into Camberley, the end of the route, and almost the ultimate point end of Dicksons' manor, where the journey must be continued by one of the big league players, Stagecoach. This town, too, is relevant to the journey, since Camberley is one of those places which has done what nineteenth-century Slough should have done, and changed its name. Originally there were twin towns here called York Town and Cambridge Town. In 1877, Cambridge Town decided to switch to Camberley, because, it was said, of constant confusions with some other place called Cambridge. Just as Bunyan is said to have caught his death of cold in Slough, so Albert, Prince consort, is reputed to have contracted his fatal illness while visiting Cambridge Town.

The journey by Stagecoach bus 200 begins drably, through York Town to a vast shopperama called The Meadows, which is what they once were but all too plainly aren't now. Beyond Blackwater, though, the landscape changes. Instead of town punctuated by shreds of country, it's country punctuated by town. The road here, skirting Blackbushe airport, is narrow and straight enough even for Lincolnshire, and heavily wooded, and two good towns occur on the way: Hartley Wintney, a village now perhaps, but studded with pubs and galleries looking out over generous greens, and Odiham, with its handsome, mellow high street, the worst of the traffic now decanted on to a thin little bypass. This is the district of Hart, rated in 2004 by civil servants in the office of the deputy prime minister as the English authority area with the best quality of life; also, by researchers at Sheffield University, as the area with the highest proportion of wealthy households anywhere in the UK. Beyond Odiham is Hook, once designated as a major new town, a decision later rescinded, which helped make Basingstoke what it is now. The schools are just out, and a gaggle of girls, twelve or thirteen years old perhaps, is installed on the back seats, romping and giggling. 'She didn't give Josh head, did she?' 'She told Marie she did.' As we pass through the village of Nately Scures they can't decide whether to spend this coming Saturday to go shopping for thongs and bikinis, or hang out at the toyshop.

Basingstoke. Look long and hard at this word. No obvious opportunities for scoffers and sneerers here. Yet W.S. Gilbert set audiences laughing at Basingstoke in *Ruddigore* (1887). It's the word that is used for calming Mad Margaret down. She needs at such times, it is said, to be addressed 'by some word that teems with inner meaning, like Basingstoke'. 'Pronounce it', is the advice, 'whenever she seems in danger of a relapse.' In what's designed as a happy ending, she and Sir Despard go off to live there. So, in 1887, this was a place whose very name was enough to soothe the agitated; but that's not how it strikes me today. Let me find what I can to say in praise of Basingstoke before its awfulness (no fault of the people who live there, as we shall see) overwhelms me. There's a comprehensive school which comes close to the top of the national tables. There are two theatres, one in the Anvil centre, which also has a good reputation for music, the other in a pretty building in the centre of town. There are fast trains out in practically every direction. It's a town which was made, initially, by the railway, which reached it in 1839. The cloth trade and the canal had pushed it to greater prominence, but the railway was the greatest agent of growth, brought to the town by the London and Southampton (later London and South Western) in 1839.

Basingstoke was never a beautiful town. In Hardy's novels, it appears as Stoke-Barehills. It features in *Tess of the d'Urbervilles*, and also in *Jude the Obscure*: 'There is in Upper Wessex an old town of nine or ten thousand souls...it stands with its gaunt, unattractive, ancient church, and its new red brick suburb, amid the open, chalk-soiled cornlands...The great western highway from London passes through it...The most familiar object in Stoke Barehills nowadays is its cemetery, standing among some picturesque mediaeval ruins beside the railway; the modern chapels, modern tombs, and modern shrubs having a look of intrusiveness amid the crumbling and ivy-covered decay of the ancient walls.' But what set it on the course to perdition was the Borough of Basingstoke (Town Centre) Purchase Order of 1965. Basingstoke was to provide 11,500 new homes (a total later cut to 9,230) to accommodate local people certainly, but mainly to house new arrivals from London. The population in 1961 had been 26,000. That was projected to rise to 63,000 in 1974 and 113,000 by the mid-1980s.

The authors of this enterprise sold it as a moment of high opportunity. Basingstoke, the *Hants & Berks Gazette* was persuaded, would become 'the showpiece town of the south of England' and 'the South's first town of the motorway age'. 'One of the most important things in the planning of Basingstoke,' said the chief architect and planner, 'is the problems of roads and traffic. We think we have found a good solution to this problem – one which we believe will mean that Basingstoke will not be destroyed.' In a farewell message when he left the town in 1968, the deputy director of development said: 'This old-fashioned country town, sitting in the path of progress, would have been obliged to face up to the pressing problems of obsolescence, traffic congestion and inadequate shopping. Town development has both accelerated the process and made it possible to find ambitious solutions that might not have been justified by less rapid growth.' All around, this vision was taking shape. Old hamlets were being absorbed. New suburbs were being created whose mildly fanciful names appear now on the destination blinds of Basingstoke's busy buses along with ancient familiar names such as Old Basing. Vast gleaming office blocks of steel and glass were erected – some now in the course of being transmuted into apartments, or 'stunning apartments', as most of the notice-boards say when one goes to admire them by way of the sodden and littered walkways under the old chief architect's then cherished, now menacing, roads.

It would not be easy, a study by the local branch of the Workers' Educational Association had warned at the outset, for this sturdy, rooted, unpretentious market town to come to terms with these vast changes which it had never asked for, and from which its present inhabitants would perhaps derive less benefit than would some others. The benefits, for those coming, often reluctantly, out of London were indisputable. In the midst of the country, a town was being created whose new commercial centre, all tidy and compact and modern, would be alluring enough to keep them happily shopping without returning to London. And certainly pitching one's sights too low can be a planning calamity, as Haverhill showed. But undoubtedly, as the WEA had feared, the casualty in this grievous collision of cultures was Basingstoke-as-it-used-to-be, much of it ruthlessly crushed, a lot of it wholly eliminated, to create this new shopping wonder ('a major shopping and leisure experience', as it calls itself). To look at Basingstoke now is to grasp an essential truth, one that crops up again and again on these journeys, about the shaping of good communities. As in so many sectors of life -- government especially, as the Thatcher years showed and some-times the Blair years too – the success of the operation depends on engineering necessary and potentially healthful change without destroying that sense of history and continuity which makes people feel secure, and sure of themselves, and at peace with the place they live in.

Before the edict was passed that Basingstoke should no longer sit in the way of progress, the centre had consisted of three main streets: one, known as the top of the town, running east–west, the two others running north, in parallel, down the hill, Church Street and Wote Street. Look at it now. Church Street at first runs as it always did down the hill, but then suddenly expires, dwindling into a footpath crossing a bridge, which seems to suggest we're about to cross a river but in fact proves to span only a service road. Beyond is what is still called Church Square, but one side of the square is the solid brick wall of Marks & Spencer, turning its back on the church as if in a symbolic display of Mammon shunning God. Yet if anything the fate of Wote Street is worse, its path imperiously blocked by the wall of the shopping centre. It's extraordinary that planners who clearly believed they were benefactors to the people of Basingstoke should have let these old streets be treated with such wicked brutality. What you see might rather suggest some disaster – a shopping centre dropped on the spot as arbitrarily and destructively as an enemy bomb.

In what used to be the town hall, but is now the free museum, you can get a sense of old Basingstoke. The old workplaces – Thornycrofts, Wallis and Stevens Engineers, Burberry, Gerrish, Ames & Simpkins. The old pubs, mown down to open the way for the showpiece town. Many old Basingstoke residents, feeling the place they lived in was no longer the town they'd grown up in, moved out, depressed and embittered. The most poignant exhibit in the museum, though, comes from a woman called Mrs Davey – not Basingstoke born and bred, but one of the early arrivals from London. This is part of what she wrote:

A new home I found as part of the Greater London overspill
Much welcomed fresh air, green fields and nearby watermill.
I watched in horror, with the motionless, sad-eyed crowd
When bulldozers knocked May St down, with crashing loud.

Tears silently shed, when schools and pubs also downward fell
Turning my new Hampshire haven into an endless,
    dirty hell.
Off with the old and on with the new
In order to make planners' dreams come true.

These lines may fall short of John Betjeman's elegance, but they certainly match his passion.

9

ISLE OF PORTLAND

Closely observed trains near the Dorchester home of Thomas Hardy – George III and his kinsmen go for a swim at Weymouth – across the shingle to Portland: its quarries, its cultural heritage, its permissive view of sex before marriage, its prisons, ancient and modern – I discover that the stroppy spirit of Portland, evoked in the eighteenth century to spur a king into action, survives in the twenty-first.

He might not have thought much of Basingstoke, but the Isle of Portland, to which I come next, fascinated Thomas Hardy throughout his life. Towards the end, he liked to be taken from his house at Max Gate, Dorchester, to a spot where he could watch the trains running by. Most of all he loved to see those that steamed towards London bearing cargoes of Portland stone. His father had been a stonemason, which may have been one reason why he was drawn to the island. 'The Gibraltar of England,' he called it, 'the stern, isolated rock in the Channel', and 'a peninsula carved by time out of a single stone'. He knew, and used in his novels, its eerie geology, its strange local customs, its separateness. Where Dorchester was Casterbridge, Shaftesbury was Shaston and Basingstoke was awarded the bleak designation, Stoke Barehills, Portland was the Isle of Slingers, reflecting the tradition that since the time of King Alfred Portlanders had repelled those who attacked the island by pelting them with stones.

My wife's grandfather, Edward Smith, took a job as a prison warder on Portland at the end of the nineteenth century. He had given up better employment on the railways in Oxford when doctors told him that the only hope of saving his ailing young wife, Rose Annie, was to move to somewhere that offered sea air. But she died, of cancer, within months. She was twenty-six. She left a son of sixteen months old – my wife's father, Charles – who lived to be one hundred. In the 1990s, shortly before Charles died, we went to Portland to look for the prison his father Edward had worked in, and to search for Rose Annie's grave in the churchyard of the fine Georgian church at Reforne.

Although it's barely separated from the Dorset coast, this island feels like another country; which is how it has always seen itself. It maintained its own distinct traditions and institutions over the centuries. Where on the mainland sex before marriage was seen as wrong and shameful and children born out of wedlock were condemned with names like 'bastard', on Portland, sex before marriage was seen as the norm. If the girl wasn't going to get pregnant she wasn't the right one to marry. If she did get pregnant, then the man must marry her, and if he tried to duck out of it, the women of Portland would stone him off the island. That tradition reflected a determination that the population of Portland must not be allowed to die out. In the twentieth century, these differences, so long and so proudly preserved, began to erode – though sometimes, as in attitudes to sex before marriage, it was the mainland that moved towards Portland's practice rather than the other way round. Yet as late as the 1930s there were people on Portland who, interviewed for a social survey, said they had never been to England.

Much of this is woven through Hardy's novel, *The Well-Beloved* (1897), an odd, unreal, even slightly kinky tale. A sculptor – a worker in stone – called Pierston successively loves a woman called Avice, her daughter and her granddaughter, the sequence of each encounter being somehow the same. Mother, daughter, granddaughter – why should this be? The 'three Avices' could not have been so alike, Hardy explains, but for the Portland customs of inter-marriage and pre-nuptial union – so embedded, he says, 'that till quite latterly, to have seen one native man and woman was to have seen the whole population of that isolated rock, so nearly cut off from the mainland'. As a novel, *The Well-Beloved* is a mess. As an evocation of the island's unique way of life, it is much more rewarding.

Hardy liked to cycle through Weymouth and across the causeway to Portland. He was fond of luring visitors to his home, Max Gate, out for rides to the island. But then, by dying in 1928, he denied himself the benefit of the X10 Sureline bus. The island's first motor buses began to run around the time of Hardy's death, and before long, bus wars developed as three drivers from the island formed a Portland Express Omnibus Company to challenge the exclusive running rights of the National Bus company – which was, as Portlanders would say, a kimberlin organization, 'kimberlin' being their word for people born off the island. In that tradition, Sureline, based on the island and run by two local men, David Beaman and Bill Landucci, began in 2002 to operate a rival service to that of the mighty kimberlin First group, which had inherited the forty-six-year-old monopoly of the old Southern National. First buses are grander and plusher, but Sureline buses rattle along with a cheerful determination and their service runs, as First's does not, from Dorchester right to the doors of the Portland museum, which is well worth inspecting if you want to get a sense of the island before you begin to explore it.

Dorchester, the county town of Dorset, is full of Hardy, though he does not have a monopoly: the statue outside the museum which houses the Hardy collection is of William Barnes, the Dorset poet.

The fearsome Judge Jeffreys, who hanged so many after the Monmouth rebellion, is also well commemorated here. Up the hill, in the district known as the top of the town, is Hardy himself, wearing a floppy hat, sculpted by Eric Kennington.

The Sureline takes a scenic route through the town, turning away from the bus station to reveal a view of a high street whose churches, courthouse and ancient inns still look much as they would have done to Hardy, though I doubt if they ran to pubs called The Bare Midriff in his day. Upwey (sometimes Upway), a mile or two out, is full of Hardy associations too: 'At the Railway Station, Upway', is one of the poems in his posthumously published work *Winter Words*, later hauntingly set to music by Benjamin Britten. Radipole, on the way in, whose chalybeate waters are mentioned in Hardy's novel *The Trumpet-Major*, used to pride itself on being a favourite haunt of George III, though others claimed the monarch much preferred a village called Nottington on the far side of town. There is ribbon development here, and gentle rain, but soon there are sumptuous views of Weymouth Bay as we rattle down into the town.

The bus stops at the waterside in Weymouth by the statue of George III, giving you time, as the holidaymakers bound for Portland clamber on board, to admire the great sweep of the bay, the golden beach, the cliffs at the eastern end, now lit up by a shaft of sunlight, and the still handsome sea front, stately but tired, its working hotels interspersed with lapsed ones. Not forgetting, of course, the statue itself, an extraordinary, garish creation (James Hamilton, architect), erected by Weymouth to commemorate the fifieth year of a reign during which royal patronage had helped boost the image and pulling power of the town. 'From 1760,' the *Shell Guide* by Michael Pitt-Rivers tells me, 'its fashion spread among the wealthy from Bath and London until royalty patronized it. The duke of Gloucester, and George III, his brother, took to regular visits. Backed to the water edge in his horse-drawn machine, the King dipped into the water to the strains of the national anthem.' In 1857, the railway completed the sequence as hotels, guest-houses, lodging houses and finally caravans sprang up all around Weymouth to accommodate the incoming hordes. It remained for a century a resort of unfailing appeal, even to some of the famous: the Labour Prime Minister Clement Attlee and his wife Violet liked to take their holidays either here or in Seaton, near Sidmouth. No jetting off to stay in the homes of rich Tuscan businessmen or in Caribbean hideaways for Labour prime ministers then.

You can see the isle, which is four and a half miles long and two miles wide, plainly across the water. There are trips by boat on offer to what the noticeboard styles 'the isle and royal manor'. Coming up towards the town bridge, the X10 has to hold back to let a horse-drawn minibus pass. The narrow streets around the colourful harbour where the little boats ride in dazzling profusion, among prettily coloured houses and the warehouses of the old Weymouth and the bars and coffee houses of the new one, are hazardous in high summer, as delivery vans stop where and when they choose and buses are forced to proceed by negotiation.

At the peak of the season some of the buses across to the island – mostly First's, though Sureline acquired one for the summer of 2005 – are open-topped, which is very agreeable as they thread their way through the streets close to the water, though rather less so as the bus ploughs on through the monotonous territory into which the old town has expanded. One can see why Weymouth attracted its royal patrons, but what can it have been about Wyke Regis, apart perhaps from its church, which persuaded some royal decision-maker to let such a drably uniform place tack this privileged suffix on to its name? Not the mark that development has left on the coastline here, for sure. But at last we are clear of Wyke Regis and on to the long causeway across the shingle which carries us on to the royal isle.

The bus comes into Portland at a place called Victoria Square, which may once have deserved this grand name but certainly doesn't now. Rather it seems to say, this place is in trouble. No doubt people used to dress up for an evening and arrive in style in their carriages at the Royal Victoria Hotel, but today it is boarded up and abandoned. The views of the sea are dazzling as the bus toils up the narrow hazardous hill through Fortuneswell, but even now that the rain is over and the sun has begun to shine like some beneficent god, there is no disguising the bleakness. The island has very few trees, and wherever you look outside the little villages the landscape is ravaged. There are great gouged-out craters where the stone used to be that has gone to glorify London and other great cities. Alongside the roads there are huge hunks of stone stacked up haphazardly, as if each were awaiting its own individual date with destiny. The oddness of this place is evident too in the roads that run through some of the villages. Why, for instance, was Wakeham, on the stretch from Easton down to the museum, built wide enough to accommodate chariot races or Wild West shoot-outs? These are dogged, thrifty, practical places. Look at the names of the villages: Fortuneswell, maybe – but Chiswell, Southwell, Easton, Weston – no flights of fantasy there. But it's easy to understand the proliferation of the pubs, in Castletown, down by the water, where sailors and fishermen and workers in the naval yards used to pitch up at the end of the day and quite often during it, or in the upland villages where the stoneworkers sought relief after their dusty endeavours.

Easton, with its square and church and cafés and congregation of small shops – there are no large shops on the island – is the nearest thing the place has to a capital. Some of the streets are bright and varied enough to be entertaining, but you rarely come across a building to stop and gaze at. One spirit-lifting exception is the church of St George, Reforne, just out of Weston, where with some kindly guidance we finally found the grave of Rose Annie. Once near-derelict, St George's has latterly been refurbished to its 1770s splendour, its twin pulpits and box pews a gleaming tribute to years of redeeming endeavour. It was consecrated in 1766 by a bishop of Bristol who was so alarmed at the prospect of reaching the island across Smallmouth Sands that islanders had to carry him there. A memorial on the wall is dedicated 'to the memories of the following islanders who were shot by the Press Gang during its unlawful raid in the Royal Manor of Portland', in what was known as the Easton massacre, on 2 April 1803. Alexander Andrews, quarryman. Richard Flann, quarryman. William Lano, blacksmith. Mary Way, who was twenty-one, died later of wounds received. Four officers and ten marines, charged at Dorchester Assizes with wilful murder, were acquitted. Of course.

The X10 runs on to the southern tip of the island, at Portland Bill, where there are lighthouses, built to diminish the fearsome hazards of this coast after repeated shipwrecks, to which the men of Portland responded with conspicuous bravery, though also with conspicuous criminality. They saved stricken crews; they looted their stricken boats. The first lighthouse was completed in 1716, the second soon after, but both were superseded by a bumper new edifice opened by Trinity House in 1789, a time which bred a fear of the French in and around Portland just as it did around Folkestone and Hythe. New upper and lower lighthouses were built in 1869. The present buildings replaced them in 1904–5. The old lower lighthouse is now a bird observatory. The upper one was bought in the 1920s and converted into a holiday residence by the eccentric palaeobotanist and much mocked champion of birth control, Marie Stopes.

It was Stopes who gave Portland the cottages which house the museum, one of which was Hardy's model for the home of Avice in *The Well-Beloved*. You will find it on the corner of a road that runs down to the sea at Church Ope, just short of the fantastical Pennsylvania Castle, built by a former governor of the island, John Penn. Its opening hours are limited, and the dark and cluttered interior immediately proclaims this to be the sort of unreconstructed museum that used to be commonplace before the days of child-friendly distractions and the domineering rule of interactivity. Crowded and under-resourced, it is full of the kind of local keepsakes which so many museums throw out when they modernize. Bottles from the Weymouth Soda Water Company. Inscribed teapot, presented to Mrs Bottomley by the mechanics of Portland Breakwater as a token of gratitude to her husband, October 1893. Radio of the early 1930s, donated by Mr J. Pearce. Photograph of warders of Portland prison, *circa* 1910. (My wife's grandfather Edward Smith among them, perhaps.) A case of septarian nodules, about 150-160 million years old. Skeleton of a cat, mummified, found in Easton. Early player organ, formerly at St George's church, plays favourite hymn tunes: the Old 100th, the Old 104th, 'Mount Ephraim', 'Luther', 'Bedford' and 'Oxford'.

There are copies of several more than competent drawings by Samuel Hieronymous Grimm. Not great art, says the caption, but evocative of the island as it was around 1790. There are tales of great shipwrecks on this dangerous coast, notably the sinking of *The Earl of Abergavenny* in 1805 in which William Wordsworth's brother, Captain John Wordsworth, and 260 of his crew and passengers were lost, although 141 people were rescued. There's a list of famous buildings created in Portland stone: the west front of St Paul's, Buckingham Palace, Waterloo Bridge, the Bank of England, Tate Britain, St Martin's in the Fields, the BBC at Portland Place, Liverpool Cathedral and Belfast City Hall. But more telling than any of this is the evocation in these dark rooms of the spirit of Portland. The sense of the isle's isolation, its fierce independence, its proud preservation of its own way of life regardless of how things were done over the water, is nowhere stronger than in some of the documents here.

The most instructive of these is a protest (kept, because it has faded, under a black cloth, but a typed copy is provided) delivered by His Majesty's 'most dutiful, faithful and affectionate servants' on Portland, headed by the rector and church wardens, to the king, demanding a bridge to the mainland; this after yet more travellers trying to cross to the mainland had been drowned. Portlanders felt that they had the right to address the king direct: William the Conqueror had held the manor of Portland in his personal domain; George III was lord of the manor of Portland as well as being king. Now, while expressing gratitude for the mild and equitable government to which they were subject, and which they were ready at all times to support and maintain even at the cost of sacrifice of their lives and property, they were making it bluntly clear that they wanted to see some action. 'Petition to King George III for Portland to join the mainland' the document is headed – and again, the urgent need to ensure that the population of Portland should not be allowed to decline is a powerful influence. The ferry now in operation, it says, 'is dangerous by reason of the strong currents and eddies, as well as the great depth of water, which renders it almost impossible to save a life in case of accident...Among other inconveniences our petitions cannot in justice omit the temporary danger attending women when medical assistance is request'd in particular cases whereby many lives have been lost, not only by reason of the delay, but the danger of crossing the ferry at all hours and in tempestuous weather, and, we submit, in a county where the increase of population is so very essential to the prosecution of the business of the island by its native inhabitants and their offspring, this is not one of the least evils deserving a remedy.' In return came not a letter from His Majesty but a rebuke from Prime Minister Pitt. In the opinion of an officer immediately about His Majesty's person, it said, no application of this sort is ever made direct to the king.

Close by in the museum is a blast by independent islanders against those in the island hierarchy who wished to thwart its bid for local government independence under legislation in 1867. 'Some of your brethren, seeing the large sums of YOUR money expended, about which you had no voice, and that you were treated as children, and not men of understanding, thought it was high time not to remain quiet any longer, but try and see if you and they could not govern yourselves.' Others had resolved to obstruct this process of liberation. Who were they? 'You know without my telling you.' At which point the pamphleteer breaks into verse:

> For our rights together we'll stand
> To each other be loyal and true
> No stranger shall govern our land
> Or spend our GRANT money too.
>
> We remained quiet long enough
> And no longer intend to be still;
> MEN OF PORTLAND SHALL GOVERN FOR US
> And none shall fetter our will.

Up, Portlanders, and be doing!
Stand by your Rights.

– A wellwisher of Portland

Portland did gets its bridge, but only after ferocious storms had destroyed much of the village of Chiswell in 1824. The first stone was laid in May 1837, too late to save two men who, missing the ferry, had tried to swim across the water the previous May. A fine procession including a detachment of guards made the first crossing in January 1839. As the text in the museum says, the bridge 'fundamentally changed Portland for ever. The old isolation was no more, the unique customs, life style and attitudes of ancient origin were slowly eroded as Portland became open to mainland influence.'

There were also the prisons. In an excellent book called *Portland, An Illustrated History*, Stuart Morris, who as a civil engineer appreciates more than most historians could how difficult and dangerous the enterprise was, records how Portland's harbour and Portland's prisons came to be built. Those who sailed around Portland, as well as those who lived there, wanted a safe refuge for ships in times of storm. Ten years before the loss of the *Abergavenny*, more than 200 bodies had been washed ashore when a fleet under Admiral Christian was wrecked in 1795: the total death toll may have been as high as a thousand. Governments saw the necessity but could not find ways to fund a solution. But in 1805 an ingenious scheme was devised to deal with two problems at once. Some 20 million tons of stone would be cut from the hill on the north-east side of the island and used to build a harbour wall. The space from which the stone had been cleared would then be enough to accommodate a great military citadel. And the otherwise prohibitive cost of this vast operation would be mitigated by using convict labour to carry it out.

The first convicts arrived in March 1848, no doubt barely under-standing the fate that awaited them. Victoria's Prince consort, Albert, who took such a close interest throughout that he was after-wards given much of the credit for the enterprise, came in July the following year to lay the foundation stone of the breakwater, presenting the convict community with a bible 'in the hope of their amendment'. By the time the work was accomplished they would have hewn out more than five million tons of stone in a process punctuated by fatal accidents, mostly to the workforce but some to over-eager sightseers. The two long breakwaters housed what was claimed to be the largest man-made harbour anywhere in the world: more than 200 ships could be seen at a time on the water. It was vast enough, even, to be chosen to accommodate Brunel's giant ship the *Great Eastern*.

What not everyone on Portland appreciated was that the presence of the convicts would be more than merely temporary. In 1869, the islanders were told that despite a petition for its removal, the prison in an area called the Grove, which had been created to house them while they were working, was to be permanent. Today, the Grove is a young offenders' institution, supplanted as Portland's premier prison by the military citadel known as the Verne – another innovation the purpose of which had not been fully revealed to Portlanders until it was finished. The Grove, where Edward Smith worked, was for many years a most notorious prison. The former Liberal MP and major fraudster, Jabez Spencer Balfour, who served part of a fourteen-year sentence there, called it in his memoir *My Prison Life*, 'a heart-breaking, soul-enslaving, brain-destroying hell upon earth'. The incidence of suicides caused outrage in Parliament. There were twenty attempts in 1884 alone; yet a further thirteen years passed before the prisons direc-torate accepted it had a problem. Feelings on Portland about the

Grove were mixed. The islanders had never wanted a prison. On the other hand, it was clearly attracting tourists. They came to stare, and sometimes to wave, at the figures in arrowed uniform. The shops sold jokey postcards: 'just arrived here' they said, over a picture of grim and disconsolate inmates trudging towards captivity. Inserts showed the gloomy gate of the prison, a distant view of the main building, and a general view of the waterfront. The Grove became a borstal in the 1920s. The military left the citadel after the Second World War. 'For a few brief years,' says Stuart Morris, 'it was a vast adventure ground for Island youngsters, exploring endless dark passages, abandoned gun emplacements and secret doorways in the cliffside.'

Then in 1948 plans were announced to make the Verne a training centre for 200 prisoners. That developed into a heavily fortified jail, housing 500. In 1997, a further prison was added: HMP The Weare – a battered prison ship bought by the Home Office from a gratified New York municipality, which had been wondering how to get rid of it. A temporary measure, the Home Office said, to be open for just three years, though it did not rule out some extension beyond that. It was not until the summer of 2005 that the Home Office accepted the strictures of Chief Prison Inspector Anne Owers, who had said of it, in an assessment that might easily have been made in just these terms before it was first installed: 'Weare is, literally and metaphorically, a container. Prisoners' living accommodation has no access to fresh air, and in some cases little natural light... Despite the best efforts of staff or managers, HMP Weare is entirely unsuitable for its present function as a twenty-first-century category C training prison.' The last prisoners were despatched. Campaigners for prison reform were elated; but Portland, once more, had mixed feelings. 'I had reservations when it first came,' said one local councillor, 'but in truth the Weare is now a tourist attraction. When people come to Portland, the first thing they say to me is, "Where is the prison ship?"' 'It had a beneficial economic impact at a time when the area desperately needed it,' said a despondent spokesman for Portland port, which owned the site.

That makes three prisons for me to inspect. The number 7 Arriva bus has taken me up the hill, past the football ground, to make what I can of the Grove. There's not much you can see from the road except the forbidding walls and the mighty fortified doors. Going back to Victoria Square, I reach the gates of the HMP Weare site by an atmospheric waterfront road through Castletown, past the Royal Sun and the Aqua-Sport hotel and the Jolly Sailor and the Portland Roads Hotel (J.A. Devenish and Co., celebrated ales, 1898, according to an inscription cut into its wall) and the Royal Blackwater. But they won't let modern-day visitors go past the checkpoint to gawp at the Weare; to get any kind of view of it, they kindly explain, you need to go to the Verne. A 7a bus does this journey. What I see from the front of the Verne, far below, is a kind of large grey metal container ('it is literally and metaphorically a container') with mean peremptory windows. It hardly seems to belong to the late twentieth century, let alone to the twenty-first. Behind me looms the huge and ominous gate of the Verne. What Jabez Balfour said of the Grove – that they didn't need to carve the inscription 'abandon hope all ye who enter here' since the whole building proclaimed it – seems even more apposite at this spot. 'You'd certainly never get out of there once they'd put you in,' I exclaim to a man who is looking over the sea towards Weymouth. But he tells me there have been two escapes in the past few weeks alone.

Hardy, at the end of his life, recognized that the strangeness of Portland was fading. Now it feels as though it is entering its ultimate phase. An island where seventy years before some had never been to England now shops at Weymouth's Debenhams, banks at Weymouth Barclays and Lloyds, goes to school in the town, pays council tax to West Dorset District Council in Weymouth, and depends on Weymouth for many essential services. 'MEN OF PORTLAND SHALL GOVERN FOR US' said the protest manifesto in the museum. Not any more. And yet the spirit of Portland, the dogged, stroppy and never easily cowed spirit of Portland, is not quite dead. On the roadside in Fortuneswell I see a plaque which says: 'Tristram Paul Baker, 18 years, taken from us on 24.10.97. Gone but not forgotten. His mates and family will always remember him as the one and only Bad Boy Baker. RIP. Will be sadly missed. From the boys.' Not quite the usual stuff of such roadside memorials. Not the way they'd be likely to phrase it across the water. Two lads who are watching me copy the inscription down ask me what I am doing. Though perhaps too young to have known him in person, they have heard all about Bad Boy Baker. As I'd guessed, he'd been killed in a road accident close to this spot. 'Now write down our names,' they instruct. So I do: Levi Moore and Lloyd Harris. Then I hop on a number 1 bus back to England.

10

TAUNTON

Brother Prince and his Agapemone, or abode of love — his
traumatic effect on congregations and his claim to divine status
— his talent for recruiting moneyed heiresses — an event of high
theological import in a chapel-cum-billiard room, followed by an
untoward birth — Prince claims to be immortal, but dies —
the end of the Agapemone — how sinners come to believe they
are spotless.

In the square in the centre of Bridgwater, Somerset, Admiral Robert
Blake, one of Parliament's heroes in its war with the king, and often
rated second only to Nelson in the annals of maritime fighting men,
stands with his back to the mildly depressing spectacle of
Bridgwater market hall, where the southern end, which in old postcards is still the salubrious Cornhill Restaurant, nowadays sports
an outsize sign which says 'Gents'. Admiral Blake died in 1657, but
they didn't get around to erecting his statue until 1900. That left a
space in the square, into which there used to emerge from time to
time in the later years of the nineteenth century a strange and exotic
procession. Outriders in purple livery surrounded a gleaming carriage which had previously belonged to the Dowager Queen
Adelaide, drawn by four magnificent horses. Bloodhounds ran
ahead. Behind them came a man who loudly proclaimed to the
people of Bridgwater: 'Blessed is he who cometh in the name of the
Lord.' There would then step out of the carriage the author and

cause of this excitement, who not merely came in the name of the Lord but, according to his theology, *was* the Lord, in that he was the agent, and later the incarnation, of the Holy Ghost.

Surrounded by reverent followers, and mocked by the rowdy unbelievers of Bridgwater, the preacher spoke insistently of salvation. His name was Henry James Prince: to his devotees, he was Brother Prince, or, in his favourite formulation, the Beloved. He and his entourage came from a hamlet known as Four Forks, just out of the village of Spaxton, four miles away, but longer if you go there by digressive service bus, where they lived in a community known as the Agapemone. The name was derived from the Greek word *agape*, meaning spiritual love, since that was the kind of love which was said to exist there, although the strong suspicion in Bridgwater pubs after the coach had carried Prince and his followers back to Spaxton was that *eros* was probably nearer the mark.

Route 18, operated by First, was running when I was there on Tuesdays and Fridays only, two journeys a day. Its destination, in so far as a circular route has a destination other than the place where it starts, was Bincombe, just beyond Over Stowey (preferably not to be confused, though it frequently is, with the more famous Nether Stowey, where Coleridge lived). The service's purpose is to pick up shoppers in the morning, give them two hours in town, and then take them home. The route for this undertaking is one of wild inventiveness: out through Durleigh and Goathurst and Enmore to Four Forks and Spaxton, then on to Over Stowey and Bincombe and back through Spaxton and different sectors of Enmore and Goathurst to Bridgwater bus station. If everything went to plan, I calculated, this should allow me some thirty minutes in Spaxton to look for the Agapemone.

The number 18, rattling and shaking, noses its way out through the suburbs of Bridgwater into the Quantock hills. There are no other passengers as it heads past pretty cottages and red stone walls and red stone houses into the glorious Quantocks. The Barford Road runs south-west out of Four Forks and there, a few hundred yards on, is the simple chapel building where Brother Prince unfolded his mysteries – just short of the Lamb public house, where the goings-on of the neighbours were a limitless source of speculation and gossip. The estate at one time ran to 200 acres. At its heart was the chapel, which strangely also served as a drawing room and billiards room. Its holy purposes long abandoned, today it looks solid, but sad. Around it are houses and cottages which, behind a protective wall, were homes to Prince and his followers, who at the peak numbered about sixty. Like so much of Prince's empire of love, the building of the chapel was an act of philanthropy by a builder impressed with the movement's teachings.

Brother Prince, the Beloved, was born in Bath to a family which had once been prosperous but had fallen on hard times. His father was sixty-six at the time of his birth. Prince trained as a doctor and worked for a time at the general hospital in Bath, but left on grounds of ill-health to become a divinity student. That brought him to the theological college at Lampeter in Cardiganshire. The cost of his studies there was borne by a woman called Martha Freeman, a well-to-do friend of his mother's who had taken a kindly interest in him. Prince persuaded her to abandon her Catholic faith and to enter with him into a marriage which, it was stipulated, would be a spiritual but certainly not a carnal union. But the education that Martha bought for her young husband was not a happy experience. He became distressed by what he saw as the laxity of those around him, the staff of the college and the principal not excluded, as well as the students. These people, in his judgement and that of a small coterie that had gathered around him – The Lampeter Brethren, they called themselves – were failing to honour the word of God. He deplored their readiness to succumb to temptation, all the more because of the pain he was suffering in resisting the wiles of the devil himself. He was tempted by the sins of the flesh – 'vile flesh, sinful flesh, rebellious flesh' he wrote in his diaries. Prayer and mortification were the chosen course of the Brethren, and the study of the Bible, but particularly, in Prince's case, a book significantly full of fleshly allure, the Song of Solomon.

Prince was appointed curate at the church of Charlinch, a small settlement on a road that runs north-east from Four Forks. It's a fine-looking church, set on a hill with glorious views across Somerset, but its doors have long been shut. The rector, Samuel Starky, was frequently ill, and Prince was soon running the parish, preaching sermons that both roused and terrified those that heard them. Where he found peace, he created discord. Wives, it was said, were threatening under his influence to leave their husbands, and husbands to murder their wives. Later there were astonishing scenes at his Sunday school, where by the time Prince had finished with them, only ten or so of the fifty children present were still able to stand: 'boys and girls, great and small together, were either leaning against the wall quite overcome with their feelings of distress, or else bowed down with their faces hidden in their hands, and sobbing in the severest agony', the architect of their sufferings recorded with some satisfaction.

Some of the clergy from nearby parishes, including the rector of Spaxton, complained to the bishop. In May 1842 Prince's licence to preach was revoked and a ban was imposed on his further presence at Charlinch. Prince found himself a curacy at Halstead in Suffolk instead. Martha had died in the month before he was ordered out of Charlinch, and Rector Starky's sister Julia accompanied him to

Suffolk. In obedience, as he explained, to God's will and at the direction of the Holy Ghost, they were married in September. His preaching got him ousted at Halstead too, and he subsequently set himself up in his own independent chapel at Brighton, where he publicly declared himself to be at least semi-divine.

By this time, Starky, now defrocked, was already preaching the message of Prince's divine calling in Weymouth. At a meeting at the Royal Hotel there, Prince had disclosed that it had been revealed to him that he was the Son of Man. Now, in Brighton in March 1845, he announced that the second coming was imminent and that he, Prince, being the agent – even, it seemed, the embodiment – of the Holy Ghost, had been entrusted with the duty of leading a final campaign to redeem humanity. At this point, some of his old Lampeter colleagues despaired of him, and departed. With the rest, who still revered with him, he moved on to found the Agapemone. This cost money, but Prince was confident that God would provide, and sure enough the movement began to attract a number of rich young heiresses. To make sure their money went where it was needed, Prince married them off to his acolytes (a wife's possessions became her husband's under the laws of those days), who obediently passed their money on to the safe-keeping of Brother Prince. Handy contributions came though three sisters, Harriet, Clara and Agnes Nottidge, whose father had bequeathed them £6,000 apiece – in today's purchasing power around £400,000. Two of them, Harriet and Clara, agreed to be married to Prince's lieutenants, though the third, Agnes, balked at instructions to unite herself with one of Prince's most trusted aides, Brother Thomas. Arraigned for her disobedience, she was soon after found to be pregnant and was expelled.

When a further Nottidge sister, Louisa, possessor of an equal bequest, declared her intention to sign up with Brother Prince, her brothers kidnapped her and put her in an asylum. But Louisa escaped and found her way back to Spaxton. Ferocious legal battles ensued, first before the commissioners in lunacy and then in a case for wrongful imprisonment, both of which went in Louisa's favour, even though evidence was given that Louisa maintained that Prince was God and that she was immortal. There were also allegations that Four Forks was the scene of sexual depravity. Other substantial benefactors came forward whom Prince rewarded with titles such as Angel of the Seventh Seal. According to one account, a wealthy London merchant gave Prince all that he had and thereafter worked as his butler.

What happened at the Agapemone was entirely decided by Prince. He made the rules, which among other stipulations forbade any contact with doctors, even for those who were dying the most painful of deaths. Some found the regime so oppressive that they fled; others, it was reported, had killed themselves. Punishment, if rules were broken, was often severe, though perhaps the worst for the faithful was the knowledge that Brother Prince was displeased. His appearance at the start of a service was greeted with the singing of 'All hail thou King of Glory'. The services in the chapel were built around sermons by Brother Prince, readings from the copious writings of Brother Prince and hymns by Brother Prince, in the tradition later made famous by Mr Toad. All were directly and divinely inspired, since, as he explained (he always wrote about himself in the third person): 'When called by God, Brother Prince was, from the very first, taken into the hands of God with a most mighty grasp. The voice of God in his word sounded in his ears like the trump of the archangel...' The rules of conventional worship were rewritten by Brother Prince. There were few formal prayers. 'They sing hymns, I think, addressed to the Supreme Being,' one contemporary source reported, in the manner of some anthropologist who has stumbled on a strange and primitive tribe, 'but as I collect, they do not, in the sense of supplication or entreaty to God, pray at all. The Agapemonians appear to set a high value on bodily exercise of a cheerful and amusing kind... It does not appear that the Agapemonians hunt, but they seem distinguished both as Cavaliers and Charioteers. They play, moreover, frequently or occasionally, at lively and energetic games, such as hockey, ladies and all. So that their life may be considered less ascetic than frolicsome.'

The rules about sexual contact were Prince's own invention too. Whatever his struggles against fleshly temptation, Prince always had an eye for a pretty woman, especially, it was said down in Bridgwater, if they were laundresses. Fleshly love was off limits for husbands and wives at the Agapemone; they were expected to live together as brother and sister. As Prince explained in one of his books, the women of the Agapemone, being the brides of Christ, lived in daily expectation of being with their heavenly bridegroom. As for the men, those who had wives now lived as if they had none, while those who had no wives did not desire to acquire them. This virgin order of life was the result of his having taken flesh and brought to light the wicked one, before concealed, as the source of all those lusts of the flesh which defiled it, to the wicked one's destruction and man's deliverance. The wives, however, were expected to serve on a panel of 'soul brides' available to the Beloved. Any husband approaching his wife while she was thus seconded was punished by Brother Prince.

Though reports of the goings-on behind the high walls were no doubt exaggerated, an event occurred in the late 1850s which was documented by a level-headed observer called Hepworth Dixon. A widow called Mrs Paterson who had joined the community had brought with her a beautiful daughter, sixteen years old. According to Hepworth Dixon's account, on this night in the chapel (which was also the drawing room and the billiard room) the congregation was invited to witness a sacred mystery in which Brother Prince (who was sixty-six) and the daughter were mystically and spiritually united in an act on the sofa which, when practised by others, was more usually thought of as sexual intercourse. The Beloved, Dixon reported, had opened these proceedings by explaining that since he was the embodiment of the Spirit, any fleshly contact in which he indulged was essentially the work of the Spirit. Or, as Prince himself described the event in his work *The Little Book Open*: 'the Holy Ghost took flesh in the presence of those He had called as flesh'.

Unhappily, whatever the spiritual significance of the occasion, it had a profoundly physical consequence. The girl, now known as Sister Zoe, was found to be with child. There was consternation when this came to light: even the faithful found it difficult to reconcile the evidence of Zoe's pregnancy with the explanations the Beloved had offered them. After long reflection, Brother Prince produced a reason for this untoward development. It was, he said, a trick of the devil, designed to discredit him. The child, he told Hepworth Dixon, was in fact the offspring of Satan (poor child, and poor Zoe!). Some of the formerly faithful could take no more. One of Prince's longest associates, Lewis Price, who had married Harriet Nottidge, left the Agapemone – according to some accounts taking Harriet with him, though others said he came back to reclaim her and was seen off by Prince's bloodhounds. That, in Prince's book, was Lewis's loss rather than the community's. According to Prince's teachings, those who left the Agapemone were doomed, since only those who made their lives there had any chance of salvation.

It was said, as he reached his seventies, that Prince was mellowing. The chapel even opened its doors to people outside the community. But in 1899 another event occurred which, being entirely incompatible with what the Beloved had told them, disturbed, dismayed and frightened them. The Beloved died. They had always believed that Prince was immortal, but here was irrefutable evidence that he'd died just like anyone else. Most accounts say the Beloved was buried standing up in his garden, according to standard Agapemone practice, although a woman I met at the Spaxton bus stop said she had known the undertaker and this was not true. Yet dominating though he was, the undeniable end of Brother Prince wasn't the end of the Agapemone. His successor was a man called John Hugh Smyth-Pigott. His father had died in an asylum, and despite having first-class results at the London College of Divinity, there were some who doubted his sanity. Extraordinarily, he was introduced to the Agapemone by the child of Satan – that reputed fruit of the act before the altar, Prince's daughter, Eva.

Smyth-Pigott was the principal figure at a church built for the Agapemone on Clapton Common in London, which is now the Cathedral Church of the Good Shepherd, primatial see of the Ancient Catholic Church. It opened its doors on Whit Sunday 1896, three years before Brother Prince died. Just as his predecessor had had it revealed to him that he was the Holy Ghost incarnate, Smyth-Pigott discovered that he was the risen Christ. News of this discovery reached the London newspapers, which brought to the church the following Sunday a crowd, it was claimed, of 6,000, with the usual worshippers having to jostle with a throng of mockers and hecklers who were keen to throw Smyth-Pigott into Clapton Pond. 'We'll see if he can walk on water!' some are supposed to have cried.

The commotion reached such a pitch that he hurried off back to the safety of Spaxton. There he presided over the community. Alongside his wife Kate he installed a woman called Ruth Preece as his soul bride. Three children were born to him and Ruth: whom they called Glory, Power and Life. Like Prince, Smyth-Pigott (plain Smyth from 1914) was blessed with a long life, though not with immortality. He died in 1927 at seventy-five, leaving everything to Ruth Preece or, as she now called herself, Ruth Annie Smyth. She lived until 1956. The community lingered on, a collection of digni-fied and respected old men (a few) and old women until it was sold by Smyth's children in 1958. In the final years, people in Spaxton insist, no one had a bad word to say about the Agapemone. For a time the chapel stood empty, until it was taken over by the people who made the TV children's programme *Camberwick Green*.

Still brooding on these mysterious events in this calm and beauti-ful corner of Somerset I return to the bus stop expecting the bus from Bincombe to be back at any moment. An elderly woman with a white stick says this is too optimistic. The drivers on route 18 keep getting lost, she warns. Their speciality seems to be going to Nether Stowey when the timetable says Over Stowey, which means that they end up going to both. Four or five other shoppers join us, telling jolly tales about their experiences of the Bridgwater bus. Today it arrives fifteen minutes late, which the group at the bus stop thinks is quite decent. 'Awfully sorry,' the driver tells them. 'I went to Nether Stowey by mistake.'

But one adventure is rarely enough for route 18, and although he has the route written out in an exercise book propped on the steer-ing wheel, as soon as we get to Four Forks he goes wrong again. 'You've gone the wrong way!' cries a chorus behind him. 'You should have turned right.' The driver stops and appeals for advice. Is there somewhere just up the road where he can turn the bus? 'No,' cries the chorus implacably. So he puts the bus into reverse; but a line of cars has drawn up behind him during the consultation, which he has to wave past. And just as the last one rounds him, a further car appears behind, and another. At which point one of the passengers – the one who is blind or near-blind – suddenly remembers a track to a farm down the road, possibly wide enough to back into. And indeed it proves wide enough for the purpose, but the track is so rough and uneven that as the driver manoeuvres the passengers are thrown about. Most take this without complaint. But others begin to assert that this isn't the first time this kind of thing has befallen them while riding on a number 18. 'We're used to this sort of thing,' cries one in a broad West Midlands accent. 'I've still got a great big bruise on my arm from last Friday!' And she rolls up her sleeve for us and the driver to see. 'Just as well it wasn't her thigh,' another passenger mutters.

But what with Over and Nether Stowey and the incident at Four Forks the bus is now running very late, threatening my chances of catching the next bus for Taunton. I have mentioned this ambition to the driver on our way out to Spaxton and now he is determined to get me there. Though the seconds are ticking away as we close in on Admiral Blake he is certain that we can do it. As we roar into the bus station, the Taunton bus is still there but clearly on the point of departing. With an elegant swerve, the driver takes his number 18 round the 21A for Taunton and stops so close ahead of it that it couldn't move if it tried. 'We've done it!' he cries.

But the ride to Taunton is nowhere near as delightful or needless to say so eventful as the Spaxton run. The Spaxton journey had something of the fantasy of Princeite theology. The road to Taunton is unremarkable, unrewarding: gritty, boring, hard professional replacing endearing amateur. The 21A sticks unremittingly to the A38 main road on a route so devoid of attraction that signs pointing back to places like Goathurst provoke a fierce nostalgia for the scenes of only thirty-five minutes ago. There are intermittent views of the Quantocks; there's an episode called North Petherton, the largest parish in Somerset, though not the most alluring.

Taunton, too, is a disappointment. The historian Macaulay said of it: 'It has not so much gone back as been overtaken', and that's the feeling it tends to give one today. It falls short of the sense of occasion of the best county towns. There is one brilliant piece of townscape, a narrow lane which brings you to the church of St Mary Magdalene, with its glorious tower (163 feet, four stages). I did not get to the top, but Macaulay did and greatly admired the view. The centre still boasts the castle, but the town makes impoverished use of its riverside. Disquieting, too, even for lovers of bookshops, to see that the fine old County Hotel is now a branch of Waterstone's. It is when landmarks like this reach the end of their original lives that you know a town is changing, and quite probably diminishing.

But it does have an excellent local studies library, with the kind of expert librarian who is genuinely engaged in what customers ask for: in my case, for the box that I knew they kept of Agapemone memorabilia. And here, brought up from some vault, are the very books which passed through the hands of Brother Prince and Smyth-Pigott and the Nottidge sisters and Brother Thomas and the no longer virginal Sister Zoe. Here are the theological writings, in book and pamphlet, of Brother Prince in several languages: *The Testimony of Brother Prince concerning what Jesus Christ has done in his Spirit to Redeem the Earth*, 1856 ('he has created a new Heaven according to His word; this was the first thing Jesus Christ did by his Spirit in order to redeem the earth; and He did it by fulfilling the gospel in Brother Prince'); *Brother Prince's Journal, or, The Account of the Destruction of the Works of the Devil in the Human Soul by the Lord Jesus Christ through the Gospel*, 1859; *The Shutters Taken Down from the Windows of Heaven*,

1877; *A Sword in the Heart of Leviathan*, 1878; *The World's Malady, its Root and its Remedy* (a far-reaching work: index entries, which start with abortion, include Paris, a whited sepulchre, Red Indian's perversion of womanhood, and statistics on unseaworthy ships, immorality and divorce; the final entry says: Young ladies, modern); a poem of 1895, on the fiftieth anniversary of his vision at Brighton; and a collection, from 1896, of hymns Brother Prince has written over fifty years. Here are books of his songs and hymns, presented 'with Brother Prince's love' to Louisa Nottidge. And a copy of Brother Prince's Journal, to dear Eva, from Beloved: very likely the same Eva who resulted from Prince's encounter with young Miss Paterson in the chapel at Spaxton; in which case, he must have come round to the view that she wasn't the child of Satan after all.

It's easy to dismiss Brother Prince as some kind of charlatan, enjoying the money and the welcome as a deity as he takes his place in the chapel, the pomp of his evangelizing descents on the square at Bridgwater, the adulation of his community, and particularly of its women – even, if pub gossip was right, the dalliances with laundresses. Yet it's hard to square that with the impression you get from these books of a kindly, reverent man who genuinely believed that the way he preached was the whole and only truth. The best attempt I have seen to make sense of Brother Prince and others like him is in a study by Aldous Huxley entitled 'Justifications', in a collection of his essays, *The Olive Tree*. Some people, Huxley argues, develop philosophies which enable them to feel morally justified in engaging in actions which otherwise they could only perform in the heat of passion and under the threat of subsequent remorse. Prince, who was one of these, would have been convinced that, in terms of his theology, his union with Miss Paterson had become a sacred duty.

Another case quoted by Huxley is that of the poet Coventry Patmore, besotted by religion and also by sex. His friend and contemporary Edmund Gosse wrote of Patmore: 'If you firmly believe that your volition is melted into God's there is no difficulty in supposing that if you find yourself wishing for something or approving something, that thing is also approved by God.' Though these words were written about another phenomenon, I think that is as near as we are likely to get to the essence of Henry James Prince, beloved leader of the Agapemone.

11

Hartland — Bude
Camelford — Wadebridge

ST ENDELLION

*Saintly King Brychan and his saintly progeny – St Nectan, in
Devon, hosts an annual get-together with Cornish siblings –
through gorgeous hedgerows to Bude – a saint crawl through
Boscastle and Tintagel to Camelford and Wadebridge – my
homage to St Endelient; also to a seventeenth-century recusant
scholar and a twentieth-century poet.*

To get from Hartland in Devon to St Endellion in Cornwall by bus
is not an undertaking I'd recommend, even in summer, and in
winter when the summer buses go into hibernation you can hardly
do it at all. Nevertheless it has to be done if you're to follow the
trail of the progeny of another unusual figure in the history of religion, St Brychan, a saint who is said to have fathered twenty-four
children, all of them saints. Just who these saints were is a matter
of some contention, but an epic attempt to disentangle them was
made in the seventeenth century by a man called Nicholas
Roscarrock, in a book now known as *Roscarrock's Lives of the Saints:
Cornwall & Devon*. It was a new edition of this book by Nicholas
Orme, professor of history at the university of Exeter, which took
me to Cornwall on a kind of bus-borne saint crawl, to see how many
of Brychan's children I could visit by bus. The evidence Roscarrock
has assembled about his various saints, of whom he charted over
400, is so confusing that sometimes he almost despairs. 'I confess

freely,' he says in one case, 'I know not which opinion I may safely follow, for remedy whereof I will truly lay down what I find written of him, and so refer it to the judicious censure of my reader that they who are able and can give better sentence than I may inter- pose their opinions and use their best means and endeavours to profit (if it may be) that of which I rest uncertain.' This is conjec- tural historiography with a built-in refutation factor.

In the case of St Brychan's family, though, Roscarrock's 'very learned and laborious' friend Mr Camden has found in the library at Merton College, Oxford, a book listing the children of Brechanus and his wife Gladwise (who some say was a saint herself) as: 1 Nictanus, 2 Joannes, 3 Endelient, 4 Memfre, 5 Dilie, 6 Tedda, 7 Nalem, 8 Wennon, 9 Wensent , 10 Merwenna, 11 Wenna, 12 Juliana, 13 Ise, 14 Morwenna, 15 Wimp, 16 Winheder, 17 Elinder, 18 Keri, 19 Iona, 20 Kanans, 21 Kethender, 22 Adwen, 23 Helie and 24 Tamalanc. Those who like to give their children distinctive names will find a few here, long out of use, which may be appealing, though number 15 is probably better avoided. All, says Roscarrock, were later martyrs or confessors who led the lives of hermits in Devon and Cornwall, but he has been unable to check any further because when Mr Camden went back for more details he found the book had been 'cut out and embezzled'. Yes, even then. And not least of his problems was that none of the authorities was entirely sure which of these saints were women and which were men. Nicholas Orme suggests where ten of them might be found: Nectan in Hartland, Devon; Endelient in St Endellion; Menfre in St Minver; Dilic (otherwise St Ilick) in St Endellion and in Landulph on the far side of Cornwall near Saltash; Tedda in St Teath; Mabon in St Mabyn; Merewenne in Marhamchurch; Cleder in St Clether; Keri in Egloskerry; and Adwen in Advent. The imperfections of public transport in this corner of England are such that to round them all up would take several days. But two places lie at the core of this story: Hartland in Devon, where Nectan, the eldest child of King Brychan, who Roscarrock thinks was responsible for his siblings' convergence on Cornwall, had his humble headquarters: and St Endellion, home to two of the others and a place rich in mementos of the Roscarrocks. I hoped to pick up one or two more on the way.

Hartland, reached by a 319 First Devon bus from Barnstaple by way of Bideford and tourist-rich Clovelly, is a calm and gentle scattered settlement containing the village of Hartland, Hartland quay on the coast, and Hartland Abbey, a former monastery, together with the hamlet of Stoke, which is where Nectan established his hermitage after crossing the Bristol Channel from Wales. His Cornish brothers and sisters used to join him there each year on 31 December. It must have been a struggle then to reach so remote a spot, and it isn't entirely easy now. The bus will take you to Hartland village, but thereafter you need to walk two miles or so to Stoke on an undemanding lane that brings you to the church of St Nectan. There's a statue of him on the front of the tower, although its head is a later replacement. Just before you reach the church, a path slopes down from the north side of the road which is signposted to St Nectan's well, 'the reputed site', as a leaflet in the church adroitly puts it, of his hermitage. My homage to Nectan, I'm sorry to say, is incomplete. It is raining so hard, and the path is so slippery that I cannot get down to the site, but at least I can feel I have reached the spot where, had I been one of his brothers or sisters, Nectan would have broken his eremetical silence to welcome me in.

Roscarrock's account of Nectan is mainly concerned with the lodging of his relics in a church and monastery set up by the wife of Earl Godwin in gratitude for surviving a sea storm or tempest. He records that Nectan, a martyr, was buried there. He does not describe his martyrdom. But according to Nicholas Orme, a twelfth-century life of Nectan written at Hartland says that after being befriended by a local man called Huddon who sold him two cows, the saint was attacked by robbers, who cut off his head. Using his saintly powers, he was able to carry his head back to the well near the hut where he lived.

Those who can't face the walk out to Stoke may make their obeisance to Nectan at the Catholic church of Our Lady and St Nectan in the village, opened in 1964. If you do go to Stoke, it's as well to return in good time. My bus on to Bude after my walk to Stoke comes into the square at least five minutes early. The following conversation ensues.

Me: When do you leave?
The driver (*imperiously*): NOW.

So much for any stragglers slogging it back from the coast. Official monitors found that 16 per cent of journeys operated by First Devon and Cornwall in 2003–4 started late or, in some ways worse, early, while 5 per cent never ran at all. Another last bus I took the next day also left early.

As must be apparent by now, the journeys in this book were not chosen for their particular beauty – more for the stories that grow on the waysides. But the roads out of Hartland in early summer are a delight. I cannot remember seeing hedgerows of such variety and such beauty, glowing with the pinkness of campion and fuchsia, as on this day in June. The 319 hums through the quiet lanes until disappointingly it comes to the main A39 – the Atlantic Highway, as whoever puts names to roads now calls it – and the journey is never again so magical. Alluring lanes near Welcombe Cross flaunt signposts to Welcombe, where a chapel, later promoted to church, commemorates Nectan, and later to Morwenstow, out beyond a village called Shop, on high cliffs above the Atlantic, where the church is dedicated to St Morwenna, another of Brychan's brood. 'Here' says the *Shell Guide* – this one is the work of the series editor, John Betjeman, who keeps cropping up on these journeys, emerging quite suddenly and unexpectedly sometimes, like the convict in *Great Expectations*, but looking much more peaceable and benign – ' here one is reaching not only the end of Cornwall, but, it seems, the end of the world.'

There are buses from Bude to Morwenstow, but not very often. Were some saintly miracle worker on hand, I would ask for this bus to be diverted, whatever First Devon might wish, to take me to Morwenstow, which as well as having connections with St Morwenna was also the home of the famous Cornish vicar, poet, anecdotalist and reputed inventor of harvest festivals, R. S. Hawker. Kilkhampton, as we flash through it, has a church with a rather good tower and a Norman door, a New Inn, and a kind of square, but all is blighted by the traffic-sodden A39.

And so the 319 descends to Bude, which has no apparent connection with Brychan, but is where I have to stop for the night to complete my pilgrimage later. This was once a port, served by the Bude canal. The railway, which reached Bude in the 1890s, finished off the canal trade but built it into a popular and somewhat genteel resort, which it still is today. For those in search of St Brychan and family, though, the chief virtue of Bude is that it's the gateway to Marhamchurch, served by a brisk little morning bus operated by Hookway Jennings – up to Marhamchurch, down to Widemouth Bay and then back into Bude. Going to Marhamchurch will entitle me to put a tick against the name of a second offspring of Brychan and Gladwise, St Merewenne.

Roscarrock, always reluctant to draw hard and fast conclusions from fallible evidence, is more than usually uncertain about Merewenne. 'There is a church in Cornwall not far from the place where St Endelient and St Minver lived bearing that name,' he says, 'which I would think it taketh of her, but I have heard it beareth the name of St Marina or Mariana, of which I wish others to inquire more, and so will I, God willing, if I live.' Having inquired more, as instructed, Nicholas Orme thinks Marhamchurch is the right address for Merewenne.

It's a glorious morning – the driver says I ought to have walked along the canal in the sunshine; it's only a mile or so from Bude to Marhamchurch – and the bus has a pleasant sense of a day getting under way, with an animated congregation of schoolchildren and young mothers with babies. As we leave the village there's a fine, if fleeting, view of the church of St Marwenne (rather than Merewenne, but there you are), perched strong and resolute on the hillside. At Widemouth (the correct pronunciation seems to be Widmouth) there's a spectacular view out to sea. The bay is lovely here, some of the buildings put up to meet the needs of the holiday trade possibly less so, but the sea is such a powerful statement that nothing else matters. And the route beyond, on the Western Greyhound bus to Camelford and Wadebridge, is better still. There are thousands of people living in Britain who go to marvel at Italian coasts and yet have never seen this one. It is never as dramatic – melodramatic, possibly – as the road, for instance, from Amalfi to Sorrento: yet those who have never travelled this stretch of the Cornish coast on a day as brilliant as this one should think of themselves as deprived.

Crackington Haven, where the bus returns to the sea, is an enticing spot, with ramblers everywhere. Then Boscastle, with its lively converging rivers, 'neither artified or self-conscious' as the *Shell*

Guide says. A substantial part of the village was beaten up by the vicious Atlantic storms not long after my bus passed through it. Then Bossiney, much reduced in significance since its days as a rotten borough, when two members were returned from here and neighbouring Trevena, which later became Tintagel. And Tintagel itself; its main shopping street hardly living up to its hugely romantic name: Avalon Crafts, Uncle Jack's Fish and Chips, Clobber – though the old post office is cared for by the National Trust. Tintagel's glory, however, is its coast, the stuff of tone poems, with its castle and a history predating even King Brychan. But I see there's also a beauty spot near here known as Nectan's Glen. And King Arthur, some maintained, was St Endelient's godfather.

Our bus does not complete the course through Tintagel. It turns away before it reaches the celebrated post office, and heads resolutely away from the coast. The landscape changes: the presence of slate says we are near Delabole. This road is not as evocative of the high days of Cornish industry as another just to the south through Delabole village, on which another service runs direct to St Endellion. But it still gives some sense of the county's long economic decline, from a peak that was reached in the final decades of the nineteenth century, reducing it by the end of the twentieth century to the poorest county in England. Where Delabole once had a slate industry it now has a slate museum. That is generally the story of Cornwall. Where there once was production, there is now only heritage. Nor can the tourist industry be relied on to fill the gap. Beyond Delabole is the Gaia centre, created at a cost of £5.5 million as a showpiece for alternative energy. A team of wind turbines, as perfectly choreographed as something by Busby Berkeley, is whirling away behind it. To me, they look like models of style and grace, though all over Britain they seem to inspire seething pockets of outrage. But the centre has closed. It opened expecting an annual attendance of 150,000 visitors, but even in its first year brought in only 20,000. New owners who bought it in 2003 from the receivers closed it in 2004. 'An exhibition on renewable energy is not high on holidaymakers' lists of fun things to do while on holiday,' said a spokesman. Another hope of regeneration lost.

From here the bus goes on to Camelford, again in my terms a mere gateway, this time, to Advent, where I hope to find another of Brychan's children. If you stay on the bus through Camelford there's a lane down a hill, just beyond the point where the road to Bodmin peels off from the road to Wadebridge, that will take you direct to Advent. But an even better plan is to get off the bus at the edge of the town and walk through the fields, dispersing the sheep as you go, and cross a little bridge, asking a lorry driver eating a large tomato if you're going the right way. If he says yes, press on up the hill through the peaceable hamlet of Pencarrow, the sort of sweet undamaged settlement which people would call unique and incomparable if they came across it in France or Italy. Just when you're starting to think you will never reach Advent, you will meet a man and his family with a battered old bus parked on the wayside who will tell you you're almost there. The church of St Adwena, my third so far of Brychan's holy brood, fell into disuse in the late nineteenth century, was rescued, declined again, was closed in 1960, then reopened, but by 2004 needed saving again. It was in the midst of refurbishment when I was there, the Cornwall Historic Churches Trust having somehow scraped together enough money to pay for it. The care and dedication with which the restorers were working was moving to see. Here I pay my quiet homage to St Adwena. Sadly, Roscarrock knows almost nothing about Adwena, though he takes the view that Adwena was male.

By this time it's clear I cannot complete my collection. There's a bus from Camelford to Launceston, destination Exeter, which will take me fairly close to two more of the children of Brychan on Nicholas Orme's list of ten – Clether (St Clether) and Keri (Egloskerry) – but each is two miles or so off the main road, and to visit Clether and Keri would rule out my tryst with the all-important St Endelient. To reach her means going to Wadebridge. But before that there's one more haunt of Brychan's children along my route: St Teath (Teath rhymes with death), on a side road just beyond Helstone. Again, Roscarrock's best endeavours have failed to turn up much about St Teath, whom he calls St Etha and is also confusingly known as Tedda; but in any of these guises, she was a woman. Further south, St Mabyn is signposted: another shadowy figure whom most authorities, including Roscarrock, make another daughter, though some say a son.

The ubiquitous Betjeman is waiting in Wadebridge, where the old station is now a Betjeman centre, though I've yet to see evidence that Wadebridge, reached by a long stone bridge over the river Camel, was one of his favourite Cornish haunts. 'Today,' he writes in the *Shell Guide*, 'the town seems mostly shops and garages and is a centre for refuelling and larder filling in the holiday season.' Not far from the old station there's a sign which says 'Camel Hire', giving hope that the place may have grown more exotic since Betjeman's day, but disappointingly the Camel refers to the river: they don't hire out camels, just cars. There's an animated discussion as the bus for St Endellion waits to depart about the whereabouts of a man in a yellow coat whom the driver and a friend who has come aboard for a chat feel they haven't seen for a while. 'He's inside,' says a voice from the back seats where a young mother sits with her daughter. 'What for?' 'Drunk and disorderly.' The discussion moves on to the question of Sid, who since he had his accident has been driving a Mercedes, but doesn't like it. But soon we are back to the man in the yellow coat. It seems he also hit someone. The driver: 'Who did he smack?' Woman at the back: 'Don't know.' The driver: 'Was it a copper? He doesn't like coppers, does he.' Woman at the back: 'He certainly hit one on Bonfire Night.' And we're off. The Camel estuary is away to the west and soon there are signs for St Enodoc golf course. The church, which is on the very edge of the golf course, is where Betjeman is buried.

The church at St Enodoc, someone aboard the bus explains, was at one time submerged under the sands, and they used to have to lower a clergyman down on a rope to keep it consecrated. I suspect this tale is untrue, but it's clearly much enjoyed by those discussing it. We are now approaching another child of Brychan about whom Roscarrock knows quite a lot: St Minver or Menfre. Of this saint – Menfre, he calls her – he says her home was not here but at a place called Tredrizzick. There was also a well dedicated to her, 'where it is said the ghostly adversary, coming to molest her as she was combing her head by the well, she flinging her comb at him enforced him to fly, who left a note behind him at a place called at this day Topalundy, where on the top of a round high hill there is a strange deep hole (as men there have by tradition) then made by the devil avoiding St Menfre'. If only, I muse, the rural police, equipped with combs, could somehow adopt this tactic when dealing with the man in the yellow coat. He would surely never smite a policeman again.

Roscarrock, I notice, is worried about his account of St Menfre. He fears critics may think him gullible. But he thinks his critics are irreverent. His method, he explains, is to set down what he finds sincerely and in conscience, 'not daring to correct that which I know not how to control'. He knows what he writes is imperfect. He wishes he knew more about the saints he describes. Yet he would not wish to be like Mr Lambert (William Lambarde, a Kent historian with a tongue which could be caustic when he was writing about the church), who has shown himself a censurer of saints, and a dogged snarler at the holies of God. 'For in these matters of saints, when we can say nothing that is good, we should in reason forbear to write that which is ill, being bound in all doubtful things to think the best.' Nicholas would not have got far in modern journalism.

The church at St Menfre is set so low on the road that it looks almost as if it consisted of a spire alone. On the road are all the signs and sights of the holiday trade, from a place called Quba Sails to Mr Grumpy's fish and chip shop. The great bay at Polzeath is festooned with signs about surfing: surf shop, surf school, surf lodge, surfside fast food. Rock, I suggest to the driver, is a place habitually troubled by the products of public schools who come here at the end of the summer term, drink themselves silly, make a great deal of noise, affront the natives and cause all kinds of trouble. He denies it. Maybe that used to happen, he says, but not now. Yet later I see that during the summer hols of 2005 the newspapers are full of reports of young people, lavishly funded by mummy and daddy, indulging themselves in Rock and Polzeath at the locals' expense. But mercifully all is tranquil today as my bus passes through. As we come into St Endellion it is beginning to rain.

Endelient is Roscarrock's favourite saint, his patroness, his muse, his life's inspiration. She lived, he says, a very austere course of life, drinking the milk of a cow only, which cow (according to old people speaking by tradition) the lord of Trenteny killed when it strayed into his ground: 'She had a great man to her Godfather which they say was king Arthur, who took the killing of the cow in such sort that he killed or caused the man to be slain, whom she miraculously revived.' Then Roscarrock describes her death and burial: 'And when she perceived the day of her death drew nigh, she entreated her friends after her death to lay her dead body on a sled, and to bury her there where certain young stots, bullocks and calves a year old should of their own accord, draw her'; which they did, to a place which was then a waste ground and a great quagmire at the top of a hill. This was the spot (across the road from the present church) where the first church was built, which was dedicated to her. There were two wells nearby bearing her name. Her tomb in the present church was defaced in the time of Henry VIII and was afterwards lodged on top of that of a Mr Batten (though some more recent authorities think it was Mrs Batten).

The fifteenth century church which stands in St Endellion now is a delight. The 'improvements' made by the Victorians – they included the removal of a Jacobean pulpit, which went to a church in Bodmin that now has no idea where it is – were undone and reversed by a rector who was here from 1932 to 1956, Gerald Murphy. It is above all celebrated for the work of a consummate master, known today as the Master of Endellion. There are bosses and little carved angels around the church, commemorating among others King Brychan and Endelient but also St Teath. Above a memorial to Betjeman is an angel that looks rather like him. But the most distinguished work is the shrine of St Endelient, carved by the Master in Catacleuse stone, worked with extraordinary delicacy, as loving a tribute as the poem Nicholas Roscarrock wrote in praise of the saint.

Two saints are remembered here: Endelient, and her sister St Ilick, or Dilic, who lived nearby. Roscarrock says that the path where the sisters walked together was greener than anywhere else, but where the path is now is a mystery even to Liz Bartlett, wife of the present rector and a knowledgeable chronicler of St Endellion, who showed me around. Of Endelient's sister St Ilick, Roscarrock says she had a church dedicated to her at St Endellion, and also a well. Local people used to say she had come out of Ireland miraculously on a harrow or hurdle. A tree grew over her well, and a man who cut it down hurt himself and died afterwards. Nicholas Orme says the church – or rather chapel – named after her fell into disuse and was later replaced by a farm, of which nothing was left eventually but a dilapidated cottage.

Down the lane to the sea at Port Quin is an Ogham stone. The inscription is no longer legible, but it may relate to King Brychan – although the fact that it described him as the son of Nadottus, which our Brychan plainly was not, makes that a continuing mystery. From here you can see, beyond Tintagel castle on its headland, the further headland glimmering in the distance of Hartland, home of Nectan, the first place of pilgrimage on my journey. Beyond that is Lundy Island, which Roscarrock believed was a haunt of his sweet saint Endelient too. And far beyond that, invisible, is the coastline of Wales, to which I go next, on the trail of an even earlier historian than Nicholas Roscarrock: Gerald of Wales. He too commemorated St Brychan: 'He had twenty-four daughters,' he says with characteristic if unjustified confidence. 'From their youth upwards they were all dedicated to the religious life, and they ended their days blissfully in this state of sanctity.'

On the way back to Wadebridge I dip into Nikolaus Pevsner's *Cornwall*. And find that this famously cautious authority dauntingly writes with Gerald-like confidence of 'King Brychan and his three wives, his concubines, and his forty-nine children.' There are even, I've since discovered, some accounts which claim there were sixty-three. Memo for any subsequent Cornish saint-crawl by service bus: next time, allow two months at the very least.

12

Manorbier — Haverfordwest
St Davids — Fishguard —St Dogmaels

NEVERN

*In the footsteps of Gerald of Wales, raconteur, man of letters
and priest with thwarted ambitions – how while attempting to
recruit Crusaders, he outpreached (he says) the Archbishop of
Canterbury – sinister disappearance of an early clerical spin
doctor – reaching St Davids, I am lectured on local morality –
Fishguard's role in our island story – the good and the bad at
St Dogmaels – how the pub at Nevern acquired an exotic
landlady, and a market gardener-turned-naturist went
beyond the permissible.*

In the year AD 1188, Baldwin, Archbishop of Canterbury, crossed the
borders of Herefordshire and entered Wales. We know this because
Gerald of Wales, would-be archbishop of Wales, ardent if sometimes disputatious archdeacon, accomplished raconteur and man
of letters, went rather reluctantly with him, and, as was his practice, wrote everything down: where they went, what they did, and
why, sadly, Archbishop Baldwin wasn't quite up to it. His great book,
The Journey Through Wales, is mainly (though not consistently,
since Gerald loves discursiveness) an account of their efforts to
enlist the men of Wales for the Third Crusade. He subtitled the
book: 'the journey of Gerald the Welshman and the difficult mission
to Wales carried out by Baldwin, archbishop of Canterbury'.
Difficult in the sense that the way was often uncertain and sometimes perilous – they passed at one point through quicksands – but

more so because Gerald felt that Baldwin should not be making this journey at all. 'He was a man,' Gerald says at the outset, 'whom everyone respected, for he was well known for his learning and piety.' He was also, however, weak: unable or unwilling to stand up for the rights of the church. Perhaps he was simply too good for this world, a quality in many ways admirable in a religious man, but a defect in an archbishop of Canterbury.

In any case the archbishop should not have been interfering in the affairs of the Welsh. Some of the canons at St David's cathedral had done their best to stop Baldwin coming, even requesting the local potentate, Prince Rhys, to forbid his visit. Gerald did not go quite that far. But he firmly and implacably believed that the Church in Wales ought to be independent and free from Canterbury's meddling. It should have its own archbishop, and that archbishop should be Gerald of Wales. On the basis of his interpretation of history (or rather, misinterpretation, since much of the evidence that he cited was fantasy) he held that the English had stolen the birthright of the Welsh church. It had once, he speciously argued, run its own show, until the English had usurped it. There were other things wrong with the archbishop's journey too. For a start, they missed out Manorbier.

Pembrokeshire is a county of castles. Stern and magnificent Pembroke, where the first Tudor king was born, built by the Norman William Marshall, earl of Pembroke, around the year 1200, to intimidate the Welsh, which it did. Carew, the most romantic of all, the saddest and sweetest of places, both ruined fortress and ruined Elizabethan mansion. And Manorbier, on the edge of the sea, cosy and homely – still now privately owned, so domestic that it even has a private house in its keep. The Manorbier that Gerald describes is still recognizable today: the castle, the stream that runs through the valley below it, and across the valley, the church.

'Of all the different parts of Wales,' Gerald wrote, 'Dyved, with its seven cantrefs, is at once the most beautiful and the most productive. Of all Dyved, the province of Pembroke is the most attractive; and in all Pembroke the spot which I have just described is most assuredly without equal. It follows that in all the broad lands of Wales Manorbier is the most pleasant place by far. You will not be surprised to hear me lavish such praise upon it, when I tell you that this is where my own family came from, this is where I myself was born. I can only ask you to forgive me.'

It is raining at Manorbier, raining as people expect it to rain in Wales, stubbornly and with passion. Children scamper around the castle, their parents plodding glumly behind them. Some families shelter in the castle's cell-like rooms. A bird flies through the great hall, recalling the moment in Bede where the flight of a bird through a banqueting hall is used to evoke the transience of life – even if in this case it's only a pigeon. In the village, close to the stop where a small drenched huddle waits for the 349 bus, is a notice commemorating Gerald as a man of letters. 'Quite right,' one can imagine him saying. 'Man of letters. The chap who wrote that knew what he was talking about.' The villages in this part of Pembrokeshire through which the 349 travels are comfortable and compact, on the pattern of southern England. The north and south of this large and beautiful county belong to quite different worlds: the two sides of a line once known as the landsker, running from Newgale Sands on the western coast to Trefgarn just north of Haverfordwest and then down to Carmarthen Bay. The north feels Welsh, the south feels English, even home counties English.

The bus takes us into Pembroke on a low road with the town massed on the hill to the north. This is merely the prelude to a fine piece of theatre as the bus sweeps around a curve and climbs a precipitate hill right below the powerful walls of the castle, before turning away from the busy, traffic-clotted main street, down a hill and over the river, where swans are parading in the continuing rain. Beyond is the planned town of Pembroke Dock, where the dockyards began in 1812 and were gone in the 1920s, leaving it looking a little drab and purposeless and downtrodden now. Still beyond that is the Cleddau toll bridge, with spectacular views of the boat-bobbing estuary. One must make the most of this display while it lasts because afterwards the route has little to celebrate. An extensive tour of Neyland follows, yet another town that boasts links with Brunel, who dreamed of making it a principal port for crossings to Ireland, a role that was snaffled by Fishguard. There are rather monotonous terraces, many pubs, and some fine views over the water.

Haverfordwest, which in the mid-sixteenth century superseded Pembroke as county town, has a Norman castle – badly damaged in the Civil War and certainly no match for Pembroke's – and a curving main street that climbs the hill to a grand market square at the top. This was one of the places where Gerald and Baldwin stopped to recruit. 'In Haverfordwest,' Gerald says, 'the archbishop first gave a sermon, and then the word of God was preached with some eloquence by the Archdeacon of St David's, the man whose name appears on the title-page of this book, in short by me.' Gerald is not content with establishing that he (as usual) out-preached the archbishop. 'Many found it odd,' he cannot refrain from adding, 'and some, indeed, thought it little short of miraculous, that when I, the Archdeacon, preached the word of God, speaking first in Latin and then in French, those who could not understand a word of either language were just as much moved to tears as the others, rushing forward in equal numbers to receive the sign of the Cross.'

Part of the charm of this book is that Gerald is out to seize on every chance for an entertaining diversion. 'I must tell you...' he repeatedly says, and you know there's no stopping him – not that you'd want to. At one moment he's digging an anecdote out of Pliny. At the next, well, here's a tale out of Denmark which demonstrates that sinister political acolytes were at work long before the late twentieth century. A priest, he says, appeared from nowhere and attached himself to an archbishop. 'He was discreet and hardworking, he had a great store of literary and historical knowledge, and he possessed a phenomenal memory. He did all he could to please the archbishop. And in a very short time the two became close friends. One day, when he was talking to the archbishop about happenings long past and events long forgotten, all of which were naturally of great interest to that prelate, he mentioned the incarnation of Our Lord. "Before Jesus Christ was born in the flesh," he said, "devils had great power over human beings; but when He came, this power was greatly diminished. They were dispersed, some here, some there, for they fled headlong from His presence. Some hurled themselves into the sea. Others hid in hollow trees and in the cracks of rocks. I remember that I myself jumped down a well." As he said this, he blushed for shame. Then he got up and left the room.

'The archbishop was greatly astonished, and so were all those with him. One after the other they asked what he could possibly have meant and put forward their own suggestions. They waited a while, for they expected him to return at any moment. Then the archbishop sent one of his men to fetch him. His name was called and he was looked for everywhere, but he was never seen again.'

The next phase of Gerald's journey is through Camrose to Newgale Sands en route to St Davids. Richards Brothers (Brodyr Richards), who run the excellent buses around here, don't take you into Camrose. But for much of the journey north, the route of their 411 bus sticks close to Gerald's. On the main road at Roch, two women wait in the rain, clutching their bicycles. 'Is it possible for us to take our bicycles on this bus?' one asks in the manner of someone translating word by word from the original German. 'We are on our way to St Davids.' The driver ponders this for a moment. 'All right,' he says, 'go on.' 'Oh, there is so much rain!' one exclaims. 'This isn't rain,' the driver replies, speaking from long wet Welsh experience. 'It's heavy dew.'

The heavy dew eases as we close in on Newgale. 'Next,' says Gerald, 'we cross Newgale Sands.' And that's that. To any sentient person who has ever come around the bend in the road above Newgale and seen laid out below the vast honeyed sands, the sparkling bay framed by the headland beyond, such insouciance seems quite extraordinary. Drivers of family cars pull into lay-bys as soon as they see it unfolding before them. Travellers on Richards buses do not have this convenient option, but I marvel at what I see, especially when I mentally edit the motorized campers and caravans out of the picture. Perhaps Gerald had made this journey so often that he took this wonder of God's creation for granted.

St Davids, long an ecclesiastical city, is now a civil one too, thanks to the grace of a London government in 1995. It's really no more than a village, but it wears the badge of city with pride. Even now, this is a lonely place, perched on the edge of Pembrokeshire, of Wales, of Britain. 'To the medieval Englishman,' says the *Shell Guide* (this time it is Vyvyan Rees), 'this was the end of the world. Two pilgrimages to St Davids equalled one to Rome.' 'St Davids,' says Gerald, 'is in a remote corner of the country, looking out towards the Irish Sea. The soil is rocky and barren. It has no woods, no rivers and no pasture lands. It is exposed to the winds and to extremely inclement weather. It lies between two hostile peoples who are constantly fighting over it, the Flemings and the Welsh.' St David chose this spot because of its very remoteness, as a place dedicated to the spiritual life, out of the noisy world.

The cathedral is astonishing. Many cathedrals have to be ascended to; this one is down a steep hill, nestling in the valley. The place has an air of uncertainty which comes from the fact that none of the floors seems to be flat: there are slopes in all directions, which gives me a queasy sense of being on board a pitching ship. The sight of St Davids fills Gerald with mixed emotions. He is fond of the place, and yet it is full of remembered frustrations. In 1176, the bishop – his uncle – had died, and Gerald, though not yet thirty, had some claim to succeed him. All four archdeacons of Wales were in line for the post, but the English king, Henry, anxious that the appointment should not foster separatist tendencies, blocked the lot of them, and a Cluniac from Shropshire was given the job. Gerald has little time for Cluniacs. 'Give the Cluniacs today a tract of land covered with marvellous buildings,' he reflects, 'endow them with ample revenues and enrich the place with vast possessions: before you can turn round it will all be ruined and reduced to poverty. On the other hand, settle the Cistercians in some barren retreat which is hidden away in an overgrown forest: a year or two later you will find splendid churches there and fine monastic buildings, with a great amount of property and all the wealth you can imagine...'

My bus from Haverfordwest gives up at St Davids, but another soon appears going on to Fishguard; but not before a very old man has buttonholed me, Gerald-like, with a tale of how evil-doing has been stamped on in St Davids. 'There is no vandalism round here,' he assures me. 'You can leave your front door open all day without fear. There were five or six bad lads round here who were causing trouble. One of them broke a seat. We stripped him and made him stand naked in the street!' Naked in the street? In the heart of this cathedral city? I mutter something appropriate. 'Bring back the cat!' he roars as if expecting instant compliance. 'Look at him!' he commands, pointing at a sturdy man crossing the street. 'He beats his old mother and steals her money!' But at this point Richards Brothers arrive to carry me out of this den of iniquity.

Coastal buses from here take you into the seaside settlements of Abereiddy and Porthgain, where there's a quite famous pub called the Sloop. Both are well worth the detour, but sadly not on the route of Gerald of Wales or that of the 411. Gerald has little to say about the next stage of his journey. Having said Mass at St Davids, the archbishop hurried off through Cemais to meet Prince Rhys at Cardigan, leaving Gerald to preach to the people, which is good for an anecdote about a man called Seisyll Esgairhir who gets eaten by toads. Gerald is on his way to rejoin the archbishop at the monastery of St Dogmaels by way of Nevern. The modern traveller intent on reaching St Dogmaels, in summer at least, has another option: a bus through to Fishguard, and then one of the ramblers' buses which now pick their way through the narrow enticing byways between the main road and the coast. The road to Fishguard offers lavish views of the sea, the best of which comes at the end of a long and lovely descent between high hedges into a place called Llanrhian, opening out to disclose a vivid expanse of ocean.

Fishguard – Abergwaun in the Welsh – was famous as a harbour and despatcher of boats to Ireland, though they now depart from an outcrop called Goodwick. In the Royal Oak pub is a document that commemorates an incident, some six hundred years after his death, that Gerald of Wales would love to have described: the last invasion of Britain in 1797, when a French landing party, led by an eccentric American adventurer called William Tate, came ashore just beyond Goodwick. (The extent of his expertise is indicated by the fact that his orders told him to land at Bristol.) Some of the older histories say his men fled when confronted with a troop of red-coats, who were not as they thought the King's military but the women of Fishguard, disguised – dressed, as it were, to kill. But the Royal Oak is not yet open this morning, and the Poppit Rocket bus is about to arrive outside.

These holiday buses are routed down lanes which can never in all their long history have expected to see a bus, and navigation – and negotiation with drivers of other vehicles which suddenly loom up in front – can be a tricky affair. The road to Pwllgwaelod by way of Bryn-henllan is as difficult to steer a bus down as these places are to pronounce – if you're English. Yet the driver keeps stopping because he is early. Whenever he gets the chance he takes out the *Independent*. 'Hutton leak inquiry,' it says, 'yet another whitewash.' There are pictures of exotic London political figures – Alastair Campbell of number 10, Trevor Kavanagh of the *Sun* – who seem quite as unreal and fantastical here on this coast as the characters in the tales of Gerald of Wales. At one point a large young man with moustache and beard gets on and asks for half-fare. He says he's fourteen. 'I think you're over fifteen,' says the driver. 'In fact' (after further study), 'I think you're over sixteen.' We wait on the edge of our seats to see how this stand-off will be resolved. 'I'm fourteen,' says the large young man in little more than a whimper. The driver sighs and accepts his money.

It starts to rain as the bus potters through Moylgrove and stops for a moment by the broad rainswept sands of Poppit Bay, often thronged but deserted this morning. As we come into St Dogmaels, down the Teifi estuary, the rain is beating imperiously on the roof. I am half an hour in a coffee shop before it abates. Then it relents, and the sun is out when I get to the monastery. This place is so mysterious now that one grumbles at Gerald for telling us no more about it than that he and Baldwin had a comfortable night there. Dogmael was a Celtic monk. The abbey was established on the site of an earlier house, in 1115, by Robert Fitzmartin, Lord of Cemaes, as a daughter church of the French abbey of Tiron, in the reformed Benedictine order. The man who runs a nearby shop is sorry to say that though there used to be histories of the abbey he can't get hold of them any more. There's an outbuilding which may soon become a visitor centre with a permanent exhibition, but at present there's no one to ask.

Beside the abbey ruins is the church of St Thomas, with a graveyard full of maritime memorials. So many from this stretch of the coast were lost at sea, sometimes in distant waters: Evan Evans, chief officer of the ship *Hawarden Castle*, lost with all hands on a journey from New South Wales to Valparaiso in 1890 (he was twenty-five); William George Evans, who sailed in the barque *Talca* of Swansea, lost at sea 1884, aged twenty-nine, on a voyage from his home port to Cape Town; Henry, son of Timothy and Anna Thomas, lost at sea off Madeira, 1896, at twenty-one; his parents had already lost Thomas, nine months, Edith, one day, Albert, one day and Lizzie at twenty-six. Many more, especially fishermen, died in waters much closer to home. Twenty-seven men and boys from the village were lost in one disaster in 1789. Also inside the church is the Sagranus stone, eased out of a whitewashed wall by a one-time vicar, who found it encased there. The inscription, like the one on the stone near the Roscarrock house at St Endellion, is in Ogham: it was the finding of this stone which enabled the secrets of that lettering to be unlocked.

The abbey, like so many, fell into ruin. The village with its long and dignified main street, and above all the abbey, have an air of unhurried serenity, especially now it's stopped raining. Yet the local paper has lurid tales of a posse of local men beating up a soldier they judged, despite a court having cleared him, to be guilty of rape. Not every peaceful village is as blameless as it looks. And people in a pub where I stop on my way on to Cardigan even confess to doubts about the monastery of St Dogmaels. They talk (perhaps to enjoy the gullibility of the visiting English) of sinful conjunctions of monks with lewd ladies, some of them possibly nuns, putting a whole new construction on that time-honoured concept, the dissolution of the monasteries.

Baldwin and Gerald went on to Cardigan where they spent two nights, then to Lampeter, and so, still recruiting crusaders, into North Wales. My journey takes me to Cardigan too, but only to mop up a bit of unfinished business. The unfinished business is Nevern – Llanhyver in Gerald's day – through which he passed on his way to St Dogmaels. It's a place full of the kind of anecdote he used to enjoy. No bus now penetrates Nevern, but the Richards Brothers/ Brodyr Richards bus from Cardigan to Haverfordwest stops on the main road a mile or so out of the village, from where it's an easy walk down the hill. At the foot of the hill you come to a pub called the Trewern Arms. Just beyond is a bridge across the river – the Trewern Arms is a favourite haunt for fishermen – from where the road leads up to the church of St Brynach. Like a good many churches in these parts, the stout tower has a hint of fortress about it. There are ancient yews in the graveyard, one of which appears to weep blood, and a fine Celtic cross.

The village is stately and, by the look of it, pretty expensive. It's the Trewern Arms, though, that would have caught Gerald's attention. The landlady there in the late 1950s was a woman called Pamela Nelson-Edwards. Before her marriage to a former RAF fighter pilot she had been Pamela Davidson, her father being the notorious Rector Harold Davidson of Stiffkey in Norfolk, defrocked for various untheological reasons but mainly it seemed because of his adventures with women. Waitresses in Lyons cornerhouses were said to be a particular weakness, though dealings with prostitutes were also alleged. Davidson always protested his innocence, and appeared for a while on the Golden Mile at Blackpool, in a barrel, complaining of a miscarriage of justice. Even now, some of his descendants maintain that his real offence was his socialism. Later he took a job in a circus at Skegness, where in the course of his duties he was mauled by an ageing lion called Freddie, and died of his injuries. Pamela alone of his family stood by him after he was disgraced, even though, according to a riproaring obituary in the *Daily Telegraph* after her death in March 2001, she suspected that her true father was a Canadian army colonel who had lodged at the rectory at about the time she was conceived. Pamela too joined the circus and became a tumbler, moving on to a theatre in London called the Windmill, where the slogan throughout the war was 'we never closed'; a formula parodied by the unseemly as 'we never clothed' since the girls appeared on stage nude.

Whether Pamela also appeared nude was not made clear by her obituarist, although her family thinks that she did. In 1938 – not the best year to choose – she signed up for a tour of Germany, where she caught the amorous eye of Joseph Goebbels. Unfortunately, as the obituary said, this did not prevent her getting locked up for a night by the Gestapo, who thought the name Davidson meant she was Jewish. Spurned though he was, Goebbels used his influence to get her released. Wartime was somewhat calmer, in that Pamela's adventures were limited to serving in the Women's Land Army and the US Red Cross. By the time she reached Nevern, her life was relatively orthodox. Even so, there were often excitements: visitors to the Trewern Arms during her reign were said to have included the Swinging Blue Jeans, Lionel Bart and George Melly; also Princess Alexandra's husband, Angus Ogilvy, not normally known as an entertainer. Although she and her husband moved away, Nevern remained a big affection: she is buried there. They still talk fondly of her in the Trewern Arms.

In November 1998, two years before Pamela's death, Nevern had been the scene of a fine scandal. A man called Roger Brett, a former major in the Royal Electrical and Mechanical Engineers, had with his wife Audrey set up a market garden in Nevern. It did not do very well. He decided, as he later explained to the police, to branch out into the world of naturism, the practice of communal nudity, but found the clientele this attracted fancied something racier. The attractions they duly provided were described in the magistrates' court in Cardigan when he admitted running a brothel and living off immoral earnings. As the *Daily Telegraph*'s reporter, Sean O'Neill, put it: 'the custom of keen gardeners who once shopped for bedding plants and potting compost was replaced by that of cross-dressing businessmen and "liberated people" who indulged in group sex in the swimming pool.' The club was advertised on the internet as 'place dedicated to the pursuit of pleasure with no limits to self-indulgence'.

In a sense Brett was unfortunate: he was shopped by the sister of one of his clients. According to Maggie Hughes, prosecuting, it was this woman's complaint which brought police to the club. Brett's client had told her sister that she had attended orgies at the Garden of Eden (for that was its name) and the sister wanted to see for herself. They were picked up at their home sixty miles away by a driver employed by Brett. On the way to the club, the driver stopped to give directions to two blonde women who turned out to be transvestites. And that was only the start. The woman and her sister, the court was told, teamed up with two men. This was much to the men's advantage, since the charge for a couple was just £30 compared to £130 for a man on his own. (Single women were admitted free.)

The first thing the visiting sister spotted when she entered the club (the court was told) was a naked man walking towards her. Then she saw a woman indulging in 'sexual activities' with two naked men on a sofa. Next the complainant was introduced to a transvestite businessman who gave his name as 'Islwyn by day and Sharon by night'. It seems to have been at this point that she went right off the Garden of Eden. She spent the rest of the evening sitting in a car outside. Brett was fined £1,000 on each count and ordered to pay £40 costs.

One would, of course, have wished to edit this down before passing it on to an Archdeacon of Wales. Yet even a bowdlerized version might well have been gleefully filed by Gerald for future use under the twelfth-century equivalent of the heading 'It's a funny old world'.

Baldwin kept his vow to go on the Crusade, and it killed him: he died at the siege of Acre in 1190. Gerald also embarked on this perilous journey, but found himself spared when King Richard ordered him home. Offers of bishoprics now regularly came his way, but all were refused. Nothing but St Davids would do. The death of the Shropshire Cluniac in 1198 revived his aspirations, but the new Archbishop of Canterbury, Hubert Walter, who was also, after the king, the most powerful political figure in the country, would not accept him. The vacancy remained unfilled for five years while wrangling continued, but even the support of Richard's successor John failed to get him enthroned. There were repeated appeals and missions to Rome, on one of which Gerald was apprehended by Walter's agents and thrown into prison. Finally Walter installed the candidate he had wanted all along – Geoffrey, prior of Llanthony. Frustrated yet again, Gerald gave up the struggle. He lived for a further twenty years, surviving Geoffrey, who died in 1214, studying, reading, but above all writing. When he died in 1223, he was nearly eighty. He had outlived the saintly but exasperating companion of his journey through Wales by thirty-three years.

And here I leave him. I am heading north – as Gerald and Baldwin did at the end of their journey – to what, though the last of their buses ran long ago, true bus devotees still think of and talk of as Crosville country.

13

Ellesmere Port — Chester
Mold — Ruthin — Corwen

BALA

Crosville, from modest beginnings, builds a mighty bus empire –
from Ellesmere Port to Chester, a town sodden with history –
I hear the call of the cattle in Mold – Ruthin comes close to
perfection, but Corwen is not what it was – Bala: a peaceful lake
and a truculent shopper – origins of the Dee and its place in
Crosvillian history.

Even the greatest empires develop from modest beginnings. Rome
was not built a day; nor was the British empire, claimed to be the
biggest the world had yet seen. 'How is the empire?' George V is
said to have asked in his dying moments; a question which, given
the empire's size and disparity, it would have taken some weeks to
answer. The monstrous media empire of Rupert Murdoch began
with a single evening paper in Adelaide. And so it was too with the
mighty bus empire which a company called Crosville established
in north-west England and expanded by bargain and conquest into
much of north and west Wales. Today, like Rome, it has gone,
surviving only in the form of a courtesy title on some of the routes
now served by one of its modern successors, First. 'Vicissitude of
fortune,' as Gibbon exclaimed in his *Decline and Fall of the Roman*
Empire, 'which spares neither man nor the proudest of his works,
which buries empires and cities in a common grave.'

Crosville began with a single service: Ellesmere Port to Chester,
in 1911. The founding imperialist was a man called George

Crosland Taylor, who started work in a family worsted mill, became fascinated by the magic of electricity after visiting the Paris exhibition of 1881, and started the company which would later become BICC (British Insulated Callenders Cables) at Neston in the following year. The income that came out of this venture was fat enough to make him one of the first men in all Cheshire to purchase and then to market that exciting new creation, the motor car. He went back to Paris several times for the motor show, and met a French car designer called Ville. Renting a building on the banks of the Dee in Chester, he set up an assembly plant to build cars on Ville's ingenious model. Five cars were built, using the hybrid brand name Crosville. Then in 1911, scenting an opportunity in the absence of any train directly linking Ellesmere Port with Chester, he moved into buses. Encouraged by the response, he began to add other routes: Chester to Kelsall; Chester to Crewe and Sandbach. The sense of pioneering excitement as he cast about for new possibilities is captured in a book called *Crosville: The Sowing and the Harvest*, by his son, W.J. Crosland-Taylor, published in 1948. 'Forty years!' the preface begins. 'A short time in the history of most nations, and a mere flea-bite out of the age of Christianity, but the *first* forty years count a great deal in the lifetime of any industry.'

Ellesmere Port is a functional sort of place, created to serve a canal cut through to the Mersey from Ellesmere in Shropshire. There's an unexpectedly imposing civic centre and a busy bus station nearby. The original Crosville journey, via Whitby (The Sportsman), Strawberry, Backford, Moston, Upton and Bache, must have been mainly through fields; in 1914, when the journey took forty minutes (it was later cut to fifteen), the fare all the way was 8d. Today the First bus route number 1, which has come from Liverpool, heads out through the usual accoutrements of arterial roads out of town

– car parks, schools with big car parks (for pupils drive too nowa-days), playing fields, and before long one of those vast out-of-town industrial parks with attendant shopping centre which are one of the most characteristic legacies of late twentieth-century life: blessed, in the way of these things, with a name that hints at tradi-tion and the ancient rural tranquillity that its coming must have obliterated – Cheshire Oaks. The usual shopping outlets are grouped around a square, and when you have finished shopping there is everything on offer from burger bars and night clubs to Frankie and Benjy's Coliseum. Beyond is Chester Zoo. One hopes as the bus passes by for a heart-lifting glimpse of natural life – perhaps a giraffe, its long neck towering poignantly over the trees. But no such luck.

Soon we are into Chester, one of the best-looking towns in England, full of good townscape, and sodden with history. The advertised attractions of Chester are legion: two miles of city walls, handsome black and white buildings, galleried shops, a self-satis-fied town hall fronting a square, the cathedral, and beyond, which makes the place such a special delight, views of a close-by coun-tryside, glimpsed down an alley or framed at the end of a street. No town, said Orwell, should be so big that a man cannot walk out of it in a morning. Better still if green fields and rivers are no more than ten minutes away.

But students of Crosville's empire must turn aside from these engaging distractions and proceed down the hill to the racecourse and the river. From here, with some help from a passing policeman, one can make one's way to where it all started: Crane Wharf, and the buildings that Crosville hired when they started from the Shropshire Union Canal Company. Today, it all looks abandoned and desolate, an area ripe for refurbishment, with new apartment blocks – described as *stunning*, of course – springing up all around.

Here, in this now crumbling place, the Crosland-Taylors, as they became, laid their expansionist plans and plotted against their enemies – those Goths and Vandals who sought to pre-empt or duplicate their routes and snaffle their passengers – and gazed, across the tranquil waters of the river Dee, at the juicily inviting prospect of Wales.

It was 1919 when they moved, like so many English conquistadors before them, across the boundary into the principality, picking out the market towns of Mold and Flint. The old Crosville route from Chester to Mold, in the hands today of Arriva, gives us a fine panorama of tasty well-to-do houses stacked up above the river bank on the other side of the Dee. The border is close – no more than a mile or so out of Chester – and we cross it with little cere-mony, at a junction with Boundary Lane in a place called Saltney. Hawarden, a little beyond, where Gladstone wrote and thought and studied and argued and prayed and chopped wood for recreation, is happily not what it might have been; its associations with the great figure who lived here have not been exploited as mercilessly as so often happens elsewhere. Gladstone acquired Hawarden Castle (a domestic building, dramatized and converted to Gothic in the early years of the nineteenth century) through his marriage to Catherine Glynne, and rescued it when the Glynne family's debts had made a forced sale seem inevitable. Sir Edward Watkin, the entrepreneur and avid would-be tunneller, whom we met at Folkestone, was a frequent visitor. Edward White Benson, Archbishop of Canterbury, father of E. F. Benson, whom we encoun-tered at Rye, was a regular visitor too and one Sunday morning dropped dead in the church just as the absolution was being said. Gladstone himself was not present, but Mrs Gladstone was, and had to take charge. The *Shell Guide to North Wales* (by Elisabeth Beazley and Lionel Brett), which I had bought half an hour before in Chester, assures me as we whip through Hawarden that the Gladstones are commemorated in the church 'in no half-hearted manner'. The Gladstone memorial, by Sir William Blake Richmond, 'depicts Mr and Mrs Gladstone in a marble ship plough-ing their way through the sea of life.'

In his history of the company's early days, I note as we rattle along, Crosland-Taylor had mixed feelings about Wales and the Welsh. 'The Welsh extensions,' he says – he is writing here of the early 1920s – 'began to give us an insight into the Welsh character that is gravely lacking in most English people who live more than a few miles from the border. They also gave us opportunities to explore that wonderful country which we should otherwise never have had. The mountains, the woods in autumn with their chang-ing colours, and the common or garden weather which is never twice the same in the same place. But to come to earth, I must say that the bus services are, with few exceptions, pitifully thin, and the houses in villages of any size are ugly and without imagination. One wonders why that is so when the people are so full of music and poetry, but there it is.' Buckley, beyond Hawarden, is perhaps the kind of workaday place he had in mind. Like so many places run up too quickly to meet a rapidly developing industrial need, in this case from clay pits, its buildings are mostly meagre, if not ugly, though the *Shell Guide* describes the church as 'hilarious'.

Crosville started running from Chester to Mold in 1921. The link from Mold to Ruthin, the next stage on this journey, had been put on the route map two years earlier. These were years of steady and sometimes bruising accumulation. By 1920, the new empire builders had around two dozen routes; by 1924, almost fifty. As Gibbon wrote in the context of Rome: 'All that is human must be retrograde if it does not advance.' Many were bought from small operators whose competition disturbed them. Crosland-Taylor's book is full of instances of underhand tactics pursued by their rivals, especially the sneaky device of sending out buses just before a Crosville bus was due to appear, so that when the Crosville bus reached its stop the potential passengers had all been transported away. But W.J. is a straight sort of guy, and he doesn't pretend that Crosville were saintly either. He even prints several pages of the testimony of one of their rivals called Hudson who, judging the Crosville service inadequate, decided to run his own buses on the Ellesmere Port–Chester route. 'What the hell did you want to start a bus service for?' a Crosville official demanded of him. 'Why did you not start some other business? I intend running you off the road.' Crosville ran buses in Hudson's colours, which turned up just before his were due and undercut Hudson's fares. In the end, his service went into liquidation and Crosville, in their moment of conquest, magnanimously gave him a job. Through a combination of wheedling backed by bullying, other operators too gave up the unequal fight. So perished over the years Lightfoots and Gregorys, J. Pye and D. M. Jenkins, Gauterin Brothers, Hooker, J. Lewis Owens, Peris Motors and Thomas John Edwards. Mona Maroon (Holyhead Motors) ceased to light up the western sky, and Busy Bee ceased to buzz.

Mold, which, rather than the less prepossessing Flint, is the capital of the old county of Flintshire, is a sensible, practical market town with a good main street. The church at the top is set at an angle which makes it look somehow kindly and protective. The old town council building, down a side street, is a particular joy. There is still a cattle market in Mold, right by the bus station, so that as you leave and rejoin the bus you can hear the prices being called and the cattle complaining. The little bus which carries me away into deeper Wales is run by a company called GHA. Some of these buses, though sadly not this one, run by way of a place called Loggerheads, where Crosville had a 70-acre site with a café and other visitor attractions. The name of the village appears to derive from a local inn called the We Three at Loggerheads, which, according to the people who run it, commemorates an occasion when two prominent local men met there to resolve a dispute, accompanied by a mediator, who proceeded to fall out with both of them, so that all three were then 'at loggerheads'. Where the word came from is a matter of deeper mystery, but it may well derive from an earlier use of 'loggerhead', meaning a long-handled iron instrument intended for use in the forge, but perhaps used sometimes to belabour an enemy.

The roads around here are a pleasure to potter through. Maeshafn, with its Miners Arms and old chapel, was the best kept village in Clwyd in 1992, I see, and looks pretty good twelve years later. Near Eryrys the driver offers so much advice to a passenger on the best route to take from her remote home to this bus route that she proffers a tip. I have never seen this happen on a service bus before. (I can't quite see if he takes it.) The route gets better and better. Every time we go over the top of a hill there seems to be a landscape full of fresh pleasures. At length we rejoin the main A road and now at last it is full speed for Ruthin on a lovely road through the most polysyllabic village yet: Llanbedr-Dyffryn-Clywd. And Ruthin proves to be worthy of the route that approached it, perched on top of a hill with a galaxy of fine buildings, mostly now the possessions of banks. In St Peter's Square, Ruthin's market place, dignified by an 1883 clock tower, old men sit in the sun, cradling their sticks, one or two reading the papers, most talking or simply observing. There's a very distinguished street to the castle, with one splendidly lopsided house with a porch room hanging – rather perilously, it seems to me, although these builders knew what they were doing – over the door. It's for sale, and a small American boy is trying to wheedle his father into buying it.

Another GHA will take us on the penultimate lap of this journey, to Corwen, on a route which Crosville first operated in 1930 when they took it over from a company called W. Edwards. This was the biggest year so far of Crosville's imperial expansionism, and it wasn't really Crosville's doing. Under the direction of Crosland-Taylor's elder brother Claude and W.J. himself, the policy had been gradualist and pragmatic. When a problem, presented itself, W.J. explains, the brothers used to go to a bridge over the railway at Madeley and watch the trains hurtling under the bridge. It seems to have made the resolution of problems simpler. It wasn't until 1930 that expansion became so headlong and, in W.J.'s view, so headstrong. The original Crosville had now succumbed to the power of a much larger group – the railway company LMS, which, like most railway companies then, was anxious to snap up buses to link with its stations. The brothers were initially doubtful about the LMS offer, but a visit to the railway bridge at Madeley soon put that right. W.J. was inclined to take the financial risk of staying inde-pendent, but Claude was set on surrendering. 'A bird in the hand,' he observed as the trains rattled through beneath them, 'is worth two in the bush.'

But the LMS knew far less about buses than they did about rail-ways and soon they were making purchases many of which W.J. thought pointless and even reckless, taking Crosville buses into territory where the natives had never seen one before. The pace scarcely slackened in the following year, bringing the total of Crosville services by the end of 1931 to a mighty 178. Familiar service names were erased from the roads or dwindled into marginal operations as the 1930s progressed: more than forty of

Western Transport's routes were devoured in 1933 alone. Brookes Brothers, Llandudno Blue, Bethesda Grey – all had to bow their knee to the conquerors' power. Claude died in 1934: he was only forty-five. 'There would be no more meetings on the railway bridge or anything like that,' W.J. was to write in his book. 'He had guided the Crosville for twenty-four years and now he had suddenly stopped doing so.'

The route beyond Ruthin is a match for the one before it. Old inns, more delicious cottages and commanding hills to the south, some of them possibly reaching the status of mountain. The road runs through the Alyn Valley, probing deeper and deeper into what George Borrow called 'Wild Wales'. The driver, who is on his way from Denbigh to Llangollen, is as gloomy as the one on the previous bus was jaunty. Those who climb abroad with a friendly greeting are met with curmudgeonly grunts. The buildings are more occasional here, the landscape more dramatic. And here, where the road from Ruthin meets the very important though frequently very frustrating A5 highway from Holyhead to London, is Corwen. 'I arrived at Corwen,' Borrow records, 'which is just ten miles from Llangollen, and which stands beneath a vast range of rocks at the head of the valley up which I had been coming, and which is called Glyndyfrdwy, or the valley of the Dee water. It was now about two o'clock, and feeling thirsty, I went to an inn very appropriately called the Owen Glendower, being the principal inn in the principal town of what was once the domain of the great Owen.' But Corwen is not what it was. Once – on the day perhaps when Borrow sat in the inn enthusiastically refreshing himself and reading his newspaper – this must have been the kind of market town that people gaily flocked into. Now it looks more like a place that people flock out of. The railway has gone, and the kind of trade which halted at Corwen on its way along the A5 now speeds on somewhere else. The faint air of melancholy is echoed in the lead story in the Corwen, Bala and Llangollen Free Press. An exclusive by Terry Canty reports that the Corwen carnival queen 'has big day cancelled'. It's the first time in almost forty years, Terry explains, that Corwen won't have a carnival, which is rotten news for the town and particularly rotten news for eleven-year-old Rosey Smith and her attendants Bethany, Ffion, Callum and Anthony. Usually these events, the Free Press reports, have been organized by the War Memorial Park committee, but this year they had handed their duties over to the local branch of the Royal National Lifeboat Institution. The RNLI launched the usual appeal for participating floats but got only a feeble response. 'The cancellation of the carnival,' the paper sombrely adds, 'comes after the postponement in November of the town's traditional bonfire after no organization would take on the running of the event from the local fire service.' Rosey, it adds, would now represent Corwen at Gwyddelwern and Carrog carnivals; but that no doubt would be meagre consolation.

Waiting at the bus stop in faded Corwen, with W.J.'s history in my hand, I reflect on the transience of so much human achievement. W.J.'s closing pages are full of apprehension. A Labour government has been elected. Nationalization looms. Can Crosville survive? It did and he was able to call his sequel *State Owned Without Tears, 1948–1953.* The 1960s were years of contraction, as heavy losses on some of the rural services doomed them to closure, a pattern that persisted through to the 1980s. But what broke the Crosville hegemony in the end was deregulation. The death blow that W.J. had feared from Labour was struck by a Tory government. The company was split into two: Crosville Motor Services and Crosville Wales. Crosville Wales became Arriva Wales, or Arriva Cymru; the rest of the operation declined, became fragmented, was sold off and sold again, and disappeared from view in 1990. 'The art of man,' writes

Gibbon in the concluding pages of his *Decline and Fall*, 'is able to construct monuments far more permanent than the narrow span of his own existence; yet these monuments, like himself, are perishable and frail; and in the boundless annals of time his life and his labours must equally be measured as a fleeting moment.'

The last outpost of empire on my journey is lakeside Bala, on a route that Crosville captured from Western Transport in that peak imperial year, 1933. It's another entrancing journey. Buses west of Corwen leave the town by a bridge over the Dee. You come out past the final houses and suddenly the landscape explodes before you: the bridge, the glorious river, meadow and forest, conveniently scalable hills: the most joyful sight, I think, in any of my journeys so far. Just beyond, the bus leaves the A5 and takes the road to Llandrillo. This road runs much of the way on the side of a wooded valley. The pattern is becoming familiar now: occasional small clustered settlements, each with its church or chapel and pub, Blue Lion to the left of you, Prince of Wales to the right of you – though at one point, to make today different, we get stuck behind a rambling sheep which contemplates escape into the hedges but then keeps blundering on. Bala looks continental: a resort town, open to all, the harbouring and entertainment of visitors swamping all previous purposes – but look around and listen to people talking, and it's deeply Welsh. The names on the war memorial are a testimony to Welshness: eight Joneses, and an Owen-Jones, six Evanses, four Davieses, four Robertses, three Thomases, three Edwardses and three Ellises. In a bread shop, an assistant whose natural language is English is doing her best to speak to her customers in Welsh. Most of them are encouraging; but one repeats a word that she cannot catch, over and over again, in relentless Welsh, until the woman behind the counter is flushed and humiliated. When a colleague comes to her aid, the word that has caused so much anguish is the Welsh word for 'sliced'.

Signs everywhere in this town point to the lake, Lake Bala, Llyn Tegid, on the southern edge. It is nine miles long – you can if you choose travel the length on a little train on the eastern shore – and it's irresistibly beautiful, even though the day is cold and windy and, for June, alarmingly dark. A single yacht rides upon it, joined in a little while by a canoe. Nothing else stirs. Stern regulations protect this vulnerable place from exploitation. No motor boats are allowed. At the southern end is the Little Dee, flowing down from a mountain called Aran Dyfrdwy, which is higher than Cader Idris. The river Dee, which rises a little to the south-west near a spot called Adualt, flows into the lake at the southern end; it is held by local opinion to make its way through the lake without ever intermingling with the lake waters. After Bala, the river moves on, ever widening, to cross under the bridge outside Corwen; it passes through the agreeable town of Llangollen, famous for its international music eisteddfod and Borrow's base for much of the time when he went exploring Wild Wales; at Pontcysyllte, it is bridged by Thomas Telford's great aqueduct, which carries the Shropshire Union 120 feet above it; and thereafter, it forms the boundary between England and Wales before crossing at last into Cheshire. And some sixty miles on, it will pass on its way to the sea beneath the windows of the building where the Crosville story began, where Crosland Taylor and his sons and associates first began to discern and develop the destiny of the empire that flourished so mightily, yet today is gone as if it had never been.

14

Matlock — Chesterfield
Bolsover — Mansfield

OLLERTON

*The old feudalism and the new – the suzerainty of the
Devonshires – their will thwarted by mere electors – through
morning mists to Chesterfield – two unique British institutions
at Bolsover – a ropy bus out of Mansfield – why Nottingham
Forest FC play in red – how old land and new money
transformed the Dukeries – Sir Giles Gilbert Scott is snubbed –
the model mining village of Ollerton celebrates the end of
feudalism, but later suffers long grass and hard times.*

Mightier even than the empire of Crosville – far older too – is the
power and influence of the dukes of Devonshire, of whom the
present incumbent, Peregrine Andrew Morny Cavendish, is the
12th. There are large tracts of Derbyshire where this family is
inescapable. Their great house, Chatsworth, is the heart of a
domain that covers some 12,000 acres and includes the whole of
the villages of Edensor, Pilsley and Beeley and the hamlet of
Carlton Lees. When the 11th duke died in May 2004, newspapers
carried extraordinary pictures of his grieving staff, many in their
uniforms, lined up at Chatsworth, heads bowed, to watch the
cortège pass by. And yet these potentates were not invincible. On
the steps of the old Matlock town hall, there was struck early in
1944 one of the most brutal blows ever addressed by the populace
to the solar plexus of aristocratic England – a portent for the over-
throw of the old order in the general election of 1945.

The Devonshires – some benign and approachable, all respected, quite a few feared – had always been the masters of this glorious swathe of England; its political masters too, for long after the great Reform Act had abolished the rotten boroughs, there were many English seats which remained in one family's pocket. The constituency of which Chatsworth was part almost always returned a Cavendish. At the end of the First World War, a local farmer called White won the seat for the Liberals, but in 1923 aristocracy resumed its reign and the voters elected the next in line for the dukedom, the Marquess of Hartington. When this marquess became the duke and went to the Lords in 1938, his successor was a man called Henry Hunloke, a son of one of the county's most famous families, the Hunlokes of Wingerworth. But the seat was still safely tucked up for the Devonshire family, since Henry was the duke's son-in-law.

But then came the grand impertinence. It began with a scandal. Hunloke, a serving officer, told the local Conservative party he intended to give up his seat. 'A bombshell!' the *Derbyshire Times* exclaimed. 'He has been serving abroad for three years,' it said disapprovingly 'but that is not sufficient reason why he should sever his connection with West Derbyshire at such short notice and force a by-election at this time.' The press was told that the duke had done his best to dissuade the MP from this course, but Hunloke could not be moved. The truth of the matter was different. Hunloke had been having an affair, and his marriage with the duke's daughter Anne was about to break up. Once out of the family, it seems to have been assumed, he must also be out of the House.

The election of another Cavendish was seen by the family – and by local Conservatives, who were not going to thwart the will of Chatsworth – as a foregone conclusion, a fait accompli. The duke's son, the twenty-six-year-old Marquess of Hartington, a captain in the

Coldstreams, seemed to them to have an indisputable claim to the seat. Under the electoral truce that prevailed at this time, Labour were bound not to oppose him. The Conservatives stitched up Hartington's nomination even before the news of the vacancy broke. But some within the constituency objected to being taken for granted. One was Charles White, leader of the county council, and son of the Liberal interloper who had briefly interrupted the Cavendish tenure at the end of another war. White's decision to stand involved some sacrifice. Fighting the seat meant leaving the Labour party and resigning his post as food officer for Matlock. The political establishment, Labour as much as Conservative, was outraged. Not only did Winston Churchill call on the voters of Derbyshire West to do the decent thing and elect the young Marquess, the Labour leader and deputy prime minister, Attlee, did so too. The hierarchies of the left and right were lined up behind the Marquess. Apart from his local support, White could count only on the Commonwealth party (a left-wing party which was running by-election candidates where Labour would not do so because of the pact) and the Communists – no great influence in rural Derbyshire.

White was determined to make the apparent attempt at a stitch-up an issue in the campaign. Why had everything moved so fast? The aim, he maintained, was 'to stop men like myself exposing the responsibility of the Tory party in bringing about the war, and exposing the lack of sympathy of the Tory party for the young men and women who are making such tremendous sacrifices that democracy shall be saved'. At his public meetings, Hartington was subjected to a level of disrespect no Cavendish would have been used to. The *Derbyshire Times* commended his patience. Heckler: 'Did you ever do a day's work?' Hartington: 'Well, I have been in the army for five years.' Even US newspapers sent reporters to cover the contest. The turnout of voters on polling day, 17 February, was at 65.4 per cent much the highest for any by-election during the war. And White's confidence had been justified. When the result was announced at Matlock town hall the following day, White was found to have won with 16,336 votes, nearly 60 per cent of the total, against 11,775 for Hartington. The fine old word 'sensation' was swiftly wheeled out. Hartington accepted defeat with good grace, went back to the war, and was killed in action, which was how his younger brother Andrew, the one who died in 2004, came to be duke. Even though the Conservatives sought to dismiss the by-election defeat as a transient embarrassment, White held the seat in the Labour landslide at the end of the war. Chatsworth remained as proud and as privileged as before, yet its old political hegemony had been shattered, and would not be restored.

My journey from Cavendish Derbyshire takes me from one kind of feudalism to another. The dukes of Devonshire in their great house were the only ones of this rank in the district. Some twenty-five miles away, across the county boundary with Nottinghamshire, great nobles used to abound – the dukes of Newcastle at Clumber, the dukes of Portland at Welbeck, the earls of Manvers at Thoresby, the Saviles at Rufford. The area became known as the Dukeries. Their finances were often precarious, but some of them were rescued by coal. They set high tariffs for letting the coal-mining companies on to their land, and mulcted the railways too, which the companies needed. Their claims and pretensions staggered humbler people. In 1919 calls for coal nationalization led to the appointment of a commission headed by Mr Justice Sankey. The eighth duke of Northumberland came reluctantly and grudgingly to testify. What right did he think he had, he was asked, to the income of over £80,000 a year he derived from the coal beneath his property? 'The fact is that I own the minerals.' And suppose science could make it possible to mine down to 20,000 feet, would he still own what was found? 'Certainly.' 'Even if it went down to the centre of the earth?' 'I understand that is the law.' 'Do you not think it is a bad thing for a man to own as much as you do?' 'No, I think it is an excellent thing in every way.' Such men were not free of greed, but were driven by necessity. Although few of those who sank the mines on these aristocratic lands could boast, like the Devonshires or the Newcastles, centuries of social command and good breeding, the pit owners became in their own way as autocratic as the aristocrats whose lives were now sustained by their industry. As Robert J. Waller writes in a fascinating history of the area, *The Dukeries Transformed: The Social and Political Development of a Twentieth-century Coalfield*, a new industrial feudalism was being erected.

The transition from the old hegemonists to the new begins with the Stagecoach number 17 bus from Matlock to Chesterfield. This will be a far from straightforward journey, because even if the roads from Matlock to the collieries of the Dukeries are fairly direct, the bus routes aren't. One has to enjoy this opening ride while one can, for what follows will mostly be far less pleasing to look at. The bus climbs the steep hill north of the town, where John Smedley created Matlock's celebrated hydro (now the county council headquarters). He also built Riber Castle, the striking ruin silhouetted on the skyline on the opposite hill. The number 17 crosses into north-east Derbyshire – solid Labour territory, which used to be represented by a tough, even mildly terrifying Labour MP called Tom Swain, about whose rough ways some hair-raising tales used to be told in Commons bars late at night when I was a new and wide-eyed political journalist. There's a big notice board here drawing attention to the presence nearby of north-east Derbyshire prizewinning herds, but there's not a beast to be seen. But that call to embrace diversity which governments constantly preach to old agricultural territories is evident too: near Kelstedge, there's a shed which claims to produce talking balloons. The bus climbs back to a summit at Three Horse Shoes which is probably very grand, but a mist with aspirations to qualify as a fog has come down and I can't see a thing. Perhaps that explains the gloominess of the occasion. Most buses you take at 10 in the morning, with shoppers going to town, are a good deal more cheerful than this one.

Another memorial to high political insolence can be glimpsed on the way into Chesterfield: the headquarters of a Liberal MP, Paul Holmes, who in 2001 seized a seat that had been safeguarded for socialism for seventeen years by no less a custodian than Tony Benn. Conversation as we come into the town has turned to divorce and the death of dogs. Chesterfield, with its crooked spire and its football ground close in to the centre of the town and its fine market space (today it's just empty trestles), is sorting out bus stops, and my chances of finding the right place to stand awaiting transit to Bolsover would be somewhere between slim and hopeless were it not for a kindly woman who says she will take me there – which she continues to do even after bumping into her sister-in-law, whom she hasn't seen for some weeks.

This bus is a double-decker, and one of Stagecoach's smarter numbers, too. Top deck at last! So many routes, like the one from Matlock, which could treat you to luscious scenery, are served by single-deckers, denying the passenger the best of the view. (The reason is often low bridges; you can hardly argue with that.) But this one's ideal for what I know will be an exciting moment: catching sight of Bolsover Castle, floating dreamlike above the valley – or, looked at from a different perspective, floating dreamlike above the roaring M1. This town can boast two of the great craggy resolute unbendable institutions of England, the other being Dennis

Skinner, Labour MP for Bolsover since 1970, and still there, defying rumours of his impending departure, after the general election of 2005. Plain-speaking and down to earth, he has the higher claim of the two to represent the essence of Bolsover – or certainly that part of it which likes to call the place Bozer. Skinner arrived at the Commons determined not to go soft on it, not to succumb to its fabled charm, to remain Mr Incorruptible. There was something about him when he arrived of the truculence of the young Freddie Trueman bustling up to the wicket for Yorkshire and England, breathing dragonlike aggression and showing respect for no one. 'The beast of Bolsover' the *Guardian* sketchwriter Michael White called him, and the designation stuck. And though he was once detected by one of the tabloids in an affair, it has to be said that through all his years at Westminster he stuck to his early principles: not pairing with Tories, which meant being there to vote far more often than most; not frequenting its bars, keeping his distance from journalists and an even greater distance from the Conservative enemy.

One of his greatest admirers in the Westminster village he tried to keep clear of was the castle-owning, louche-living Tory MP Alan Clark – just the kind of rich aristocratic *flâneur* that Bolsover Castle was cut out for. Like Chatsworth, Bolsover and nearby Hardwick were essentially Cavendish houses. The present castle, on a site originally picked out by the Normans, was chiefly the work of Charles Cavendish, son of the legendary and frequently married Bess of Hardwick. Charles's son William, a besotted horseman, added the riding school and the westward terrace. It was he, too, who built the delicate, fantastical, extravagantly devised, decorated and furnished inner castle, a venue for inventive parties held amid scenes soaked in symbolism, often of an overtly erotic kind. The two final rooms are designated Elysium and Heaven. A recorded guide is available to explain the castle's history as you go round, narrated by an actorly re-creation of a steward of William's called Andrew Clayton. The trouble is, he's a creep. Half a minute of him would make Dennis Skinner vomit. He speaks with a local accent, and he calls the place Bozer, but he's still an obsequious creep. It's a joy to discover towards the end of the tour that Clayton was eventually sacked for dishonesty.

The most telling sight at Bolsover Castle is the view from the western terrace. William Cavendish looked down on green parkland stretching out to the boundaries of the next great aristocratic estate. But today it is Skinner's England that laps at the bounds of Cavendish England. The view today is of the scars of industry, much of it now shut down, and of rows of industrial terraces, built as a model village for colliers. Industry has left its mark on the castle too. Pollution has eaten away at the stonework. But the castle's days of greatness were over even before the dirt and smoke took over the valley. Many of its treasures had been sold, and an eighteenth-century writer recorded systematic plundering of building materials and furniture. A book published in the 1870s by the inveterate guidebook writer and assembler of wayside facts, John Timbs, describes a range of apartments now roofless and rent into fissures, and of which only the outside walls are standing. 'The whole pile is wearing away,' Timbs reports. 'Trees grow in some of the deserted apartments, and ivy creeps along the walls, though the remains have little of the picturesqueness of decay.' And now, as you roam the ruined rooms, you hear at all times the relentless pounding drone of the motorway.

A good honest road runs east out of Bolsover heading directly to Ollerton, a distance of fourteen miles. Unfortunately, no bus runs that way. This means a journey that takes two hours, by way of Mansfield. This bus is a double-decker and two small boys are trying to coax their grizzled granddad into letting them go upstairs for a better view, but he won't, perhaps because he has travelled these dull roads before. This is not a route for aesthetes. Little relieves the monotony. Now and then there are splashes of upmarket housing – at Scarcliffe there is even a spate of double garages – but most of these roads consist of streets run up cheap in short years of industrial expansion to house a burgeoning workforce. Some are called in this life to have their horizons bounded by Matlock, Chatsworth and Edensor; others by Palterton, New Houghton and Pleasley. Earth, as Wordsworth so nearly said, has not anything to show more unfair.

At some arbitrary point we cross the county boundary into Nottinghamshire, but this makes for little amendment of life. The Miles Hill Garage, which looks as if it might once have been a cinema, promises 'miles of smiles' but I can't see any in or out of this bus. It is, of course, raining. At some point Pleasley has ceased and we are now on our way into Mansfield, which I've seen described as a rough, tough, mining capital where they spend hard and fight hard. It's certainly uncompromisingly rugged. 'There's more to Mansfield', says a visitor brochure I pick up at the bus station. More of what, precisely? A daily market, a museum and art gallery, two theatres, a Harry Ramsden's, a McDonald's, a swimming and fitness complex, two shopping malls – they are doing the best they can. Still Mansfield, for the purposes of this exercise, has only one role of consequence: as the gateway to the small pit town of New Ollerton.

The bus, a Stagecoach route 13, is filthy; on the top deck, cigarette ends are scattered everywhere. 'Don't tell me this is a crap bus,' says the driver who is moving in. 'Oh yes it is,' says the driver whose duties are over, gleefully, 'It's really, *really* slow.' 'Oh well,' says the incoming driver settling into his seat, 'at least I haven't got schoolkids on the way back.' 'Oh yes you have,' says his predecessor triumphantly. 'The Garibaldi. They'll all go upstairs and rip the seats off.' Just putting on the frighteners, no doubt. The sun comes out as we head north-east out of town past an old mill and a good public park and a shop that offers 'the ultimate sandwich experience' and Celestial Cycles (closed), into a vast estate in the midst of which are the Garibaldi school, the Garibaldi sports complex, the Garibaldi estate information point, and the Garibaldi training centre.

Why all this Garibaldi? It seems to reflect a wild enthusiasm which swept through this part of the world when the great Italian patriot and part-author of the unification of Italy visited England in 1864. Nottingham Forest football club, formed the following year, decided in Garibaldi's honour to play in his colour, red – as they still do. The club treasurer was sent to a local shop called Daft's to purchase gear in the appropriate colours, while the young players pledged themselves to play in the same dashing spirit which their hero had shown in his conduct of war. Their results in the season 2004–5 suggest that this tradition has lapsed.

A couple on the front seat are having a row, one of those rows which starts quietly and suddenly escalates into something bigger and darker. She starts by being conciliatory; he doesn't respond. Raising her head from the *Daily Mirror*, she says: 'Have you heard that Man United are getting rid of van Nistelrooy?' He does not reply. She begins, very haltingly, to read him the story. She offers the paper to him. 'Want to read it?' 'Ner.' We pass the Squinting Cat pub. 'We need two different central defenders,' she says. 'Do you think we could get them from Liverpool?' No reply. Clipstone has a country park and a derelict colliery. 'Have you got your goggles?' asks a notice outside its rescue room. You can still see figures still posted for weekly tonnage. Beyond there's a very upmarket development with a posh pillared gateway: Cavendish Park. A man who got on at the Dog and Duck now tries to get off, slides down the stairs on his bottom and totters out of the bus towards a fresh hostelry. We divert into Edwinstowe, a pleasant, essentially pre-colliery village. 'Robin Hood's village' a tourist noticeboard claims. Nearby is Ma Hubbard's hotel and eating house and Maid Marion Way, incongruously one along from Lansbury Way, presumably named after the old Labour hero.

The couple on the front seat are not, as I first assumed, about to break up. They cannot break up. They are tied together for ever, brother and sister. The girl has given up on conciliation and a torrent of fierce resentment is pouring out. 'When mam died, you never cried!' she storms at him. For the first time the lad comes to life. 'No,' he says ,'because I was happy.' The girl is in real distress. The boy, I think, must be drugged. Along the way, signposts tell of the hybrid history of this area: ducal homes, almost all now abandoned; old collieries, almost all now abandoned too, though Thoresby and Welbeck made it into 2005. And here is the first of two Ollertons.

People who live in Old Ollerton, someone has warned me, don't like you to call it Old Ollerton. It was here before the pit village arrived, so plain Ollerton ought to suffice. It is flauntingly pretty: the sort of favoured village you'd expect to find a couple of miles outside Guildford, a green with a river (the Maun) and a stream (Ranworth Water), a watermill, a tea room, and comfortable houses looking out upon flowery gardens with Guildfordy names (Ropemakers Cottage, Bee Gem Cottage), and good-looking pubs (the Hop Pole, the Snooty Fox). A real butcher's shop ('special agents for haggis') survives and at least the Olde Curiosity Shop doesn't say 'Ye' or 'Shoppe'. Ollerton Hall was built by George Markham, standard-bearer to Elizabeth I. It later became the house of Lord

Savile of Rufford, lord of the manor and principal landowner here, and later still was the home of one of the senior managers of the Butterley Company which owned the Ollerton pit. It was derelict when I saw it, festooned in bright red warning notices and apparently ready for demolition.

What transformed this area in the years from 1918, as Robert Waller establishes, was a convenient and on the whole successful alliance between old land and new money. The noblemen who lived in the Dukeries had the land and needed the money; the colliery owners had, or were going to make, the money, and needed the land. In ten years after the war, seven pits were opened in east Nottinghamshire and close by in South Yorkshire. Most of these Nottinghamshire pits prospered so well that by 1980, just before the industry fell into traumatic decline, more coal was coming out of this coalfield than from the north-east and South Wales together.

This transformation alarmed established communities. The expansion was thought to be driving up rents and saddling the original householders with high rates to pay for new services. But a lot of the tension reflected a class divide. An Edwinstowe resident from the mining side of that chasm told Robert Waller: 'They were they, and we were us, and they tended to look down on us...I can remember going into one of the shops at the top of the High Street, it was Woodhead's actually, he owned a toffee shop then, and unless you were old village, he didn't want to serve you.' There was none of that kind of tension in New Ollerton. Where Edwinstowe had uneasy commingling, the two Ollertons had something close to segregation.

The Butterley colliery company was, by the lights of such companies, benevolent. It sought to create what it hoped would be seen as a model town, with houses built to a far higher standard than most of those who came to Ollerton in search of employment could ever have experienced before. (The management, though, looked after itself even better: see, for instance, the houses in their part of New Ollerton, entertainingly named Savile Row.) The coal-owners offered sports and entertainments and seasonal treats, but at all times made sure that the workpeople who lived in Ollerton knew who was boss. There were rules, and penalties could be severe when they were broken. The town, Waller says, was 'essentially an integral part of the manufacturing process rather than a blueprint for a balanced society, however "benevolent" the paternalism involved'.

This new industrial feudalism, much like the older aristocratic variety, had the ultimate sanction: if you alienated the management and it cost you your job, you would lose your home as well; or, if for some social infringement they threw you out of your house (and 'living in sin' was regarded as such an infringement), you would lose your job along with it. A rigid regime was imposed which the workforce could not resist. The company ordained which shops should serve the community; if you failed to pay their bills, the money was stopped from your wages. If you failed to trim your lawn to the standards required, the company sent in a man with a mower and levied a charge of 2d. The keeping of dogs was forbidden – a tough imposition, this, on families from traditional mining areas. 'Nobody was supposed to walk on the lawns,' an old Ollerton resident told Robert Waller, 'where you can see cars on them now. And there used to be a chap, we used to call him Bobby Healey, and if he caught anyone walking on the lawns, he used to prosecute them, he used to fine them at the pit.' ('Bobby' in this context implied a policeman: Healey dressed in a uniform that made him look like a policeman.) Drinking was frowned on: the company initially built no pubs in the town. And no use trying to take all this up with the union. Initially, all trade union activity – any kind of party political activity too – was banned. When union membership did begin to develop, it was mainly through the Nottinghamshire Miners Industrial Union created by George Spencer, which worked on the basis of seeking collaboration rather than conflict with the mine-owners. The Spencer Union had been instrumental in organizing the return of Nottinghamshire miners to work after the 1926 strike: a local tradition that would be maintained when the Nottinghamshire miners set up their own rival union to the NUM during the Scargill strike of the 1980s, and continued to work while the pitheads elsewhere remained silent.

The sublime self-confidence, long since swollen to arrogance, of the Butterley company is beautifully caught in Waller's account of the building of the church of St Paulinus, New Ollerton. The company liked to set its sights high, and what it proposed in this case was nothing less than 'a cathedral for the new coalfield'. Sir Giles Gilbert Scott, one of the nation's most famous architects, who had built Liverpool cathedral, was invited to send in plans, and came to inspect Church Circle, one of the few departures from a rigid grid pattern. He might have been good enough for Liverpool, but apparently he wasn't up to the standard required for New Ollerton. The company rejected his plans, and gave the work to a firm from Derby. St Paulinus opened in 1931. It's an odd and somewhat clumsy creation, unlikely to be taken even by the unwary as the work of Sir Giles Gilbert Scott.

At the time when West Derbyshire was defying the will of the Devonshires, the dictatorial powers of the Butterley company were eroding too. Deference was on the retreat, even in company towns like this one. In June 1943, eight months before the West Derbyshire upset, the Newark division of Nottinghamshire, of which Ollerton was a part, was faced with a by-election. For years it had been returning the duke of Portland's heir, the marquess of Titchfield (Conservative) to the Commons – but only, some local opinion maintained, because people respected his mother. Titchfield was known as 'the silent MP'. But now the duke had died and Titchfield and his silence were being translated to the upper chamber. As in West Derbyshire, no Labour candidate stood because of the electoral pact, but an 'Independent Progressive' and a candidate of Richard Acland's Commonwealth party polled 45 per cent of the vote between them, against the successful Tory's 44.2. Few assumed at this stage that results like these presaged the defeat of Churchill's Conservatives by Attlee's Labour nationalizers at the end of the war. And yet it was plain that the mood was changing. Post-war Britain was likely to be a less easy environment for old and new feudalism when the men returned from the war. Sure enough, although the Tories kept Newark, the Dukeries mining villages went solidly Labour in 1945. The nationalization which that victory ensured meant the end of the road for both kinds of beneficiary of the 1918–28 Dukeries transformation. The colliery owners were swept away; the noblemen lost the one source of income that could help pay the enormous bills incurred by their great estates. Most sold their estates and left the Dukeries. The duke of Newcastle's Clumber was demolished. Rufford Abbey, home of the Saviles, crumbled away into ruins and became a country park. The Manvers house at Thoresby was subdivided into apartments.

There were always those at New Ollerton, including men who had worked in the Butterley pits for most of their lives, who feared that nationalization would demean the place; and soon they were feeling vindicated. The old regulations, backed by the old punitive sanctions, were diluted or abandoned. People walked freely all over the grass. They left lawns unmowed without punishment. They even lived in sin. 'Vesting day,' one old resident told Robert Waller in 1980, 'was the day when the rot set in for this village.' So the village now was a lot less tidy and neat? 'Oh, it's scruffy. Scruffy compared to those days.' 'Ollerton itself,' said another, 'was a beautiful place, no hooliganism. No, nothing of that sort...The colliery village at Ollerton was the best colliery village I've seen in my life, and I've seen a few, for its layout and everything.'

Much worse was on the way. The National Coal Board's plans to run down the industry, the NUM strike, the resistance to that strike of Nottinghamshire mine-workers and the contentious creation of their breakaway union, the UDM, the acceleration of closures thereafter, in line with Arthur Scargill's darkest forecasts – all blighted places like Ollerton. Two weeks into the strike, one of the flying pickets sent to try to get Nottinghamshire miners to join the strike was killed when a brick hit his head. In 1994, ten years after the strike, the closure of Ollerton pit was ordered. So much for the UDM. In the end, it seemed that compliance had been no better protection than militancy in staving off the inevitable.

An old miner sitting in the sun in the centre of Ollerton is downbeat about the place. They had their money, he says of his fellow miners. They could have done something with it. They blew it. They never learn. And just look at the place today...The problems which beset these mining communities – which did so before the closures, even before the strike, but grew worse, often very much worse, when the jobs had all gone – are evident here. 'Crack down on drugs', say the posters near the town hall (two semis knocked together to form the headquarters of Ollerton and Boughton town council), 'rat on a rat'. Yet Ollerton hasn't the air of hopelessness that hangs over Grimethorpe. The thumping great Tesco is open twenty-four hours. Although when I was there it still felt like a place with its purpose shot out of it, out at the back, on the wide swathe of land between the supermarket and the railway, where the pit used to be, something hopeful is happening. They're creating, at a cost of £100 million, a Sherwood Energy village – new housing, opportunities (if they are taken up) for commercial development, new leisure attractions, a hotel and a bio-mass power station – all designed to be green and alternative. A lot of the money comes from central government and from Europe, but the local council insists that this has been from the start the community's project. And this time, no duke, no colliery boss or manager, no agent of feudal power, old or new, will have any say in deciding Ollerton's destiny. A cheerful thought to take with me as I catch my bus on towards Lincolnshire.

15

LOUTH

*How a Lincolnshire school took on a famous roué – Paul
Verlaine, seeking new pastures, unwisely settles on Boston –
why Woodhall Spa would not have been right for him, nor
Horncastle even – I arrive by a devious route in the fine town
of Louth – a death, a benefaction, and fireworks.*

One day in early spring in 1875, there arrived at Sibsey station in
Lincolnshire a French schoolmaster, thirty years old, striking in
appearance, though some said strikingly ugly, who had been
engaged to teach French, Latin and drawing at a school in the
nearby village of Stickney. He was met at the station by a pony-
chaise, sent by the school's headmaster, and driven by a lad whom
he took to be twelve years old. Twenty years later, in still faltering
English, he recalled that first journey across the flat fenland in an
article for the *Fortnightly Review*: 'Twilight was about to fall...The
last rays of daylight were shedding lustre upon a landscape which
was exquisite in its sweetness of pasture and trees – those English
trees with their branches capriciously twisted and "intricated" if
I may be allowed the barbarism, which the Bible somewhere says
are those to bear the best fruit; both sides of the road, which was
flourished with thick hedges, were studied, so to speak, with big
sheep and nimble colts rolling free...'

He made a sketch of the scene, which he later developed into a
poem, published in a collection called *Sagesse*. This book, perme-

ated by expressions of the deepest piety, would certainly have commended him to the congregation at the Anglican church of St Luke, which, though himself a Catholic, he often attended. Indeed, he became so enchanted with *Hymns Ancient and Modern* that he translated some into French. But his name can have meant very little to most of those who lived in this remote and antique corner of England, which was just as well, for had he submitted an honest and comprehensive CV he would never have found this suitable employment in Lincolnshire – or indeed virtually anywhere else.

Paul Verlaine, it might have read, poet, romantic, notorious drinker (an alcoholic at twenty-three), bisexual lecher, and all-round reprobate. Married a girl of seventeen whom before long he started to knock about, just as he'd previously knocked about his doting mother, sometimes threatening her with knives when desperate for money. Took up with another poet, a lad of sixteen, who believed that great poets needed to taste degradation. When his wife, now pregnant, objected that the young man whom Verlaine had taken into their house had been stealing from them, he threw her out of bed. Later, after the child was born – a boy in whom he took little interest – he tried to set fire to his wife's hair, threatened to kill her, and threw their child against the wall.

The name of the young poet with whom he became besotted was Rimbaud. They lived together in Paris and London, at first, as his biographer Joanna Richardson says, with Verlaine initiating the younger man into a life of depravity, though subsequently becoming the pupil as 'Rimbaud plunged his teacher into depths of vice he would not have explored alone'. The lovers were drunk a lot of the time, and when drunk were frequently violent. They broke up, but were soon reunited. Before long, Rimbaud was trying to end the relationship again, and treating Verlaine so brutally that he left and headed for Antwerp. Rimbaud, full of remorse (they were both rather good at remorse), pursued him to the quayside; but Verlaine, though he saw him there, stayed on the boat.

Verlaine wrote to his wife demanding a reconciliation, saying he would kill himself if she refused. She refused. He begged Rimbaud to join him in Brussels. Rimbaud arrived, but insisted they live in Paris. Verlaine refused. Rimbaud said he was leaving. Verlaine locked the door, pulled out a revolver and shot him, wounding him in the wrist, then handed over the gun and told Rimbaud to kill him. (All this time, grotesquely, Verlaine's long-suffering mother had been in an adjoining room.) Fearing Verlaine would shoot him again, Rimbaud called the police. Verlaine was arrested and charged with attempted murder. Although the charge was reduced to criminal assault, this pious applicant for the teaching post at Stickney was sentenced to two years in jail with hard labour, with a fine of 200 francs – the maximum sentence being imposed, it was deduced, because prison doctors had told the court they had found evidence of sodomy. On 16 January 1875 he was freed from his cell at Mons – and his mother was at the gates to collect him. Just over two months later he arrived at the doors of Stickney grammar school.

Stickney's new schoolmaster emerged from Mons prison believing himself to be a changed man. While in Lincolnshire he wrote a poem expressing his gratitude for his imprisonment. This had been a time of penitence and piety: much of *Sagesse* had been written in Mons. Having served eighteen months in prison, he wished to put the ways of the world behind him.

Verlaine seems at this point to have been genuinely anxious to mend his undisciplined ways, to find a fresh way of life which would keep temptation at bay. There could scarcely have been a more penitent and redemptive journey: from the depths of depravity to the decorous plains of east Lincolnshire. True, there were good-looking boys to teach; there were also two pubs. But the population was only 800; there was little chance of meeting another Rimbaud in Stickney. The Post Office directory for 1876, which I found in the county library at Lincoln, provides a convenient snapshot. The most important figure in Stickney was Canon Coltman, MA, of Brasenose, Oxford, who lived at the rectory. He was also one of Stickney's two biggest landowners. A school for the poor had been established in 1678 by one William Lovell, who left 51 acres, producing £126 annually. This was where the poet would teach. The Wesleyans and Primitive Methodists both had chapels. There was good grazing land, and the chief crop was wheat. The village had two butchers, two bakers, two grocers who also were drapers and another who was also a tailor, a wheelwright, four retailers of beer besides the Rose and Crown and Nag's Head, two blacksmiths, two tailors, two shoemakers, a bricklayer, a farrier, a carpenter, a plumber and glazier, and several farmers. It must have been a much busier and livelier place than it looks today.

The school had a good reputation. William Andrews, the head, was a graduate of London university. He and Verlaine met in the playground: 'a man in the thirties,' Verlaine noted, 'with a large moustache and enormous whiskers, whom I could just distinguish in the dusk as he raised his felt hat and greeted me with the words, "Welcome, moussou."' In erratic English and halting French, they managed a conversation. Next day, Mr Andrews introduced M. Verlaine to his new charges. 'Monsieur Verlaine, who is a Bachelor of Arts of the University of Paris, is willing to assist me in the French language and the art of drawing. He knows English as well as an Englishman, and most certainly far better than all of you put together, but of course he cannot pronounce it. Should any of you take advantage of his foreign accent to show him the least want of respect, I shall lose no time...in correcting the error.'

The days passed pleasantly at Stickney; this was, the poet would later conclude, one of the best times in his life. He taught and wrote and read English writers – Marlowe, Addison, Fielding, Macaulay – walked the flat Lincolnshire country and even learned to play football. But he did not stay as long as he had intended, nor indeed, subsequent events suggest, as long as he should have done. His mother arrived from France at the beginning of 1876 and wanted to live somewhere better than Stickney. Verlaine also felt he might make more money in a place with a larger population. Since arriving in Stickney he had been regularly to Boston to make confession at the Catholic church on the Horncastle road, sometimes taken there by a carrier, sometimes walking the best part of ten miles. Boston was where he decided to go. In March 1876, just a year after his arrival at Sibsey station, he was bidding goodbye, 'almost in tears'.

I reach Stickney on a ramshackle Brylaine bus out of Boston: the sort of bus where the destination space on the front is empty and the route is announced on a piece of cardboard stuck in the front window. The final phase of the journey, from Sibsey, is the one that Verlaine would have enjoyed in his pony-chaise. Although there is no trace of Verlaine, the church is full of associations. George Coltman, rector from 1835 to 1883, whose company the poet so much enjoyed, is commemorated in a gold plaque: 'served his generation and fell asleep 19 July 1883'. By the organ there's a gold plaque remembering headmaster Andrews, who was also lay-reader and organist at the church. Coltman's rectory, next door to the church, has become the Old Rectory Rest Home. Though it has been gravely extended, you can still discern the original house amidst the additions. There is still a William Lovell school, lineal descendant of the one that Verlaine taught in, though in a different building, and still a pub in the main street; and still something left of Stickney windmill. The shops are almost all gone. Through it all runs the snarling A16, carrying Celsius First and Argos Direct and Taylor's Transport of Mansfield from Boston to Grimsby and back. But walk out of the village, on the road past the village hall and the long low cottage block of Steepings Charity (founded 1600; rebuilt 1883) and a curious and characterful 1830 concoction called Bull Pastures, and you may begin to see why Verlaine loved this uneventful landscape: long views across flat lands, bathed in a blissful light, with mild, untaxing hills beyond.

Verlaine should not have left Stickney for Boston. Boston did not work out: few came to be taught, and soon he moved on, to Bournemouth, with the promise of wicked France just across the water. Where should he have gone? Lincolnshire has so many delightful small towns that it should not have been a difficult choice. The Brylaine bus north out of Stickney takes me eight miles or so through a tranquil country of vast fields, small rhines and a distant church crowning a hill, where happenings, catastrophes and strokes of fate seem barely imaginable, to the small but fetching market town of Spilsby, 'pleasantly situated', the Post Office guide for 1876 reported, 'on an acclivity overlooking vast tracts of marsh and fen'. It's a well-appointed, comfortable sort of place. In the square is a statue of Spilsby's great hero, Sir John Franklin, the sailor, explorer and sometime governor of Van Diemen's Land (later Tasmania), who died in a bid to discover the North West Passage in 1847. There's a pleasant collection of buildings around and beyond Sir John, of which the most inviting is the White Hart hotel. There is also, on the way out of town, an extraordinarily grand theatre, once a court house, an essay in classical architecture which looks as though it might have escaped from somewhere three times this size. And Spilsby, a town of 1,600 souls to Stickney's 800, certainly had a well-established free grammar school, founded by a local benefactor in 1611, that Verlaine might have taught in.

Better still, though, he could have pressed on to Horncastle, a journey accomplished from Spilsby these days on the number 6 Lincolnshire Roadcar service, heading for Lincoln, a bus as smart as Brylaine's was shabby. This route takes you off the fen and into the wolds, which makes for a really enjoyable ride. Along the way there are unexpected incidental pleasures like Raithby, where the bus leaves the A158 and explores the kind of village where one might happily linger for several hours, particularly if the Red Lion pub is as good as it looks. A horse looks inquiringly over a fence. A field of sheep flees from the sound of the bus, too noisy and urban a creature for Raithby. The hall, in whose stables Wesley is said to have preached, looks, from a momentary glimpse, very grand and exciting. Hagworthingham, beyond, could, despite its unprepossessing name, be a treat as well, but the heart of the place is now bypassed: a boon to Hagworthinghamians, true, but disappointing for those of us confined to the number 6 bus.

There's a very strong sense in Horncastle of the place as it must have been in Verlaine's day. The Post Office directory lists sixty-eight villages for which it served as a centre, some of whose names might have been picked to appeal to a poet: Asgarby, Ashby Puerorum, Asterby; Bag Enderby, Baumber or Bamburgh, and Belchford; Cawkwell and Claxby Pluckacre, Gautby and Goulceby, Mareham-le-Fen, Mareham-on-the-Hill, Miningsby, Minting and Moorby; Salmonby, Scamblesby, Scrivelsby, Somersby (where the Tennysons lived), Thimbleby, Tumby and Tupholme, and in a final flourish, Waddingworth, Wilksby, Winceby, Wispington, Wood Enderby, Woodhall and Wragby. The town, the 1876 Post Office directory tells us, had been greatly improved in recent years, with the coming of the canal (1801), the butter market (1853) and the 'handsome' corn exchange (1856).

Horncastle is close to the confluence of the rivers Bain and Waring, suggesting a firm of superior drapers. If you take the road over the Bain to the west, it will bring you to the grammar school, now a specialist science college, founded in 1562, and therefore solidly established by the time that Verlaine arrived in these parts. Horncastle's population then was over 4,900, suggesting a fair opportunity for additional freelance teaching. The school, the directory says, 'is of high repute and eminent persons have been educated within its walls', which sounds promising too. On the other hand, a book I found in Horncastle library says the grammar school had fallen on such bad days that in 1886 it had only sixteen scholars; a crisis to which it responded in 1903 by letting in girls. So probably better not Horncastle.

So what about Woodhall Spa? Lincolnshire buses are organized on a very sensible system where the spine bus, the number 6, runs though several main centres on its way from Skegness to Lincoln, while feeder buses serving surrounding areas ferry passengers up to route 6 and collect them from it and take them home. One of these feeder buses will take you to Woodhall Spa. That might seem an ideal location for Paul Verlaine to make a new life, since Woodhall Spa oozes respectability. Everything about it is tidy, neatly brought up, and demure. It is full of genuflections to royalty, with pleasure gardens and a swimming pool created in honour of the jubilee of King George V; also to golf, of which it is the administrative capital within England, the nearest thing it has to St Andrews.

The building which housed the spa is distressingly derelict, but the cinema next door is happily still in business. The Kinema in the Woods, they call it, and to look at it you would imagine that nothing had changed since the 1920s, and that this week's attractions would probably star John Gilbert and Greta Garbo. It has to be said, however, that, disconcertingly, on the two occasions I've been there, the Kinema was showing first, *The Spy Who Shagged Me*, and the second time, *Meet the Fockers*. The spa was a kind of accident. In 1811 a man called John Parkinson, steward to the wealthy Hotchkin family, thought he was going to find coal here. He dreamed of sinking a pit and creating a city around it, and a forest beyond. The coal eluded him, and the exercise left him bankrupt. But the shafts he had to abandon filled up with water, seeping in from a nearby stream, and the water was found to be rich in iodine – rich enough to alleviate the complaint of gout-ridden Thomas Hotchkin, lord of the manor, who seized the chance of creating a spa. In 1849 the family opened its first good hotel and the coming of the railway in the 1850s provided a further boost. Yet it never fulfilled Hotchkin's hopes. It came close to collapse in 1920, and faltered on through the 1930s, when doctors ceased to prescribe the waters. The closure of the railway in the 1950s virtually finished it off. But for all its endearing gentleness, Woodhall Spa would not have made a base for Verlaine: it was still only barely developed in the 1870s. Even had he found a school to employ him, opportunities for extra tuition would not have been much better than Stickney's. Louth, to the north of Horncastle, looks a riper prospect.

The feeder buses that link with route 6 Skegness to Lincoln have a further attraction: you can ring up and ask for one to come to your village – even, if you request, to your door. If you wanted to go to Somersby, for instance, and see the house where Alfred Tennyson spent a very difficult childhood with his very difficult father – a priest who had to continue to preach the faith though his own faith had ebbed away – one of these buses would gladly divert down the lanes and take you there. Mine took me at one point down what was hardly more than a rutted track to deliver a shopping-laden customer to her gate. Even if there are no such callers and the bus sticks firmly to the advertised route it's a pleasantly eccentric journey. Deviations from the main road made Spilsby to Horncastle enjoyable: but this bus is all diversion. It might say Louth on the destination blind, but there are moments when it seems to respond with enthusiasm to every available signpost except those that point to Louth.

The little 6C can thus introduce us to Greetham, with impressive houses at each end of the village and a good-looking church, and Salmonby, which is big enough to be twinned with somewhere in France. Here Brian gets on in a fine Russian hat and everyone says they just love that hat, Brian, and Brian looks suitably pleased, and when Brian gets off they fall to discussing the strange way he dresses. 'He knits them himself, I suppose,' says one observer. 'Gives him something to do,' says another. Somewhere near Tathwell the bus catches sight of a sign that says that Louth is straight on, and shoots away to the left as if terrified of ending its journey. Part way to Cadwell it turns, reverses, again shoots past the sign to Louth and makes towards Legbourne. But soon the moment of reckoning can no longer be avoided. We come over the top of the hill and there before us is Louth.

For years the first thing travellers saw when they made this journey was the spire of Louth church, which was as exhilarating in its way as the first sight of Salisbury cathedral; all the more so, perhaps, for travellers coming from Horncastle, where a truly feeble spire has been stuck on the top of the tower. Louth's spire had unchallenged command of the town. And then the malting factory was built, and the spire had an ugly, thuggish competitor: 'fancy a fight, mate?' it seemed to be saying. This building is the only real blot on what ought to be universally recognized as one of Britain's finest small towns, up there with more celebrated places such as Ludlow, Cirencester, Beverley, Bury St Edmunds and Devizes. It was recognized from the start as a grievous eyesore, although it brought work to a town that must have needed it. And now it is empty, abandoned and due to be razed. When it goes, the bells of a church thus restored to undisputed pre-eminence should ring loud and long in celebration.

'A fine structure,' the Post Office directory of 1876 says of St James's, 'the East end having exquisitely beautiful windows.' I have never got into this church. Once when I went to Louth, as I do on the slightest excuse, it had shut around twilight; on both other occasions, funerals were in progress. I do not regret this, since while the problem persists I shall never be short of a good excuse for visiting Louth. In 1843 St James's was struck by lightning, and investigations showed it to be unsound and unsafe. Restoration, completed in 1846, cost £1,746, 19s 3d. The great spire is with you wherever you go, disappearing and reappearing at every turn, unifying the town. The centre now is Mercers Row, and the market place immediately north of it, with enticing cut-throughs and alleys in between. Many shops look as if they are still truly local. Spencers, the booksellers and newsagents, was shut while I was there because of its founder's funeral. Seeing a man at Trevor Fairburn's, the butchers, working the slicing machine, I sense there's a decent chance that it might be Trevor. The market hall, now in the hands of a single company and a topic of contention for years in the town after East Lincolnshire district council, which now governs Louth, resolved to sell it, is a pleasingly wayward construction, opened in 1866 when Samuel Trought was mayor, and adorned with a fantastical clock tower topped with a spire – echoing, just a touch mockingly, the spire of St James's. The Corn Exchange – written off by the *Lincolnshire Shell Guide* as rather ridiculous – has gone, but the town hall in Eastgate is a splendidly boastful creation, bursting with that characteristic Victorian local pride which says: 'We are Louth, and in every way we're as good a town as anywhere else; and quite probably, come to think of it, better'. Close by is the stately 1835 Wesleyan chapel, now the Methodist church. But wherever you go in Louth – down the hill from the church to the river, or up the hill on the further side, where streets have names like Gospelgate (don't in particular miss number 15), or north-east, up Ramsgate, beyond the abominable malt monstrosity – you will come across something to delight and surprise. Louth is the architectural equivalent of someone who never set out to be charming but simply grew up that way.

And then there's the grammar school, with which the search for the place to which Verlaine ought to have gone is complete. This surely would have been perfect. The free grammar school, my old friend the Post Office directory tells me, was founded and endowed by King Edward VI. Alfred Tennyson, whom Verlaine greatly admired, went to school here. It even lists the staff, and yes, they employ a specialist French master. The present incumbent is called Monsieur Pahud. At first sight, that seems to indicate that there would not have been a vacancy for Verlaine. But further acquaintance with Louth tells a different story.

If it's a pleasant summer evening you can catch a bus south out of town to the gates of Hubbard's Hills, where Louth takes its evening pleasure: a sequence of parklands which bring you, alongside a stream, through to Westgate Fields and into Westgate itself, the best-looking street in the town, and so back to the church. This was private land, presented to the town in 1907 by a resident who had recently lost his wife and wished to honour her memory. His name, it says on a notice just inside the park, was Auguste Alphonse Pahud. Pahud? Where had I seen this unusual surname before? In the 1876 Post Office directory. Pahud was the man who taught French at the grammar school. According to local accounts, his time in Louth was for a while unhappy, and by the mid-1870s he seemed likely to leave. But then he met a woman called Annie Grant, the daughter of a farmer who lived in one of the best of the fine houses in Westgate, and found that he wanted to stay. They married in 1877; their devotion ever after was famous through the town. But in 1899, in London, at the start of a planned visit to Norway, Annie was taken ill and died within a few hours. Auguste never recovered. One day in July 1902 he went to his room after lunch in a state of depression, so the married couple, valet and housekeeper, who looked after him judged. After a while the house-keeper knocked on the door. When he did not answer she assumed that he must be sleeping. The valet, more apprehensive, summoned the doctor and together they found a way into the room. Pahud had hanged himself with the cord of his dressing gown.

M. Pahud had come to be an important and respected figure in Louth, as a county JP and a man with an established reputation as a writer and translator. He left what must have been a sizeable sum of money for seven trustees to fund local religious and charitable projects in memory of his Annie. They used some of this money to save Hubbard's Hills, then threatened with a plan to fell its trees, and in 1907 opened it to the public. Nine thousand people came to the market place to march in procession, accompanied by the Babbington military band and the bugle band of the Church Lads' Brigade. At the end of the evening, fireworks spelled out the message: 'May Louth enjoy Hubbards Hills. Goodnight.'

So Louth never had the honour of entertaining Verlaine. Yet had he by some timely manoeuvre replaced the unhappy Pahud, Louth would never have got Hubbard's Hills. Paul Verlaine or Auguste Alphonse Pahud? You would not need a referendum to establish which outcome present-day Louth, wandering at its ease by the stream on a summer evening, would have chosen.

16

Malton — Eden Camp
Thornton Dale — Langdale End

WEST AYTON

I return to Yorkshire – incarceration in Eden – an audience with
Neville Chamberlain and another with George Formby – a
Sunday ride though an autumn forest – how to toughen men up
in the back of beyond while invoking Nelson and Wellington –
history collected but left unchronicled – at the Moorcock Inn –
how a coachman soared above Brompton Dale and gave in his
notice on landing.

And so back to Yorkshire, where I began these excursions. Of all
the fine buses that swept in and out of Leeds city bus station as I
looked down upon them from the great glass windows of the West
Yorkshire Playhouse months ago, few were as grand and gleaming
as those about to embark for the eastern seaboard. These are the
Coastliner services, their coachwork decorated with pictures of
invigorating water splashes, which take you through York to the
market town of Malton. Here the route divides, one service running
east to Scarborough and the other by even more glorious roads over
the moors to Whitby. Grand though they look in Leeds, their arrival
is even more of an event in the little bus station close to the railway
at Malton – or rather, Norton, since the south side of the river
Derwent preserves its cherished separateness by insisting on being
addressed by its ancient name. Malton comes in three flavours.
Norton is one; the centre of town, with its bold atmospheric market
place is the second and much the largest; and then north-east-

wards, up the hill but following the line of the river, is spruce and dignified, not to say posh, Old Malton, with its stone cottages, priory church and institutional buildings with important cars parked outside, and signs to the site of the Roman fort of Derventio. Beyond is the throbbingly busy roundabout where the roads to Scarborough and Whitby divide: and within a minute or two we are at the gates of Eden Camp.

There was no convenient and comfortable Coastliner for the first prisoners of war, 250 or so Italians, who arrived here in 1942 from a camp at Oldham. They were marched up the hill from the station by yapping NCOs. This was camp 53: one of some 1,500 camps established to hold Italian and German prisoners during the Second World War, around 400,000 of them by the time the last went home as late as 1948. Many of these camps have now vanished as if they had never been; others have been so drastically reshaped that they are hardly recognizable as what they once were. But partly by accident, Eden Camp has become a place of commemoration, of the world war in general, of the POWs in particular. After the last prisoners left in 1948, it became in turn an agricultural holiday camp, a Ministry of Agriculture depot, and a grain store for the Fitzwilliam estate, which had owned the land before the POW camp was created. After that it housed a prefabricated concrete unit and a car workshop. Then in 1985 a local entrepreneur and self-made millionaire called Stanley Johnson bought it to set up a crisp- manufacturing business. He was still in the process of planning it when a letter arrived from three Italians who had once been prisoners there, asking if they might come back and see it once more. Johnson himself showed them around, and was so impressed by the experience that he resolved to forget his crisps and re-create the place as a museum of wartime: a 'people's war museum', as he called it, which would evoke for future generations the conditions of war both at the front and at home.

So here you can listen to Neville Chamberlain's grave announcement, on a whistling radio, on 3 September 1939, that no answer having been received from the German chancellor to his ultimatum, Britain was now at war. No matter how often I hear these words they are chilling, bringing back the moment I heard them as a small child and knew that something dreadful had happened. The announcement was hardly completed when the sirens sounded in London and we hustled out to the shelter which my father had dug in the back garden. Here too, in Eden Camp, are the sounds of the Blitz, with the eerie wail of the siren; and, at the other end of the scale, the voice of George Formby, in the camp music hall (performances daily), keeping us cheerful. Even ten-year-old feet tap to the music of sixty years ago.

And here is the *Daily Express*, a newspaper as full of bombast and fiction then as it is today: 'The *Daily Express* declares that Britain will not be involved in a European war this year, or next year even' (30 September 1938). Here are soldiers' service records and ration books and identity cards for Frank Broadbent of Pudsey and the Booths of Pitt Street, Barnsley, and all the other paraphernalia of wartime existence at home. Elsewhere, there are the sounds and signals of battle: bombs falling, a U-boat moving in to attack. From the other side of the firing line, there are enemy instructions to troops. 'A gentleman', Italian admiral Gino Birindelli instructs his men in 1940, 'always shaves before going out in the morning. If we are to sink a British battleship today, let us make sure we are properly shaved.' How very British! Then there is the ironmongery of war: tanks, and torpedoes, guns and ammunition, right down to the humblest of items that squaddies packed in their kitbags. There is evidence too of PoWs and local people beginning to commingle. The *Malton Gazette* reports that Dorothy Richardson has married Hans Kock, whom she met at the fun fair.

One hut is devoted to evoking the conditions in which the prisoners lived. The double bunks hug closely together. Lili Marlene plays in the background, to make you feel how homesick they must have been. Toys and puppets and carvings which they spent their evenings making after a tough day's work are on show. Heinz Knop was here, Kurt Kraftzig and Herbert Koenig – Eden Camp has got their service identity cards – and Hans Baldes has offered his testimony that Eden Camp was not a bad place to be; certainly the best of all the camps he was in. There is only one recorded escape: an Italian prisoner tried to scramble under a wire, got hooked up on it, and was found by guards, stuck firm and impotently weeping. That in itself is remarkable, for escapes from these camps often occurred, and it tends to confirm the impression that Eden was one of the better ones.

What happened in Britain's prisoner of war camps is well documented. Much less is known about a system of camps established between the wars by the British authorities, about which little was said, and what was said was often evasive and designed to mask their true purpose. One such camp was established on the outskirts of a little moorland village called Langdale End, only fifteen miles and a couple of bus rides away from Eden Camp. The Whitby Coastliner runs on through Pickering, another solid and self-contained market town with a bigger tourist pull than Malton, perhaps, since it is closer into the North York moors and offers trips on a reclaimed railway through wonderful landscape to Whitby. I am making for Thornton Dale. Or possibly Thornton-le-Dale. Some indications give the one and others the other. This is one of those beguiling North Yorkshire villages which deserve to be rated somewhere between pretty and preposterously pretty. With its cottages and cottage gardens and the stream that flows at the side of the road – always a reliable turn on for trippers, whether here or in the Cotswolds – it might have been created for devotees of days out. There are numerous cafés: ice cream is sold copiously but decorously. Remarkably too for a place of this size it has two second-hand bookshops, handily placed for those who are changing buses close to the main village stop.

Coastliners come through the village all year round, but some of the buses which make scenic journeys through lanes and byways operate in the summer only. The bus which goes to Langdale End is one of these, running four days a week in high summer, but dwindling in early autumn to Sundays only. Mine, in late October, is the last Moorsbus of the year. The driver, whose name is Ann, is one of those people who radiate competence. Had twenty more people tried to get on, she would no doubt have coped, though goodness knows how. Indeed, had she announced at some point, 'I'm sorry, but because of adverse weather conditions this bus will divert via Siberia', there would not, such was our trust in her, have been even a glimmer of panic. The general verdict aboard Ann's bus is that this is the best day all year to have done the journey. October is late enough to give you the autumn colours; and despite the lateness of the season no one can remember a day this year when the sun was more bright and benign. The ride through the forest is punctuated by green open spaces laid out for picnics, with neatly appointed car parks and tracks winding out through the trees: we lose a few of our contingent at each of them. Part way along this wandering road we come to a block post where a charge of £5 is levied. The country now feels remote. At Dalby village, deep in the forest, new passengers present themselves and every seat on the bus is occupied. Cyclists pedal devotedly past, some wearing numbers: one feels a pang of pity for the struggles of number 472, so far adrift of the rest. At last the road leaves the forest and comes out into the sun. 'Shall we open the skylight?' solicitous Ann inquires. 'It's getting a bit hot and stuffy.' But here is a pub called the Moorcock, which is where I get off.

What was once the Langdale End work camp is now a scout camp – Birch Hall. I come to it down a long track into the hills, north-west of the village. Only birdsong disturbs the silence, until a platoon of quad bikes appears, racing away towards the village. Then all is quiet again. There is no one about at Birch Hall. The gates are locked; notices ban intruders. But something remains of the work camp, which is true of few of the rest of them. There is one long green corrugated iron hut, and a shorter grey one, and various concrete bases where other huts must have been. The architecture has an air of mean-eyed deterrence which incongru-ously recalls the prison ship off the Isle of Portland. There is no sound now except the wind in the trees. This place is eerie. And must have seemed eerier still to the men who were brought here, against their will, to be toughened up.

In 1928 Stanley Baldwin's Conservative government resolved to create a network of training centres to assist the unemployed to transfer to places with better prospects. The Labour and National governments that followed continued the policy. 'I am convinced', Margaret Bondfield, Ramsay MacDonald's minister of Labour, told the Commons in January 1930, 'that young men and women – and middle-aged men and women too – who have been subjected to compulsory idleness, week after week, month after month, without any hope, lose their powers, they deteriorate in their quality of their minds and the skill of the hand which was theirs. The centres...are for the purpose of keeping them alive, of giving them something to think about and of making them feel they have the capacity and that some time or other the nation will badly need them, and we have to keep them fit and well and sound in body and mind.' But some men who might otherwise have qualified for inclusion were thought to require a rather tougher regime: the work camp. In his book *Labour Camps – the British Experience*, Dave Colledge reproduces a memorandum sent by a civil servant called Bowers to a counterpart in the Treasury in December 1928. 'I think I ought to warn you,' Bowers writes, 'that we have under consideration here a proposal to deal with the class of men to whom our existing training schemes do not apply. I refer to those, especially among the younger men, who, through prolonged unemployment, have become so "soft" and temporarily demoralized that it would not be practicable to introduce more than a very small number of them into our ordinary training centres without danger to the morale of the centre...It is essential to the success of the transference policy...that only the best material available be sent forward for any given job. It is obvious, therefore, that the class of whom I am speaking cannot be considered by our local officers for transfer until they are hardened.'

The notion of work camps was neither new nor malign. The Salvation Army leader William Booth had established one long ago at Hadleigh in Essex. The Fabians instituted a few; so did the Quakers. But the impetus in the case of the government camps was predominantly defensive. The numbers of those who could not be described as 'the best material' and were vulnerable to the kind of demoralization described by Bowers must have seemed to some in Whitehall to be immense. In 1930 some 2.3 million were out of work; by 1931, 3.25 million, by 1932, 3.4 million or 15 per cent of the workforce. And in many areas it was far worse than that: 36 per cent were jobless in Wales. Some were inevitably 'softened'; others were seen as troublemakers, drawing and disseminating conclusions about a political system which inflicted so harsh a fate on so many. Whitehall thought that it knew the answer. Take such men for three months, on a voluntary basis, of course (but backed by the threat that benefits would cease if they did not comply, leaving their families destitute), subject them to military discipline (most of those running these camps came from the services), keep them at a safe distance from the nearest large town, and disorder, even a developing taste for revolution, might be averted. Getting them back to work – almost any work – should begin to sort them out. In practice, some of the work struck those who had been dragooned as insultingly pointless: today, dig a trench; tomorrow, fill it back in. Attempts to educate the inmates were sometimes resented too. 'The first week in the training camp,' one recipient recorded, 'is spent at school. Lessons are given in the tying of knots, in mathematics, and in the benefits conferred on the nation by such men as Nelson and Wellington.'

Some who went there did so rebelliously, and found the camps as hostile as they had feared. Concentration camps, they called them, even slave camps. Standing in the remoteness of Birch Hall now it is easy to imagine what this exile was like for men who had lived all their lives in the noise and company of great cities: even the stillness must have been menacing. In a distant spot like Birch Hall even escape must have seemed a frightening prospect. The one consolation seems to have been that those in the better camps were properly fed: some of those who came to the camps had not eaten so much in years.

Although more than 100,000 men may have passed through them in a little above a decade, life in these camps is barely documented. It is clear that in some, notably at Peebles in the Scottish borders, there was unrest which had to be quelled. In another camp, in Northumberland, some of the Glasgow contingent objected to the running up of the Union flag each morning and demanded that the Red flag be hoisted instead. Some Labour MPs asked awkward questions in Parliament. At one point *Challenge*, the newspaper of the Young Communist League, published a double-page spread alleging that a man had died for lack of care in one of these camps, at Redesdale in Northumberland. The MP for Glasgow Maryhill demanded a public inquiry. Wal Hannington and Harry McShane, leaders of the National Unemployed Workers' Movement, toured the camps to investigate conditions. Hannington collected and published evidence of inadequate food, of dirt and lice and lack of heating and lighting, of petty tyrannies and sometimes full-blooded assaults by staff on prisoners. Dave Colledge, fifty years later, collected more such testimony from veterans of the camps. One who had sampled camps both at Brandon in Norfolk and Kielder in Northumberland recalled that in his time young men at both had killed themselves. But Colledge also reproduces part of a novel by an inmate called William Markall which presents a more varied picture of life in the camps than Hannington did. Some found their time there humiliating. 'To the outsider,' the novel reflects, 'to the tourist, the camp was negligible, a thing of a day, something root-less, unworthy. How like a large proportion of those within it, the same observer might have thought. The unwanted cogs of machines no longer working; the unsatisfactory pieces, the too-perdurable, the still-unmoulded, the cracked, the rusted...' Others, though, quite enjoyed their exile: one of Markall's characters rejoices in his escape from a nagging wife. There was pleasure to be found in the sense of companionship, the occasional trip to the pub or a village dance hall (even if they only had pocket money of four shillings a week to pay for it), and the sing-songs – although such evenings, as one of Colledge's witnesses sadly reflects, frequently seemed to end with a fight.

So far as I could establish, no record of life at Langdale End has survived. The county library at Northallerton could find nothing at all. When the camps were abruptly closed at the outbreak of war, many of the records were sent to the camp at Weeting Hall in Norfolk where they were destroyed in a fire: deliberately, Dave Colledge suspects, for fear that parallels might be drawn with the concentration camps which the British authorities now vehemently condemned. In 1998, Warren Lakin and Jane McMorrow, who were running an organization called Workers' Republic, suggested to the trade union Unison that the memories of men who had been through these camps should be collected before it was too late. The then general secretary, Rodney Bickerstaffe, was enthusiastic and wrote to local newspapers appealing for information both from men sent to the camps and from people who lived around them. 'We feel this episode is an important part of our country's history which needs to be fully researched and acknowledged,' he said. The response was said to be good. Yet seven years later the evidence that the appeal produced was still languishing somewhere in the vaults of Unison's London headquarters, uncatalogued and unpublished.

There is not a lot to the village of Langdale End: a church, a couple of farms, a scatter of cottages and a village hall which looks suspiciously like a hut from the work camp, liberated by some means or other. A notice board announces that Piers and Jasmin Turner are running a bus, subsidized by the county council, from Bickley through Langdale End to Scarborough. The Moorcock Inn trades heavily on nostalgia, with advertising signs for Turf and Woodbines and White's lemonade. Ada Martindale, it says over the door, six days only, licensed retailer of FOREIGN and BRITISH spirits, wines, ales and tobacco. A new sign, lettered to look like an old one, says the Yorkshire Penny Bank will open here every Thursday. There is plenty of time before the next bus back for a meal and a drink and perhaps a taste of the local gossip. Although there's sunshine outside, there's a welcoming fire in the rustic grate this lunchtime, and some lively and affectionate banter about the likely effects on property values of the new airport at Doncaster and the gratifyingly high level of house prices in Weybridge, Surrey. But the wait for Ann and her Moorsbus is unsettling. What if it's full? What if this late autumn sunshine has brought out so many ramblers that the bus sails past and leaves me in Langdale End till Piers and Jasmin come by?

But Ann's bus, just as if she'd organized these matters down to the last detail herself, has a couple of seats for the journey onwards to Ayton on the Pickering to Scarborough main road, through Hackness village and down into the enchanting Forge Valley by the side of the dappled Derwent. You would never guess it to look at the place, but aeronautical history was made a few miles from here, at a place called Brompton Dale, where in 1853 Sir George Cayley, aristocrat and engineer, then well past eighty, constructed and flew, as it says in the reference books, the first successful man-carrying glider. However he didn't exactly fly it himself; that honour went to his coachman, who having landed, told his employer: 'Please, Sir George, I wish to give notice. I was hired to drive and not to fly.' At West Ayton, one of a pair of villages on either side of the Derwent, and a mile or two from Brompton by Sawdon where Sir George lived and worked, the Moorsbus turns to make the beautiful journey back to Thornton. Only a handful of people get off. So they must have come, not for the ramble, but just for the ride through the autumn forest, knowing that at the moment when the last of the season's buses pulled into the car park at Thornton, the summer was finally over. This summer of 2004 has seemed to most of the people I met on my journeys – and painfully so to those who make their living from B & Bs – relentlessly sunless and drab; but this was the kind of day people pray for. It won't be like that, I fear, when I get to Gateshead.

The Angel, and Gateshead resurgent, but only bits of it – what
John Dobson, Tyneside architect, did for exhilarating Newcastle
– Byker: triumph or tragedy? – North Shields, a Dobson town –
Tynemouth, its festive station, its windswept priory, its Grand
Hotel and its outsize tribute to Nelson's number two.

Ask people in Newcastle or Gateshead – or to use the form invented
when they joined in a bid to become the European City of Culture:
NewcastleGateshead – if they know who Antony Gormley is, and
they may well be able to tell you he created the Angel of the North,
that symbol of the North East resurgent that floats above the A1.
Ask them who John Dobson was, and what he created, and though
he was once esteemed as one of the great men of Tyneside, they
may be rather less certain.

The Angel of the North is essentially an angel of Gateshead,
thought up by Gateshead and put there by Gateshead, the poor rela-
tion across the water, without reference to mighty Newcastle. When
the plans were proposed a lot of people in Gateshead thought it a
great waste of money. It's more difficult to find such opinions now.
Twenty metres high, with a wingspan of 54 metres, made with 200
tonnes of steel, the Angel is something to marvel at. And thousands
do. A North East firm, Hartlepool Steel Fabrications Ltd, constructed
it, but essentially it's the creation of Antony Gormley – of London.

In the wake of his Angel have come the Baltic galleries, a con-
version from a 1950 Rank flour mill; the millennium footbridge

across the Tyne, an inspired addition to what must already have been about the best collection of bridges in any British city, built by a Gateshead company, Harbour & General, who brought it by floating crane from Wallsend, to designs by the London architects Wilkinson Eyre; and the Sage music centre, constructed by Laing O'Rourke of Dartford, Kent, whose architect is the Manchester-born, London-based Norman Foster. The Baltic and Sage are Gateshead, not Newcastle; the millennium bridge, though it prudently lands on both side of the Tyne, is the Gateshead Millennium Bridge. All around them the Gateshead side of the river thrums with activity. As in Newcastle before it, smart flats for smart people are appearing in fair profusion, the odd celebrity is moving in, and estates are being built for the kind of purchasers who like to think that they live in villages. The great names of British development and construction – Laing, Taylor Woodrow, Ove Arup – are out in force. Nearly all London-based, of course, but it's good to see, as one wanders the area, that one formidable piece of earthworks is being carried out by Thompsons of Prudhoe. There has, however, to be one reservation about this exhilarating renaissance. We have yet to see the rebirth of the rest of Gateshead. It was never entirely clear how the rest of Gateshead was going to benefit from this glamorous cultural enclave camped on its shores. How many of those who walked across the bridge to hear the Northern Sinfonia in its brilliant new headquarters would go for a meal or a drink or an hour or two's shopping in the rest of Gateshead? How many would even give the rest of Gateshead a thought? Few have deluded themselves that mere trickledown from the riverside cultural enclave would have more than a marginal part in that resurrection.

There's a visitor centre between the Sage and the Hilton hotel by the main road bridge into Newcastle in the former St Mary's church. It was ravaged in 1854 by a fire so severe that substantial damage was done on the Newcastle side of the water. The architect John Dobson, who was based in Newcastle, was called in to refurbish it, which he must have done with a heavy heart since his eighteen-year-old son Alexander, who he had hoped would follow him into the practice, was burned to death in the fire. After further fires in 1979 and 1983 it was closed for worship. Both within and without there are monuments to Gateshead's industrial past. Outside are the tombs of the Greenes, for instance, colliery owners. George Greene, 'viewer and owner of collieries', died in 1796 aged twenty-seven: 'saved from the world of greif [sic] and sin with GOD eternally shute in'. Inside, one exhibit records that in 1831 industrially versatile Gateshead dug coal, made paper and tobacco pipes, and built boats. It had glassworks and ironworks and gasworks and dye works, lime kilns, rope works and cinder ovens, chemical works and works where they made colliery staithes. It had oil mills and vinegar manufactories and plants that made glue. Between them they made their owners tolerably well off or better, kept the plebeian classes in work, and vilely polluted the land and the atmosphere in Gateshead and all around it.

Simply to imagine the air in Gateshead as it must have been in those days is enough to dispel any sentimentality about a world of manufacturing now largely gone. An enterprise called the Kittiwake Project solicits comments about the past and present condition of the Tyne. 'I was an apprentice at Vickers Armstrong, Elswick,' John Bishop of Corbridge writes. 'On a sunny lunchtime break we would go down to the Tyne. It stank, as many sewers emptied directly into the river. Newcastle and Gateshead can be proud of the transformation which has refreshed and rejuvenated the area during the last fifty years.' Yet refreshed and rejuvenated are hardly words one could use about the present-day centre of Gateshead. Its most celebrated building, surpassing in public attention the charming Victorian town hall with its attendant clock tower presented by a subsequent mayor, and the new and imposing complex of civil buildings of 1987, and the excellent road and rail interchange opened in 2004, is the car park by the market, which must rate as one of the ugliest buildings in Christendom (though some would rate the now demolished Tricorn centre in Portsmouth as even fouler: they share the same architect, Owen Luder). And yet there was outrage when the local council proposed tearing it down, since it was within these gloomy portals that a famous episode in the movie *Get Carter* was staged in which Jack Carter (Michael Caine) pushes Cliff Brumby (Bryan Mosley) off the top, which, not surprisingly, kills him. That is still regarded as something for Gateshead to boast about; something, even, that feels more authentically Gateshead than the Sage or the bridge or the Baltic.

But the shopping streets here are mostly mean and dismal, with that proliferation of takeaways and charity shops and amusement arcades which signals a town where money is tight. 'Discount,' they howl at you, 'DISCOUNT'. If you want to get from here through to the new Gateshead, you must do so through graffitied walkways littered with broken glass, while above you important traffic roars into Newcastle, invading Gateshead territory to satisfy the needs of its mighty superior. Gateshead, these arrangements seem to announce, knows its place: underneath.

There are seven bridges into Newcastle. The swing bridge of 1876 was built because big vessels could not get under the road bridge of 1781. A high-level bridge was opened for rail traffic in 1849 and for road traffic the following year. At the eastern end of the sequence is the lovely new invention of Wilkinson Eyre. But the best-known bridge, the Tyne Bridge of 1928, is one that is used by the 301 Go Coastline double-decker bus, Gateshead to Whitley Bay. There are not many journeys in this book where one bus does all the work, but this is one. It gives you a taste of Newcastle, pushing briefly into the district named after its creator, the inspired developer Richard Grainger, as Grainger Town. But even this brief encounter is enough to demonstrate how a combination of fortunate geography, an enlightened developer working with talented architects, and a dazzling late twetieth-century makeover have made this today one of Europe's most visually ravishing cities.

The architect John Dobson was not a Newcastle man – he came from North Shields, down the coast – but his work is a crucial part of the city's nineteenth-century legacy. It is not as rich a memorial as it should have been. Enlightened though Grainger was, there were plans that Dobson proposed which he found too extravagant and declined to adopt. The central station building and train shed, commissioned by the North Eastern Railway in an era when Newcastle would not have, possibly could not have, turned to a great London architect when something of high importance was to be done, were probably his finest achievement. Yet Dobson's expensive design for the station was never entirely completed; the portico, based on modifications by Dobson, was added by one of his pupils. And some of the best work he did was wantonly erased in the redevelopment craze of the 1960s and 1970s.

Dobson was no Wren or Hawksmoor. His output is generally rated competent rather than brilliant. A book by Thomas Faulkner and Andrew Greg, published in 1987 to mark a Dobson exhibition in Newcastle, judiciously sums him up as 'an immensely respected and important provincial architect of considerable national renown'. But he left his mark on a city and a region as few architects have done, and only rarely worked outside it. Faulkner and Greg list over 380 assignments undertaken by Dobson – some completed, some uncompleted, some never even commenced, of which 90 per cent were within the North East, and just one overseas, in Germany.

The 301 bus taking us out towards Dobson's attributed home town, North Shields – in fact he was born in the nearby village of Chirton – comes first to a suburb with little or no mark of Dobson, but an honoured place in recent architectural history. The Byker estate is admired and vilified, lauded and mocked, but whichever of these judgements may be preferred, it displays an ingenuity, an attempt to create new patterns of living unmatched by other post-war estates on Tyneside or most other conurbations. It is listed by the UN as one of the most important architectural innovations of the twenty-first century. One can catch just a glimpse of it as the 301 ploughs its way along Byker's main street – on the southern side, behind the new library. You come into it through a great wall, strong and irregular, rising in places to four or five storeys, punctuated with little sniperish windows, sealing it off like the wall of a medieval city from a hostile world outside. The specific enemy the architect had in mind was a motorway, which was never built. Beyond the walls, the houses of Byker village are more modestly scaled, pleasingly landscaped, gathered in friendly squares and crescents with the motor car kept at bay – almost cosy, were it not for the notices: 'Warning: anti-climb paint'. Who's been climbing, and why? It's encouraging, as I wander the Byker's walkways, to catch sight of the spire of a church. It is always reassuring when a church or a favourite pub is saved from some bout of redevelopment. They give new arrivals the sense of an older, settled community, and older inhabitants a reassuring feeling of continuity with the place they grew up in. But when I reach the church by a mazy route past abandoned shops and the boarded-up Stag's Head pub ('All items of value have been removed'), the church is no longer in business, graffiti artists have been at work on the windows, and old suitcases and mattresses litter the churchyard. The view from up here, though, over the city and river and the bridges with the hill beyond, of St James's Park football ground, where Jackie Milburn and Malcolm Macdonald banged the goals in for Newcastle United (and Alan Shearer, in 2005, was doing so still), is comprehensive and thrilling.

The architect of the Byker was Ralph Erskine – from London. He is named in the RIBA's list of great buildings for Byker and for the Greenwich Millennium Village. His work, says the citation, is partly inspired by Swedish empiricism (Erskine himself was part-Swedish) and partly by British community planning. Erskine died in 2005, enthusiastically obituarized. John Dobson gets one entry on the RIBA list, for Newcastle station.

The 301 bus moves on through the suburb of Walker into a territory full of reminders of Tyneside as it used to be when still a power in shipbuilding and engineering and coal-mining and when yuppies in search of a stunning apartment had not yet been dreamed of. Here are the old C. A. Parsons engineering works, subsequently taken over by Siemens in 1997, and beyond them an inn called the Colliery Engine. At Wallsend, the end of the great Roman wall, the Swan Hunter shipyard is briefly visible down a side road: today, I see from the evening paper, much of the workforce has gone up to London to urge government intervention to save their jobs. In one street, every one in a row of five or six houses is up for sale. The conversation aboard this bus is full of disappointments and dis-satisfactions. 'How is Lisa?' 'She's really not well, and Jack's not well either.' This somehow provokes a discussion about inadequate cleaning. 'People don't clean. I've never seen her do the front step. I've never seen her do the stairs.' (Short, disconsolate silence.)

'Mind you, that's one thing I can say for Jenny. She does move the furniture.' There are cranes on the river skyline. A moment later we pass Burnside Community High School, in the process of being wrecked. 'It's a shame,' says a woman who sees me gazing at it. 'It's the old grammar school,' she explains. 'Mind you, there just aren't any grammar schools left.' An appropriate silence follows.

But soon we are into North Shields. The bus stops at the doors of an unalluring shopping mall. Down the hill you come to the river-front. There are trendy new stunning apartments here with balconies, and a handsome building by another of Grainger's favoured architects, Benjamin Green, commissioned by the fourth duke of Northumberland to accommodate visiting sailors. A ferry across to South Shields plies from the other side of the road, picking its way judiciously through the paths of bigger shipping; there are afternoon river cruises advertised, some specifying that they will pass under the Gateshead Millennium Bridge. Eastwards along the waterfront is the fish quay, punctuated by old-fashioned pubs, the last of the hundred pubs that once lined this waterfront. Up the hill, away from the water, there is still a lot to admire in North Shields, and constant reminders that Dobson was here. The north side gives a strong sense of planned new town, late eighteenth century and early nineteenth, especially in Northumberland Square, which is home to firms of solicitors, accountants, estate agents and similar professional persons. The statue in the square proves to be not one of the dukes of Northumberland, whom I expected, but a troubled old woman with a pack on her back. Emblematic, I think you'd call her. Certainly not one of the duchesses. Howard Street, leading into the square, has good older buildings and some neatly harmonious newer ones. The Scotch church here is Dobson's, as is the Baptist church. He built or reconstructed almost a hundred churches across Northumberland. He also built or rebuilt a variety of country houses, the most successful of which, in the judgement of Faulkner and Greg, was Longhirst Hall, in 1824, which is well off my route, near Morpeth: 'Dobson's finest classical design,' they say, 'and thus, as Dobson was always a classicist at heart, his best building.' Behind Northumberland Square is Christ Church, originally (1668) the parish church of Tynemouth, a fact that establishes well-appointed heavily Dobsoned North Shields as a mere parvenu compared with its next-door neighbour. Without modern-day street signs you could scarcely tell where one place ends and the other begins.

The best way to see Tynemouth is to disembark from the 301 bus at the Master Mariners' Asylum, designed by John and Benjamin Green of Tyneside for the third duke of Northumberland. A narrow path on the left takes you to one of the glories of the town: the once magnificent station, for years a showpiece of the line. But when Tynemouth ceased to be such a lure for day visitors from urban Tyneside it fell into disrepair. There was even talk of pulling it down. A local outcry saved it; it was given the necessary protection of a grade 2 listing and a rescue operation began in 1989. One obvious money-devouring problem was the filigree iron roof, and despite all the work that was done on it, it looked far from happy again when I was there in 2004. When you look at the parts that are best preserved a vision swims up of the cheerful noisy crowds that used to debouch from excursion trains under great glass roofs which must have seemed to echo the Crystal Palace, all decorated with lavish displays of flowers in hanging baskets. There's another powerful evocation of those days in a map painted on tiles on a wall near the booking hall, charting the routes of the North Eastern Railway. So many of these journeys, given up long ago, must have been as enchanting as the names make them sound. Wearhead to Wear Valley Junction, via St John's Chapel, Wolsingham, Harperley and Witton-le-Wear. Hexham to Allendale, via Langley and Staward. Barnard Castle via Romaldkirk to Middleton-in-Teesdale ('gateway to High Force and Cauldron Snout'). Others sound grittier: Ferryhill via Shincliffe, Sherburn Colliery, Pelaw, Felling and Gateshead East to Newcastle. Doncaster to Selby, via Moss, Balne and Heck. The lines of the NER are set out in big bold colour: those of rival companies are given pitifully thin black lines which make them seem no more substantial than rivers.

Garibaldi excited Tynemouth as he did Mansfield. The station has a Garibaldi restaurant. 'Giuseppe Garibaldi. 19th century patriot', says a plaque on a nearby house, now part of King's School, 'stayed in this house in 1854, while visiting Tynemouth to brief local political and industrial leaders on his plans for a united Italy. He was hailed throughout Europe as a true idealist and an honest politician.' How many political figures, apart from Nelson Mandela, would be saluted so admiringly now? Beyond is another nineteenth-century patriot treated throughout Britain to an even greater degree of reverence. Queen Victoria sits at the top of Main Street, head bowed and not looking happy, as if she resented the way that the curve of the street ahead denies her a view of the sea. Erected after her death and unveiled by the mayor, the statue, which is very competently done, commemorates what its inscription calls a 'beneficent, wise and glorious reign'. If you mentally edit out the garish stonework of the Tynemouth Social Club, this is a pleasant, harmonious scene.

This isn't in any way routine Tyne and Wear. The town grew up around the priory and castle, out on a headland where the Tyne completes its journey from Cumbria and at last meets the sea. The eventful past of this site is well summarized in an English Heritage guidebook by Andrew Saunders which they sell at the priory gate. Its first fame was as the burial place of St Oswin, King of Deira, slain by his brother and later venerated as a Christian martyr; also, to a lesser extent, as the last resting place of a murdered king of Northumbria, St Osred. The original monastery, destroyed by the Danes, was refounded in 1085 as a dependency of St Albans Abbey. Monks who had got into trouble at St Albans were packed off to Tynemouth to reflect on their errors and imperfections. Thereafter it developed as a curious combination of the religious and the military, exemplified by the requirement that the prior had to pay for the maintenance of the fortress and garrison. When the priory fell victim to Henry VIII, this place became a part of the king's defence network. In time the castle fell into ruin too, though the fourteenth-century gatehouse substantially survives. But the place never lost its usefulness for the defence of the realm. It was the military's need in the 1780s for extensive alterations to the site that swept away much of those parts of the priory that were still standing at the end of Henry's reign. The floor of the chapter house, says Saunders, was dug up to make cellars for a regimental canteen, while the Percy Chapel was converted into a powder magazine and remained so for forty years until John Dobson restored it. There were guns still in place here until 1956. Even now, beyond the ruined priory, of which the high east end is the most complete survivor, there are modern military installations.

This is one of these places where the emotional pull is strongest when the weather is bleak. Saunders reprints a letter from a thirteenth-century monk who had been banished from St Albans and clearly wished he was back there. 'Our house,' he writes, 'is confined to the top of a high rock and is surrounded by the sea on every side but one…Day and night the waves break and roar and undermine the cliff. Thick sea fret rolls in, wrapping everything in gloom. Spring and summer never come here. The North wind is always blowing and brings with it cold and snow; or storms in which the wind tosses the salt sea in masses over our buildings and rains it down within the castle...' 'See to it, brother,' he counsels, 'that you do not come to this comfortless place.' Yet the church, he has to accept, is 'of wondrous beauty'. And the fishing is good. But that bleakness persisted. The eighteenth- and nineteenth-century gravestones on the headland tell a consistent story. Many of those buried here died young. Quite a number died old. There are fewer than one might expect of deaths in between. A man called Clark lived to seventy and his wife to eighty. They lost one daughter at nineteen, and another in infancy, while a grandson died at four; but another daughter lived to be seventy-three. If you survived your early years here, you were strong enough to give you a chance of what counted then as a long life.

Much of Tynemouth belongs to the nineteenth century. Take the coast road north from the priory and you come to a crescent, called, after one of the great North country families, Percy Gardens, which seems to have aimed for a grandeur it didn't achieve – although clumsy unfeeling additions to some of these houses must take a fat share of the blame. Beyond, on the curve of the bay, there used to be a pleasure drome called the Plaza, destroyed by a fire in 1996 (there's only now a Plaza tandoori, which isn't quite the same thing). But here is a joyous discovery: a Grand Hotel which really looks and feels like a grand hotel, which it didn't when I first came here back in the 1990s. The first sight that greeted me then was an act of desecration: through the centre of the fine curving staircase, created for gorgeous women to float down on glittering evenings, someone had stuck a lift shaft. The present owners have taken that out, redecorated it in the style it deserved, and generally made it once more the place its name pronounced it to be.

It is evening now, and there's one more essential Tynemouth sight still to be seen. There's a lane which becomes a track leading down from the priory towards the sea. And there at the end of the track, starkly outlined in the twilight, is a statue, twenty-three feet high on a plinth of fifty feet. It salutes the memory of a great Northumbrian hero, who was born in Newcastle in 1749 and died on active service in 1810. He is Admiral Collingwood, colleague and comrade of Nelson, buried beside him in St Paul's. The inscription says that Collingwood 'led the British fleet into action at Trafalgar, and sustained the sea fight for upwards of an hour before the other ships were within gunshot, which caused Nelson to exclaim, "See how that noble fellow Collingwood takes his ship into action"'. Four guns which belonged to his ship, the *Royal Sovereign*, are stationed around him. He stares vigilantly through the encroaching darkness out towards the sea, while lighthouses flash on either side of the mouth of the Tyne. The first view of this statue on the water's edge must have seemed as amazing to people coming upon it for the first time as the Gateshead Angel does now to travellers on the A1. The statue is the work of John Graham Lough. And which prolific local architect was called on to devise and direct this colossal performance? At the end of this Tyneside journey, does one need to ask?

18

Kirkcaldy — East Neuk of Fife
St Andrews
DUNDEE

Kirkcaldy, Adam Smith's town, though the council prefers not to say so – Smith's views not entirely as Thatcherites would wish them to be – Pittenweem, Crail and other undersung pleasures along the Fife coast – I spend an hour in St Andrews, none of it devoted to golf – Dundee, its opulence, its squalor, its wasted opportunities.

'No society', wrote the great economist Adam Smith in his immortal book, *The Wealth of Nations*, 'can surely be flourishing and happy, of which the far greater part of the members are poor and miserable. It is but equity, besides, that they who feed, clothe and lodge the whole body of the people, should have such a share of the produce of their labour as to be themselves well fed, clothed and lodged.' This teaching may well have been relevant to the town of Kirkcaldy, on the banks of the Firth of Forth, where Smith was born in 1723; but it came to be even more true of another town, for which I am heading on a sequence of buses along the Fife coast, through the city of St Andrews and over the river Tay: Dundee. It is also a useful reminder that the hero, even some would claim the founding father, of the economic doctrines that came to be known as Thatcherism was not the granite and heartless figure that some devotees have portrayed.

There used to be signs on the roads into Kirkcaldy proclaiming it as Adam Smith's town. But in 1998 Fife district council had them removed and replaced with the information that Kirkcaldy is twinned with Ingolstadt, Germany. The council's critics alleged that this was as a punishment for Smith's contribution to the development of Thatcherite teachings. The council denied any such petulant motive. There was simply a limit, its leaders said, to the amount of information that a council could cram on to a road sign, and Ingolstadt deserved its acknowledgement.

When Smith was a child he was kidnapped by gypsies who, after some thought, kindly handed him back. There are clearly some who believe that had the gypsies only hung on to him, the subsequent doctrines of Thatcherism might have been lost to the world and the sum of human happiness increased accordingly. And it's true that *The Wealth of Nations* is packed with pronouncements close to the core of Thatcherite preaching: the belief in the benign operations of markets, the cheerful assumption that the pursuit of self-interest tends to lead, through the operations of an 'invisible hand', to the enhancement of the general good, the conviction that governments intervening to make things better frequently make things worse. And yet Smith is no uncritical champion of the ways in which capitalists operate. He is constantly on the prowl for the misbehaviour of the successful and prosperous. At times he attacks fat cats pawing in excessive profits in language New Labour would never dare utter. The rate of profit, he says at one point, is always highest in countries going to ruin. It's a shame that Smith's more perceptive defenders failed to stay the erasing hand of Fife district council. But at least I can take a swig of him now and then on my journey to Dundee.

Certainly Smith has not disappeared from Kirkcaldy. There's an Adam Smith cultural centre ahead as you leave the railway station, and a plaque in the high street which marks the site of the house, demolished in 1834, where he lived with his mother while writing *The Wealth of Nations*. Shops converted with different levels of expertise from former banks and offices and houses ramble along the street, with here and there a really distinguished contributor to the scene. To understand how the high street became what it is, you need not only the teachings of Adam Smith about how market economies work, but a book called *The Kingdom of Fife*, an illustrated architectural guide by Glen L. Pride, which should never be out of the curious traveller's hand between here and the Tay Bridge crossing. It not only tells you all about what you see in Kirkcaldy; it also tells you what you would also have seen had it not been knocked down. It will help you understand the extent to which Kirkcaldy in former times was suffused with linoleum. Michael Nairn began manufacturing floorcloth here in 1847. By the end of the 1870s his new linoleum had become the town's staple industry, covering floors all across Britain and subsequently across much of the world. The great days of linoleum are over; only one product, marmoleum, persists here. But old factories survive, some, like the one that is now Fife College, adapted for new purposes; there are also magnificent wrecks, including one thunderous building which looks less like a place of work than a prison, on Nairn Street. Many jobs perished with these old linoleum works, but so did an aspect of Kirkcaldy almost as famous in Scotland as the product itself: the smell that resulted from the boiling of linseed oil. It was everywhere inescapable. There is even a poem about it, appropriately engraved on linoleum, displayed on Kirkcaldy station.

Another part of the town's tradition is enlightened patronage and philanthropy. Ravenscraig Castle in its fine park set above the Forth, bestowed on the town by Sir Michael Nairn in 1929, is one powerful instance; another is the sequence of museum, art gallery and library by the railway station, also given to the town by the

Nairns in the 1920s. There is, however, one truly dreadful disfigurement in this town – a crime against the environment, though committed for good environmental reasons. It is what has been done to the waterfront. The motive was fine: to get the traffic out of the narrow and winding main street. But this was achieved by building a brutal relief road along the waterfront by the Firth of Forth, thus comprehensively wrecking one of the town's best natural assets. The planners have had the gall to call the result an 'esplanade'. An esplanade, says a good Scottish dictionary (*Chambers*) means a level space for walking or driving, especially by the sea. Well, it's level all right, and it's certainly fine for driving, often at rather excessive speeds; but who could derive even the tiniest drop of pleasure from walking here? Most of the buildings along this stretch are horribly appropriate. The back of the Mercat Centre, the main shopping mall, the back of the indoor market, an uninspired swimming pool building, and car parks, one of which looks as if some aesthete speeding along the Esplanade had lobbed a bomb into it. Glen Pride makes a kind of defence of it: 'the walls...said to have been conceived deliberately as a ruin, achieve spectacular irregularity'. But maybe it simply symbolizes the ruin of Kirkcaldy's waterfront.

At the eastern end, and beyond beneath the shadow of Robert Hutchinson's flour mills, there are bursts of aspirational flats like the ones now colonizing the banks of the Tyne; one, inevitably, is named after Adam Smith. So at least some citizens of Kirkcaldy, though probably not the more seasoned ones, get the chance to enjoy the view across what seems like the sea, though as yet it is still the Firth. Perhaps what is needed now is some mighty philanthropist in the tradition of that famous son of Dunfermline, Andrew Carnegie, to roar 'This cannot continue!' and recruit the ingenuity of twenty-first-century designers to give the riverfront back to the rest of the people.

Ten miles or so to the east of Kirkcaldy, one comes to the enchanting East Neuk ('neuk', as *Chambers Dictionary* confirms, is a Scots form of 'nook') of Fife. Did Adam Smith ever travel this route? I wonder as the first of my buses pulls out of the bus station. Even by accident? He was famously absent-minded. According to a publication called *Kirkcaldy's Famous Folk*, he once strolled in his dressing gown to the end of his garden, forgot what he was doing, set off along the coast, and did not stop walking until he got to Dunfermline. This stage by stage journey is served by Stagecoach Fife. The quickest way to begin is to take the X26, a powerful creature which runs from Glasgow right through to St Andrews, which takes one in plushy comfort to Lower Largo, the first big East Neuk attraction.

At the edge of Lower Largo is an authoritative viaduct of 1856–7, built to take the old line from St Andrews to Leven and Thornton over the valley. The Crusoe Hotel, down by the water, was built at about the same time. There is also a vestigial pier. From here a narrow street with houses and the occasional shop crowding around it runs parallel with the water. All is calm and restrained, even the traffic. Even tourists are doucely wooed. The whole place has a withdrawn feeling about it. The most famous attraction is the Selkirk statue, erected in 1885, 'in memory of Alexander Selkirk, mariner, the original of Robinson Crusoe, who lived on the island of Juan Fernandez in complete solitude for four years and four months. He died 1723. Lieutenant of HMS *Weymouth* aged 47 years'. In 2004 Lower Largo was twinned with Juan Fernandez. The Chilean ambassador attended the ceremony. It must have been an unusually exuberant moment for Lower Largo.

From here, a Stagecoach 95 will take me all the way to St Andrews, but with many opportunities to stop and browse on the way. There's a sense along this road of intruding into the fine estates of great landowners, obediently served by pliant inferiors. Here is the glimpse of a great house, Kilconquhar Castle, and a church with a perfect churchyard, and an inn, and a lake. The view of the church as you look back across the lake is the best moment of all. Beyond, as the bus returns to the firth, there's a close succession of villages from Elie across to Crail. People fly hundreds of miles out of Britain to enthuse over fishing villages no more attractive than these. At Elie, the 95 puts me down outside the parish church, a Georgian reconstruction with a clocktower attached to the front: it looks like a church designed by a pastrycook. Some of the buildings in South Street, between here and the water, and once the principal street of Elie, have marriage lintels – stones on which newly married householders had their names jointly inscribed. Gillespie House has a splendid carved and decorated doorway transplanted from a famous Elie house, now demolished.

From here on, the 95 bus serves for a time as a kind of mobile watchtower from which to observe the sea. Two miles on – these villages are mostly only a couple of miles apart – is St Monans, otherwise St Monance. Little seems to be known of this saint. A complicated network of little streets spills down the hill to the waterfront. Although the sun has been shining all day, the wind is cutting. Small boats bob and clank in the harbour. The seafront is a joyous assortment of variegated brightly coloured cottages; yet St Monans has an air about it of a place that has known hard times. There is not much fishing left here, and the last substantial employer, a boatbuilder, shut his doors in the early 1990s. The church, perched on the edge of the sea and claiming to be the church built closest to the water in Scotland, is irresistibly historic, but locked. King David II ordered its building in 1362, the English knocked it down in 1544 and 1560; for a time it was little more than a ruin, but nineteenth-century Scots rescued and restored it. Generations of Reekies and Robertsons, Aitkens, Fyalls and Fernies sleep in the windswept graveyard. St Monans past is as real here as St Monans present.

Next down the coast is Pittenweem, a bigger place altogether. As at St Monan's, the bus stops at the top of the hill, here by the Tollcross, and leaves me to find my way down to the waterfront. The high street might have been built for a film set. There's a good collection of local shops, a grocers (except that now it calls itself a convenience store), some galleries, and then, at the eastern end, blocking off the end of the street with brutal authority, a building that combines the kirk with the tower of the old Pittenweem toll-booth (the tollbooth in Scottish towns was the municipality's headquarters, often incorporating a small prison). Turn east at this point down Cove Wynd and you come to the cave of the seventh-century hermit St Fillan; a dark and inhospitable spot, though less so perhaps for the saint, whose arm (it is said) lit up to help him write in the dark. Below is the harbour, expansive enough to confirm Pittenweem's status as the biggest of the fishing ports on this coast. *Unity* is moored here, and *Rebecca*, and *Incentive*, *Just Reward*, *Quo Vardis* (sic) and *Sea Spray II*, alongside *Solway Provider*, *Crusader of Pittenweem*, *Shalimar*, *Wet Ardgour* and *Winaway*, rocking and jangling together. And again, on the water's edge, there's a gallimaufry of houses, more demure in colour here than at St Monans, from East Shore to Mid Shore to West Shore, the best of the lot. I meet a man on West Shore who's a refugee from Hackney. He and his wife did not want their children to grow up in Hackney, so they gave up their jobs, sold off their home, said goodbye to friends who thought they were mad, and made a new life on the Fife coast. Did he miss London at all? He looks at me as if he thinks I am crazy.

At Anstruther the bus comes down to the harbour and halts near the Anstruther fish bar, an institution over which lips have been licked as far away as Fleet Street. This, more than Pittenweem, certainly more than St Monans, is a tourist spot, with a fisheries museum and workshop, and boat trips out to the Isle of May, gleaming in the distance across the water, and proving on closer inspection to have a ruined priory and one of Robert Stevenson's lighthouses. Anstruther has a lighthouse too. Saltires flutter over boats in the harbour. Beyond, off the tourist trail, is an eerie place called Cellardyke: long narrow wandering streets, with relentless irregular terraces, giving the place a claustrophobic, conspiratorial feeling. The sounds are of echoing feet, and the lapping sea, and occasionally a burst of muffled conversation. Where James Street changes to John Street one comes upon Cellardyke town hall, erected in 1883 by Stephen Williamson and David Fowler 'for municipal and other purposes'. There's a strong air of other purposes in this place, some of them in Williamson and Fowler's day no doubt extremely nefarious. There is not one boat in the tiny harbour off Shore Street, only squawking and chuntering gulls. Beyond, at a place called the Cooperage, there are modern holiday huts.

The 95 bus climbs out of Anstruther back to the main road and on through rich farmland to the last of these communities, Crail. This is the oldest of the East Neuk burghs, whose former importance is demonstrated in Marketgate, a broad and imposing street which continues the line of the high street. In the churchyard there's an ominous battlemented fortress-like building, 'erected' it says ' for securing the dead'; almost as if someone feared they might try to escape. Below, down steps from the walkway around the site where the castle once stood, or down tumbling Shore Street, is the little compact harbour. 'Lobsters cooked while you wait', says a notice, 'also dressed crab'. These are ancient trades in Crail: a house on the harbourside is decorated with effigies of lobsters and crabs.

From Crail we leave the Neuk on an inland road across fields where the Kingdom of Fife seems to transmute into the Kingdom of Golf. 'I used to walk to St Andrews,' a middle-aged man complains to the passenger beside him, 'but it's all golf courses now.' Beyond Kingsbarns, the bus surges over the top of a hill and there laid out before us is the sparkling Tay, the city of Dundee on its northern side, and behind it, the Grampian hills. And in the foreground below us, the skyline of St Andrews, now in unstinting sunshine: the roofs and spires, the big houses and bigger hotels, the ruins of the cathedral, the dazzling bay.

St Andrews has three traditions: religion, scholarship, golf. The strongest of these is religion. People died for religion here; they did not die for scholarship or even for golf. The streets are punctuated by churches and martyrs. The cathedral was for centuries the centrepoint of Scottish religious life. Like Tynemouth, exposed on the edge of the sea, it survived savage storms in the thirteenth century and even, though extensive rebuilding was needed, a fire in the fourteenth; but it fell into decay with the Reformation. The tower of the church of St Rule, older even than the cathedral, stands intact among the ruins. The churchyard makes the link between church and university. St Andrews is the oldest of the Scottish universities, here since 1413, long predating Edinburgh. Around the ruined cathedral the graves of celebrated professors are arrayed as if in some kind of posthumous academic procession, often with long and fulsome epitaphs. But local tradesmen have their place too. Here is a stone set up by a candlemaker who, within the years 1814 and 1819, lost four of his children and then his wife.

Unexpectedly in the midst of dead academia, there's the effigy of a golfer, now in eternal mid-swing amidst the professors.

There are famous clubs and courses down by the sea, of which the Royal and Ancient is the most influential of all. These are places of pilgrimage, the first sight of which for some must have matched the first sight, for others, of Karnak or Niagara or the Taj Mahal. 'Provided', says a plaque on a bench where I eat my lunch, 'by the widow and daughters of Robert E. Byrne of San Mateo, California, for whom the reality of St Andrews surpassed even his dreams.' St Andrews has golf clubs like some people have mice – at least nine of them, a man on my bus computed. And one was even proposed quite recently which would not have bunkers: painless golf, a pastime only tenuously related, one might have thought, to the original. Once, Protestant Scotland – and not only its golfers – would have risen in wrath against such a notion, calling it decadent.

A 99 bus takes me on to Dundee. The road runs through marshland towards Guardbridge, which has a fine medieval bridge and a papermill, and towards the airfield at Leuchars, where the jets are flying so low one is thankful that the 99 is not a double-decker. It is not until we are close to the banks of the Tay that Dundee appears before us. Its location – south facing, on an estuary, with a ring of protective hills behind it – might have made it one of the best-looking cities in Europe; yet here is a brutal skyline, dominated by menacing tower blocks. The city's great days were largely founded on jute. It built ships which would carry jute home from India; it had whale oil derived from the town's whaling fleet, which could be used to soften the jute; and it seems to have been well stocked with spirited entrepreneurs. Industrialization transformed Dundee from a town of handloom weavers into one of great factories. The employers who ran them became the dominant class in the town. They were known as jute barons; Dundee was jutopolis. Their mansions still span the town, from the west along the road to Perth and eastwards along the road to Broughty Ferry towards Arbroath and Montrose. Baronial performances, set in well-tended gardens, announce to the world that Dundee is a place of high importance, and they are Dundee.

These families lived lives of God-fearing ostentation. The parade of their riches continued even in death. A number 39 Strathtay bus out of the centre will take you to the Eastern necropolis, a place of law clerks and schoolmasters, true, but mainly of shipsmiths, merchants, and manufacturers. It was the grand manufacturers who gave this city its great institutions. Sir James Caird of Ashton Works found £100,000 – perhaps £6 million today – to build a city hall and concert hall – the Caird Hall. Sir David Baxter of Dens Works, whose company was reputed to be the world's largest linen manufacturer, gave the town Baxter Park. The largest jute mills of all were at Lochee: their site is marked by the 86-metre-high chimney known as Cox's Stack, another proud demonstration of jutocratic authority.

But, as Adam Smith might have warned you, their philanthropy was selective. One of the old factories, Verdant Works on West Henderson Wynd, is now the museum of jute. On its walls the limits of jutocratic philanthropy are sardonically noted. The wage rates here were among the lowest in Scotland; not just ungenerous, not even adequate. Adam Smith's advice about liberality to labour was left unhonoured. Terms of employment were often brutal. Boys were laid off when they reached the age where they would have to be paid full wages and new boys brought in to replace them, leaving them out of work at eighteen with little prospect of finding further employment. Women in the workforce outnumbered men by a steady three to one. The men were the kettle-boilers, who stayed at home and minded the children. Only in times of war did they have the chance to find reliable work and a tolerable wage. Yet many who volunteered were rejected. More than half the men who turned up at army recruitment offices in 1904 were considered too weak for service. And whether those accepted would ever return to Dundee was another matter.

When I first went to Verdant Works in the mid-1990s I was shown around by people who had worked in the industry. Some were deaf, through years of subjection to the infernal racket of the machinery. The work in the days of Dundee's greatest success could often be perilous. Mill fever was one problem; the other was industrial accidents, some fatal, many others ensuring that the victims would not work again. This was a town of conspicuous, even awesome, poverty (as parts of it still are today). The great philanthropic jutocrats did not build the new houses needed to accommodate their burgeoning workforce. Nearly all the Dundee tenements were two-roomed at best. In the early years of the twentieth century, a third of children in Dundee died before their first birthday. Had Adam Smith been listened to, things might have been different. Manufacturers ought in their own interest, he said, to see that workers should be paid a proper return, simply to ensure a further supply of workpeople. 'Our merchants and master-manufacturers,' he wrote, 'complain much of the bad effects of high wages in raising the price, and thereby lessening the sale of their goods both at home and abroad. They say nothing concerning the bad effects of high profits. They are silent with regard to the pernicious effects of their own gains. They complain only of those of other people.' Contemplating the great merchants and master-manufacturers of his day, Smith mourned, like the Preacher in Ecclesiastes, human vanity: 'The marriage bed of James the First of Great Britain,' he says at one point, 'which his queen brought with her from Denmark as a present fit for a sovereign to make to a sovereign, was, a few years ago, the ornament of an alehouse at Dunfermline.'

The legacy of the great manufacturers is as evident now in the mean streets as in the grand ones. Hilltown, north-east of the city centre, was a place of weavers. James Cameron arrived in 1928 to start work as a journalist with D. C. Thomson. Later, in a book called *Point of Departure*, he wrote of 'the opulence of the jute-wallahs in Broughty Ferry, the hopeless hovels of Hilltown and Blackscroft'. 'Dundee in the early thirties,' he recorded 'was a place of singular desolation...It had, for a start, the air of a place that from the beginning of time had reconciled itself to an intrinsic ugliness. This struck me even in my youth as being odd, even anomalous, since of all the cities in the kingdom Dundee had been placed with the greatest potential for grace and charm: it was set on a firth of breadth and grandeur; it was built around the slopes of a small mountain, the Law hill; it backed on to a hinterland of fields and glens – at one time or other, Dundee had the makings of a kind of Naples, which, forgetting the punitive nature of its climate, it geographically resembled.' Now its defining qualities seemed to be 'its brutal melancholy, its façade of unparalleled charmlessness, an absence of grace so total that it was almost a thing of wonder'. Even now, the city is rotten with inequality. A Save the Children survey in 2002 claimed that 96 per cent of children on its Whitfield South estate were living in poverty.

Not surprisingly, Dundee became a radical town. For a time, as in everything else, the jutocracy was firmly in charge. One of the Baxter daughters married a Russian merchant. Though he could speak little or no English, her father ensured his election to the House of Commons. But Dundee was a stroppy place. The word 'heckler', used to describe a person who asks aggressive questions at political meetings, is said to derive from the hecklers who combed out flax or hemp, some of whom would use their combing-out skills on the pronouncements of the politicians they mistrusted. Dundee was a great, even rabid, supporter of the French Revolution. George Kinloch, whose statue can be seen in Albert Square, was a laird and a yeomanry officer who resigned his commission because he came to the view that standing armies ought not to be permitted in peacetime. In 1832, his city sent him to Westminster as the first of its Reform Act MPs. Winston Churchill, then a Liberal, was elected here in 1908 but was ousted fourteen years later by a man called Scrymgeour, representing the Scottish Prohibition Party. Churchill wept when he heard the result and vowed never to set foot in Dundee again. Scrymgeour's success reflects another famous aspect of Dundee – its drunkenness. Many women would gladly have voted for anyone who might possibly curb their men's drinking.

The city that jute built had to learn surprisingly early to accommodate to a life without it. The expansion of a home-based industry in India, a process which the jute barons had fed, did for them in the end. The going rates for Indian workers were a tiny fraction of what the workforce was paid in Dundee. In 1924, 41,000 worked in the industry; in 1945, 20,000; in 1991, 1,806; in 1995, 400. Hillside works, in Hilltown, is now an Islamic centre; Eagle Mill is Kitchen and Bathroom World; Camperdown works at Lochee is a supermarket. But at least the men who ran Dundee in the nineteenth century left behind a city centre of style. In mid-century a city engineer called William Mackison erased much of the pre-Georgian town, planning a centre influenced by the work of Haussmann in Paris, with wide straight uniform streets. Developers were required to build precisely to the pattern he wanted, with high ground floors and three complete storeys with attics. Reform Street, leading up to the high school, the square in front of Caird Hall, the McManus galleries in the Albert Institute in Albert Square, with its statue of Burns – all these give the place the feel of a serious city.

Down by the waterfront, close to a railway station which looks to be made of plastic, a battery of tourist attractions has been deployed with the return of Scott's ship *Discovery*, built in Dundee. The city has awarded it an honoured site near the Olympia Leisure Centre. Yet all this is swamped, not to say mugged, by what deserves to be called the second Tay Bridge disaster.

The first Tay Bridge disaster was the one commemorated in the most famous of all poems by William McGonagall when on 28 December 1879, a night of fearful storm, the 5.20 p.m. train from Burntisland was hurled into the river as thirteen central spans of the bridge collapsed. The bridge had become so crucial to Dundee that an immediate decision was taken to replace it, although the new one was not ready until June 1887. McGonagall had been apprehensive about the first bridge:

> Beautiful railway bridge of the Silvery Tay!
> I hope that God will protect all passengers
> By night and by day,
> And that no accident will befall them while crossing
> The bridge of the Silvery Tay,
> For that would be most awful to be seen
> Near by Dundee and the Magdalen Green.

Now he wrote, with much greater confidence:

> Beautiful new railway bridge of the Silvery Tay,
> With your strong brick piers and buttresses in so grand array,
> And your thirteen central girders which seem to my eye
> Strong enough all windy storms to defy...

As they have. But a road journey from St Andrews to Dundee involved a detour of around forty miles until the first road bridge opened in 1996 and gratified traffic streamed across. There was nothing wrong with the bridge. There was everything wrong with where it landed on the Dundee side of the water. The original plans had it coming to earth on the edge of the city centre. Traders were horrified: did the planners want to destroy them? So its route was altered to disgorge its traffic at the centre of the Dundee waterfront, from where it gyrates around a confusing whirlpool of roads. At the centre of this wheeling confusion is an office block, Tayside House, built to be home to Dundee council, which apart from its intrinsic ugliness also succeeds in blighting the view south from the city centre. And this is not the only place in which Dundee dishonours its river. Just west of this dire concoction, there's a stretch of waterfront which in most European cities might have served to create a parkland, punctuated by restaurants and bars, where the city could stroll on a summer evening. Despite what Londoners think, Dundee does have summer evenings, even warm summer evenings, when the light is benign and the river dazzles and the hills behind are a glory. But this stretch of the riverside is the story of Kirkcaldy all over again. It's a retail park.

Adam Smith, my companion throughout this journey, must have the last word. In a chapter in his *Wealth of Nations*, which I read as I left Dundee, he points out the particular advantages of inhabitants whose city is by the water. Its inhabitants, he says, can draw on the materials and means not just of the surrounding country but of the most remote corners of the world. A city might in this manner grow up to great wealth and splendour, while others around it were left in poverty and wretchedness. Dundee, in its heyday, had the glory and the splendour that Smith foresaw. Unhappily, it had the poverty and wretchedness right alongside it. And still has.

Lairg — Altnaharra — Tongue
Bettyhill — Thurso — Golspie

DORNOCH

*The first duke of Sutherland: benefactor or beast? – scenes from
the Highland clearances – mysterious disappearance of a
postbus from Altnaharra – I am rescued, and taken to Tongue –
the odious record of Patrick Sellar, and Bettyhill museum's
revenge – the coast road to Thurso, and on to a castle reeking of
reverence – the duke on his plinth on Ben Bhraggie, confronted
at last – how he came to take second place to Madonna.*

Imperious in death as he was in life, George Granville Leveson-
Gower, first duke of Sutherland, master of more than one million
and a half acres here in the north of Scotland, gazes out from the
top of Ben Bhraggie as if in search of fresh territories to conquer.
He is thirty feet high, this duke, on a plinth more than twice his
height – all paid for with money collected from an allegedly grateful tenantry after his death in 1833. Some people say he ought not
be there. Some nationalists, inspired by the cull of statuary in
Eastern Europe after the fall of communism, petitioned for him to
be dynamited. A spokesman was quoted as saying: 'The gentleman
on top of this pillar is perhaps one of the most evil men there ever
was. Like Stalin and Hitler, he destroyed people's homes without
cause. He was guilty of enormous cruelty. He has no honour in
Scotland, and he is despised in the Highlands.'

His offence? Ordaining and presiding over the Highland clearances, a process in which, in the first half of the nineteenth century,

thousands of men, women and children were brutally evicted from their homes in the duke's domains. His other offence: he was an Englishman, whose right to the name of Sutherland was bestowed only six months before his death. He was Marquess of Stafford and before that Earl Gower of Stittenham. He had been MP for an English seat. His own great estates were in England: Trentham in Staffordshire, Lilleshall in Shropshire, Stittenham near York, all inherited with his marquisate in 1803. His London home, Stafford House, now Lancaster House, was of such distinction that Queen Victoria is supposed to have said when visiting: 'I have come from my house to your palace.' His Scottish dominions were his only by marriage – to Elizabeth, Countess of Sutherland, who on the death of her father when she was six had inherited the greatest estates in Britain.

The village of Lairg, on the road from Inverness to the north coast at Tongue, is close to the south-western corner of the duke's vast domains. It was also the scene of the first of the clearances, at Whitsun in 1807, when some 300 Highland people were ejected to make way for sheep whose wool would go to manufacturers, to the benefit of the economy of this remote and undeveloped land, and for the enrichment, of course, of the Sutherlands. The Highlanders were promised new homes and work on the north coast, but they did not like what they found and could not settle. Many chose instead to emigrate to the New World. The ship on which they set out was lost off Newfoundland.

In the summer of 2004, Lairg looks a little depressed. Its big hotel, the Sutherland Arms, at the point where the two roads of the village meet, is shuttered up and forlorn. There aren't many people about. 'You should have seen the village last year,' says the cheerful woman who drives my postbus north. 'It was teeming.' This bus, on its way to Durness, will drop me off at the western end of

Strathnaver, scene of one of the most grievous, destructive and bloody of all the events which swept the old Highland population out of these lands in the years after 1807.

The postbus service is an anxious experience for newcomers. Some of these buses have only three or four seats and there's always the risk that one may turn up at the stop to find half a dozen eager young ramblers toting enormous backpacks already at the front of the queue. But today there is no competition. It's only me and the driver. She is feeling immensely cheerful since this is her first day back on the road after several weeks stuck in the office, and though Highland weather is notoriously fickle it looked like a promising day. Soon our stalwart old postbus, many thousands of miles on the clock, is bounding over the hills into a country fringed by blue mountains, with scattered white cottages, occasional grey, more substantial houses, cattle grids and sheep. Friendly walkers along the road wave to the driver, who waves energetically back. At one point an oncoming car stops to ask 'anything for us?' and letters are handed over. On a day like this, I say, this job must be hugely enjoyable. Indeed, says my driver, but it isn't always like this. Postbuses ply their trade in all weathers, and in winter these journeys can be tough and exhausting. The postbus does not always get through. There are days, she says, when only Hamish Macnab is capable of getting the bus through to the coast, and even he has sometimes been defeated.

There's a pub on this road called the Crask Inn, which must at one time have been one of the loneliest hostelries in the kingdom. Here the scenery changes, the softer landscape south of the inn giving way to rough open moorland with promiscuously wandering sheep. The sense of an otherworldly remoteness is dissipated by the number of cars we meet, though perhaps even more by the fact that road signs around here have German translations. Like most of the roads in these parts this one is single track, but with places where you can pull off – sidings, the driver calls them – to let others get through. It's astonishing how many drivers along this route don't comply with this elementary etiquette. When bus and car come face to face at a point without sidings, they sit at the wheel with implacable faces and won't reverse. A signpost announces, or possibly warns, 'You are entering Mackay country', as if to do so might be a hazardous business. A formidable clan, the Mackays, not much given, if I remember, to reversing either.

Some forty minutes on, we pull up at the Altnaharra hotel, my driver to take the road to Durness, and I to set off in search of the great Strathnaver clearance. It was all done in the name of improvement, moral as well as economic. The Highlanders in their primitive homes on Strathnaver simply occupied the land, scraping the meanest subsistence from it, apparently content to do little or nothing. A kind of dreamy romantic inertia reigned. True, they seemed to live in harmony, in contentment – even some of those who most despised them noted the absence of crime – and yet it seemed to improvers that this indolence was a kind of depravity.

It was different in times of war. Inert though he was at home, your Highlander made a fine fighting man. His courage in engagements such as Wolfe's fight for Quebec in 1759 was legendary. These Highlanders had a double appeal: they were brave but they were also expendable. 'They are hardy, intrepid, accustomed to a rough country,' Wolfe wrote, 'and no great mischief if they fall.' But in 1799, when the traditional appeals were issued for volunteers, they hardily and intrepidly declined to die abroad. That dereliction may have helped to settle their fate in the next two decades. This land, the improvers urged, could so easily be made productive. The Highlanders, once shifted, could be made to work. A pit would be opened at Brora. Industrial opportunities, as well as useful employment in agriculture and fishing, would be offered at Golspie and Helmsdale. That was the meaning of progress.

The little settlement of Altnaharra is dominated by a white hotel bedecked with the flags of the nations. An inviting loch is virtually at its doorstep. 'Famous for salmon and trout angling since the early 1800s' its signboard proclaims (or, to put it another way, since the time of the clearances). It is open all year. There are two or three bed and breakfasts in the village, self-catering cottages, the kirk, the primary school (reopening in 2005 to serve just three pupils) and a notice that warns 'lambs ahead'. You would hardly think this was the twenty-first century, until you notice the black dishes that bring *Sky News* and *The Simpsons* into the homes of Altnaharra; or until, even more, you flinch from the screeching, scraping sound of a low-flying jet, the first of many this morning.

The walk on the Strathnaver road – mostly along the loch, though here and there you are separated from it by outcrops of forest – is an episode of almost infinite peace, mildly marred, this being Scotland, by midges. It's a kind of provisionally sunny day, but the weather can change in a moment around here, and the landscape with it: at one moment benign and full of solace, at the next majestic and wrathful, like the Old Testament God. Yet in either manifestation the place is so beautiful that it isn't hard to see why the early nineteenth-century Highlanders loved life in this lonely region, for all the poverty and the squalor and the knowledge of the world's disdain. And wasn't their simple and primitive lifestyle the precursor of the dreams of alternative back-to-nature existences which tempted so many around the millennium?

In time, the road arrives at Grummore. In 1813 Grummore and its neighbour Grumbeg housed some thirty tenant families. By the end of the decade, everything had gone. A man called Patrick

Sellar, the factor (managing agent) of the duke's estates, ordered the first of the families to be off the land by Whitsun 1814. When they did not comply, he resolved to force them. The most famous account of what followed is that in John Prebble's *The Highland Clearances* – a passionate book, influenced and enraged by the writings, mainly in newspapers of the region, of a Strathnaver stonemason called Donald Macleod. Rambling and erratic though it is, Macleod's book, published in 1892 as *Donald MacLeod's Gloomy Memories in the Highlands of Scotland*, deserves a place on the shelves of working-class writing somewhere between Samuel Bamford and Robert Tressell.

Here, as elsewhere where Sellar operated, the houses of the evicted were set on fire. They were even denied the right to take with them the wood known as bog fir, a constituent of their simple houses, to help them build homes elsewhere. 'Many deaths', Macleod wrote, 'ensued from alarm, from fatigue, and cold; the people being instantly deprived of shelter, and left to the mercy of the elements. Some old men took to the woods and precipices, wandering about in a state approaching, or of absolute insanity, and several of them, in this situation, lived only a few days. Pregnant women were taken with premature labour, and several children did not long survive their sufferings. To these scenes I was an eye-witness...' Macleod's indictment, taken up by several Scottish newspapers, caused alarm in Edinburgh, which spread to the London Parliament.

Sellar was arrested and imprisoned at Dornoch. He came to trial at Inverness in April 1816 on charges which included culpable homicide. Among the jury of fifteen men, as Prebble notes, there were eight local landed proprietors, two merchants, two tacksmen (middlemen between the landowner and his tenants) and one lawyer: most were magistrates and justices of the peace. Lord

Pitmilly, president of the court, told the jury not to consider any of the charges except one relating to the death of a woman called Margaret Mackay, and even here he told them they must carefully weigh the source of the evidence – a tinker – against the established character of the accused. The jury may not have needed that cue: they already knew the difference between a man who was one of themselves and a mere tinker. They took fifteen minutes to dismiss the charges. Sellar wept when he heard the verdict, and was tenderly consoled by the judge. Sellar returned to carry out – albeit rather more cautiously – a further eviction, but now on his own account. His service with the Sutherlands was finished; they dismissed him in 1818.

The fortunes of the estate were entrusted to a man called James Loch, a far more sophisticated operator than Sellar, who later became a Liberal MP. Loch was critical of his predecessors. The Highlanders had been decanted too precipitately to the new locations chosen for them. Such people were likely to settle and work much better if they moved in a more cheerful frame of mind. Yet intrinsically his attitude to the Highlanders was not so different from Sellar's. 'Such a set of savages', he once wrote, 'is not to be found in the wilds of America. If Lord and Lady Stafford do not put it in my power to quell this banditti we may bid adieu to all improvement.' In 1818–20 he ordered what one historian of the clearances, Eric Richards, calls 'the most sweeping removals ever seen in the Highlands, and possibly one of the largest single coerced relocations of rural populations achieved in modern British history to that time'. The clearances of 1819 to 1821 saw less violence than Sellar's initial foray. Yet Loch went even further than Sellar into social engineering, ordering restrictions on the Highlanders' right to marry to keep down the population and avoid the sub-division of landholdings.

Beyond Grummore is Grumbeg, where you can see a burial ground going back to the early years of Christianity in Scotland, and beyond that are Rossal, one of the largest of the clearance villages, and Syre, near where Sellar once lived. But Syre is a good ten miles on from Altnaharra, and Bettyhill, which houses the Strathnaver Museum, to which I am heading, is twenty-three; and the furthest any buses go (and they are rare ones) along this road is Grumbeg. So every mile so far walked from Altnaharra will have to be walked back. It is time to head back to the postbus.

The hotel at Altnaharra is not of the backpacker kind I had rather expected, but quite a smart one – not a billet where a rough per-spiring walker can feel completely at home. But they do a good solid soup to sustain you through the afternoon, which in my case merely entails a second journey by postbus, to Tongue. Accordingly, half an hour before the bus is due, I station myself outside the hotel. No bus appears. It begins to rain, first tentatively, then insistently. I begin to sense that something must have gone wrong. And then from the Altnaharra hotel there come the thundering feet of the barman, crying out with some urgency, 'You've missed it. It's already gone.' 'But it can't have,' I wail. 'I've been standing out here at least half an hour.' 'Well, it seems to have called extra early today,' says the barman. Is there any way I can get to Tongue by public transport? 'Can't help you there, I'm afraid.' Or by taxi? 'A taxi? Not around here.'

A signpost stands at the crossroads beyond the hotel: 'Tongue 16 miles' it mercilessly announces. Sixteen on top of the ten or so I have done already along the loch. Walk until you fall down, I tell myself, and then someone may offer a lift. I have trudged perhaps a quarter of a mile when I hear hooting behind me, which I take to mean 'get off the road'. So I do, but the hooting continues. Inside the car are two women who had been in the bar at Altnaharra, and had witnessed the barman's rush into the yard. Would I like a lift? They happen to be going my way. The rule for this book, until this moment piously honoured, was that every journey in it would be travelled by bus. But no further bus to Tongue will run until tomorrow. Like a lift? Yes, I very much would.

The driver is Scottish; her passenger, a friend from France. As we bowl up a lovely valley of loch and forest it becomes increasingly clear that, however much they deny this, they hadn't been going this way, but had generously diverted to get me to Tongue. This is an even more glorious route than Lairg to Altnaharra, sweeping on past Loch Loyal, and Loch Craggie, and the Borgie Forest, planted after the First World War on land gifted, as the Scots say, by the then duke of Sutherland. To the west is a jagged mountain which the driver says is Ben Loyal; far below, a splash of lush land, impossibly green, with a loch encased in it like a jewel. This is the most beautiful of all the roads I have travelled so far. Tongue, which I reach with some reluctance at the end of such an approach, is a small and apparently prosperous village (or by my preferred standards of measurement, little town) and the capital of a remote and thinly populated country. The view inland to the south is dominated by Ben Tongue: to the west and north is the estuary of the Kyle of Tongue, spanned by a fine new causeway with the road to the west swinging across it and curling away into the hills. Outside the post office, which seems an appropriate place to leave my bus-substitute, I say a fond farewell to my rescuers and go inside to ask the Post Office people why my postbus let me down. But the postbus has not arrived, they protest. It isn't due in for nearly an hour. Is it possible, someone suggests, that the Altnaharra hotel had seen the southbound bus – this morning's driver on her way back from Durness – and assumed it was the one on which I planned to go north? There seems to be no other possible explanation. The Royal Mail leaves the court without a stain on its character. The culprits who deserve to be thrown, bound and gagged, into Loch Naver, I conclude, are the Altnaharra Hotel.

Another brilliant morning, another postbus, more like a rudimentary minibus this time with the passengers fenced off from the driver. Even so there are only three of us, me and two German girls who only want a lift of a mile or so up to their B & B. The cheerful and sweet-natured driver points out some of the sights of Tongue on the way: the outline of the castle ruins to which I had tramped last night, but also a palm tree in a roadside garden, elegantly refuting the notion that the climate here is cruel and inhospitable. The rest of the journey is simply me and the mail as the bus hurries along the coast road with new views at every turn of dappled trees, white luxurious sand and deep blue water. Because it's a postbus we keep stopping, sometimes to collect one letter, often none. The postbus is the paper delivery service too. One tries not to think what this service must cost the Royal Mail; or what hard-headed accountants will make of it, if and when privatization arrives.

When we turn away from the sea there are dazzling lochs and distant mountains, some of them cloaked in what I call mist but my driver describes as low-flying cloud. He lives on this route, at Skerray: no wonder he seems so contented. These buses, he says, have been running for three years or so. Before, the service west out of Thurso ended at Bettyhill. He never tires of the journey. The seasons change, the landscape changes: over one hill and everything's blue, over the next and the whins make it yellow. Too soon the signposts announce that we're nearing Bettyhill. The bus passes Torrisdale Bay and the mouth of the Naver where the road swings north. The sun, which has been abating, disappears, and a spotty rain begins.

The village of Bettyhill after this journey seems almost metropolitan. 'Court shame of Bay City Roller' says a billboard outside the Post Office. The museum is on the edge of the village, on the Thurso road, in the former church of St Columba at Clachan in the parish of Farr, declared to be surplus to requirements in 1954, and rescued from deroofing by local protesters. (Farr itself was one of the early victims of the Sutherland clearances, in a parallel operation to that at Lairg in 1807.) I get to the door past rank upon rank of dead Mackays, interspersed with Munros and Macleods. Inside is an enchanting clutter of mementoes of every kind: as at Portland, yet to be steamrollered out by the march of interactivity. A late neolithic beaker pot. A pram, *c.* 1900. A very old gramophone. A frockcoat. An early concertina. A vacuum cleaner. A box bed, a tin hat, a bowl decorated with a picture of Kitchener, a violin. An adjustive candleholder. But most of the collection, marked by notices composed and written in the simplest of terms for children to absorb and remember, commemorates the clearances: 'Between 1812 and 1819,' says one, even-handedly, 'thousands of people were evicted from their blackhouses (so named after their dark interiors) and holdings to make way for sheep. Ever since, controversy has raged over two issues; whether life was better or harder as a result of the evictions, and the manner in which the evictions were carried out.' A text from the John O'Groat Journal of 1963 lists the casualties of the clearances. On the east side, 39 townships, 212 families and 1,000 acres of arable land; on the west, the side of Grummore and Grumbeg, 24 townships, 126 families, over 600 acres of arable land.

Nearby is a model of one of the townships as it might have been before it met Patrick Sellar. And here, perhaps the culminating evocation of what happened when the fires burned in Strathnaver, are portraits of Sellar himself and his wife. He is sharp-featured, with a pointed nose, stern, supercilious. She, bonneted and busy with her knitting, looks kindly but cowed. These portraits, when I was there, did not hang on the wall as they would in most museums, but were placed on the ground, so that Sellar's implacable mouth was roughly level with the toe of a visitor's boot.

After Altnaharra, every wait for a postbus is an apprehensive affair, and particularly so at Bettyhill, since I know my next bus will be small. But what arrives is a car: a Vauxhall saloon, big enough to take three passengers in reasonable comfort, and four at a pinch, but no more. 'Surely, this is a car not a bus,' I observe factually to the driver, who replies with impeccable logic that it must be a bus, since the word 'bus' appears in quite large lettering on the door. Here beside me as we head off towards Thurso is another contented man: like the two postbus drivers before him, this one says he never tires of driving this route. The terrain is harsher and rockier. Strathy, where we stop, is the northermost point of my journeys. From here you can walk out to Strathy point, which, despite the reputation of John O'Groats, is the very top of the kingdom. The roads are better here, mostly dual track, with no need to pull off the road or dodge into sidings. The driver's one reservation seems to be that Caithness has less of a sense of adventure than Sutherland. And sure enough when we cross the boundary into Caithness, the urgency goes out of the landscape; everything seems duller and flatter, and an importunate rain begins. By the time we say our farewells in Thurso, people are running for shelter. A man in a kilt stands by the bus stop, braving the rain as a true Highlander would: his is the very first kilt I have seen in Scotland.

Thurso is a Sinclair town. Sir George and Sir John have principal streets named after them, while another is Sinclair Street. Later there was Sir Archibald, who, as leader of the Liberal Party, was incorporated in Churchill's wartime coalition. The greatest of the three, I deduce, was Sir John, since his is the statue in the main square looking down towards the river. He qualifies, in a back to front way, as a hero of the clearances, since he refrained from ordering any. That is certainly how he seems to John Prebble. 'He was probably the only Scot of his age who used the word "improvement" objectively. Had he been listened to, had his example been copied, the half-century of evictions, burnings, riots and exile that followed might have been avoided.'

Thurso is set on the edge of the sea, but hardly anyone seems to notice. The sea front is not so much undeveloped as unconsidered. The Marine Inn, equipped with a terrace where one can imagine sitting, drink in hand, looking out towards Orkney, is boarded up, abandoned. I meet a man walking his dog who says he came from North Wales. And what brought him here? 'I'm a fireman,' he says; which I take to mean, I have the kind of job where you can live wherever you like. He liked North Wales, but likes Thurso even more. I ask why Thurso does not make more of its sea front. He says he lives in a house that backs on to the bay. 'In winter, you try to open the door and the wind just blows it back in your face.'

My route next morning, after a night in a fairly disgusting hotel, lies down the coast to Golspie, to inspect the duke of Sutherland's castle, Dunrobin, and then to visit his eminence on his eminence. Today's conveyance is a Citylink bus, route 958, Thurso to Inverness. Soon we are purring along on a journey which will take a good two hours (it's three and a half if you are going all the way through to Inverness). 'Nice day!' a passenger observes to the driver as he gets on at Castleton, but by soft southern England standards it isn't, and within five minutes the windscreen wipers are busy. By a bay (Sinclair's Bay) just short of Wick the road comes back to the sea, but it's still monotonous. A line of sun appears and glows briefly on the distant water. Illuminated signs warn in German and Italian that round here we like to drive on the left of the road. At Wick we stop a wee while in the supermarket car park that also serves as the bus station. We flash though Thrumster and Ulbster, Occumster and Lybster. After an hour and a quarter the weather is getting worse, although the scenery's getting better, a sure sign that we're about to cross back into Sutherland. But before that, there are signs to Badbea, where victims of the clearances at Langwell, Ousdale and Berriedale took refuge in a terrain so hostile that families are said to have chained their children to the cliffs to save them from falling. The road twists and climbs and falls in a series of switchbacks, and more placenames appear which recall the clearances: Helmsdale, which Loch once claimed was developing like some pioneering American town; Port Gower, planned to be a substantial settlement based around a fishing port; Brora, where the Highlanders were promised work in the pit. And a moment or two after Brora, we are at the gates of Dunrobin Castle.

Done robe-in, it's pronounced; not, as some might have hoped, done robbin'. Parts of the castle date from the early 1300s. Much of the rest dates from the seventeenth century, with additions by the countess Elizabeth, wife to the first duke. The family has continued to own it and still pays occasional visits, but essentially it's a tourist attraction now. It's a fantastical place on the very edge of the sea, decorated with turrets and spires. People who like this kind of thing, as Abraham Lincoln is supposed to have said of a book he reviewed, will find this is the sort of thing they like. But for those who have just read John Prebble, or almost any other account of the clearances, or who do not in any context much take to ostentatious self-adulation, it may be a rather more limited pleasure. From the moment you enter the majestic hall, hung with tributes to the first duke and his successors, the place reeks of reverence. The portraits make a rewarding study. The duke (while still a mere marquess) by George Romney, is a classic study of arrogance. The countess is painted by Thomas Lawrence, twice, and by John Hoppner. If she wasn't a fetching – though probably spoiled – creature in her youth, her portraitist has certainly made her look like one, though in her maturity she looks strong-willed and potentially frightening. There's a different duchess in the library who is an absolute stunner. A family portrait by Landseer is a masterpiece of emetic art. The most endearing aspect for me is the house's collection of books, unexpectedly modest, and not the kind of array you so often find in such places, all expensively leather-bound and packed so tightly into the shelves that you doubt if they've ever been opened. Here is *Anne of Green Gables* shelved alongside *At the Point of the Bayonet*, *Celtic Scotland*, *British Moths* and a history of Torquay.

From the castle it is a walk of a mile, according to the castle's brochure, into Golspie, but my feet suggest it is closer to two. Behind the street, to the east, the sea is lurking, again largely un-celebrated. The road to the duke runs westward under a railway bridge. A memorial fountain commemorates his duchess. From here I take a wandering track up through the forest until at last, gasping for breath, I am out again under the sky, and there he is, towering above me. No chance of addressing him face to face, man to man, when he's sixty feet higher than I am. Face to plinth is the best I am going to get.

'Of loved, revered and cherished memory' the inscription says of the duke. 'Erected by his tenants and friends.' Ought the duke to be toppled in the manner of Saddam Hussein, allowing the ghosts of those he displaced to dance on his ruin? Perhaps the duke was guilty more of sins of omission than sins of commission. He rarely visited Sutherland: the angry stonemason, Donald Macleod, describes both the duke and, more surprisingly, the duchess as absentees. Nor did he ever make money out of the clearances; indeed, he drained the revenues of his English estates to pay for them. Even the duchess is not utterly damned in Macleod's indictment. 'Had this great, and (I am willing to admit, when not misled) good woman remained on her estates,' he writes of the banished Highlanders, 'their situation would have been materially bettered, but as all her charity was left to be dispensed by those who were anxious to get rid of the people, root and branch, little benefit resulted from it, at least to those she meant to relieve.' Maybe he is being ironic. Or maybe, cocooned in their power and their arrogance, the duke and his duchess were never fully aware of what was being done in their name. As even Prebble accepts, the duke was indeed 'the Great Improver' his admirers claimed him to be. Thirty-four bridges and 450 miles of road constructed across the Highlands – without which my journey would not have been possible – would not have been there but for him.

Yet he cannot be completely exonerated. In his scholarly and balanced assessment of the clearances, the historian Eric Richards concludes: 'A peasant society and a distinct culture were, in many places, razed from the face of the land. The Highlands of Scotland were transformed as much as any colony in the Empire in that age, fully incorporated into the role of supplying the metropolitan economy and routed by the forces of change. The benefits which accrued from this great upheaval did not flow in the direction of the people who inhabited the region. The central historical question is...why the Highlands underwent this appalling experience, and why this tragedy was not ameliorated or tempered by a nation which had become the richest and most dynamic the world had ever seen.'

I have one final call to make on this expedition – the last journey the duke made himself, after his death in 1833. The 958 Citylink bus, on its way down to Inverness, stops close to Dornoch cathedral, a sandstone building in a pretty sandstone town. In July 1833, says Donald Macleod, the duke of Sutherland, who had been in bad health for some time, breathed his last in Dunrobin Castle, and was interred with great pomp in the family burying-place in Dornoch cathedral. The day of his funeral was ordered to be kept as a fast day by all the tenantry, under penalty of the highest displeasure of those in authority, although the herring-fishing season had just begun, and the loss of a single day's work was a calamity.

The final journey of George Granville Leveson-Gower, first duke of Sutherland, second marquess of Stafford, was an occasion that all who saw it remembered for the rest of their lives. For years it remained the greatest event in the history of the cathedral. And then, in 2000, an American singer and actress took it into her head to hold her wedding at Skibo Castle, once the home of Andrew Carnegie, four miles out of Dornoch, and to have her young child baptized the previous day at Dornoch cathedral. Ask almost anyone now what they know about Dornoch, and it's Madonna that they will remember – not the final words spoken by the minister over the bier of the loved, revered and cherished first duke. We have different notions of aristocracy now.

20

BALFRON

*Glasgow, city of style – the testimony of a letterpress printer
called Shadow – riches next door to poverty, then and now –
the death of Parkhead and the death rates of Shettleston
– Easterhouse, a dream that became a nightmare – I ride the
Friday night bus to Balfron and am deafened; but no one is
sick over me.*

A good-looking couple lean against the wall of an arch. He seems
to be speaking; she to be listening, entertained by what he is saying.
Their clothes are smart casual. In this case, expensive smart
casual. They're outside the gallery that houses the Burrell
Collection. Above their heads, a caption floats in the air: 'There's
an art to relaxing in Glasgow.' The message is spelled out in smaller
print underneath: 'There's something about our city that makes
you feel good inside.' Several possible explanations are offered: the
warmth of the people, the luxurious hotels, the seriously seductive
shopping, the renowned galleries, the Charles Rennie Mackintosh
legacy... 'Whatever increases your feel-good factor', the advertisement promises, 'you'll find it in a city that's not short on style. It's
called Glasgow.'

And it's true. New millennium Glasgow is a brilliant and sparkling
city, set on a steady upward curve by its successful campaign to
become the European city of culture, when £20 million was spent
on a year-long programme of music, dance, theatre, opera and exhi-

bitions. Even before that, the process of rebranding Glasgow had begun with the garden festival staged in 1988. In the arts, from the Citizens Theatre and classical music through to rock and pop – this is the city of Franz Ferdinand – to its poets and its colonies of painters, Glasgow aspires to match any city in the UK outside London. The main square in the town, George Square, is all that a big city square ought to be, presided over by the gloriously exuberant and boastful city chambers, the city's chief civic building. The square is filled with statuary: Queen Victoria, inevitably; her prince consort; Sir Robert Peel, sharing the honours with Robert Burns; Lord Clyde, distinguished soldier, buried in Westminster Abbey, and Thomas Campbell, poet, and Sir John Moore, who died at Corunna and was buried at dead of night in a poem that everyone once had to learn; James Oswald, long-serving Liberal MP for the city and a champion of parliamentary reform; Gladstone; Thomas Graham, chemist, physicist, master of the mint; the Greenock-born inventor James Watt – as fine an eleven as ever turned out for Rangers or Celtic. Towering above them all is the writer who reinvented the romance of Scotland's history, Walter Scott. Old institutional buildings around the city have been found twenty-first century uses. The Royal Exchange has become the Museum of Modern Art; the former headquarters of the Scottish Provident Institution, a Slug and Lettuce pub. The river, though still a fine sight at night, is, by the standards of great European cities, neglected and unexploited. But everywhere in its new-found confidence Glasgow seems to be saying: this is one of the great cities of Europe. All those who love cities will love this city. It makes you feel good inside.

This is one version of Glasgow. There are others where trendy young people do not lean against walls exchanging their views on Cezanne; where levels of deprivation, as recorded in the 2001 census, are among the worst, and sometimes the very worst, anywhere in the nation; where crime statistics still afflict this city with a title not advertised in the Sunday supplements but freely bestowed elsewhere in the Sunday papers: the murder capital of Western Europe, with a homicide rate twice as high as London's. The bullet-riddled corpse on the pavement is not *le tout* Glasgow; but the doorway of the Burrell is not *le tout* Glasgow either. If you want a cross-section of the city, in all its glory and squalor, its riches and poverty, you could start by riding the number 40 First bus.

You can pick up the number 40 in the heart of the city, near the station on fashionable Argyle Street. All the familiar names are here: Glasgow has been Dixoned and Debenhamed. Stores which flourished when Sauciehall Street was the top street in town – Daly's, Copeland & Lye, Trerons – have gone, although Watt Brothers in Hope Street survives. My bus makes a minor detour to pass the Museum of Modern Art, where in the best Glaswegian tradition the duke of Wellington's statue has a traffic cone on its head. For a time, the authorities used to remove them, but they were always replaced within hours, so now they've become a fixture. There are temples of opulence, with swish new hotels, and the Great City feeling is maintained until we reach Trongate, where a grittier everyday world begins to appear. Stanz Leather is here, and Mitchells Amusements, and Seasportz Brand Clearance, and the ATM discount store. Beyond the clocktower, the diminuendo continues: Snack Shack, Smoking Ideas (novelty lighters and pipes), Cost-less, Stanley Racing, Discount Motoring, Discount Fabrics. Beyond Bellgrove station the once proud premises of the Glasgow Abattoir Company Limited are a wreck. Duke Street is lined with four-storey Victorian tenements and Quality Discount, Pricerite, Graham's Amusements, Ladbrokes, charity shops, and places to escape dismal everyday life for a tan.

Poverty on the doorstep of opulence has always been a hallmark of Glasgow. In 1858 the Glasgow publishers Thomas Murray produced a book called *Midnight Scenes and Social Photographs*, being sketches of life in the streets, wynds and dens of the city, by a writer who used the name Shadow. It depicts a city of squalor and misery orchestrated by all-conquering drink. Shadow – the alias of a letterpress printer called Alexander Brown – describes appalling scenes in and out of doors in Trongate, the High Street, Bridgegate (where 'nearly every shop on both sides of the street is a public house') and not least Argyle Street, where he stops a policeman. 'Did it ever strike you,' he asks, 'to count the number of drunken people on this great thoroughfare of an evening?' 'No; I never did count', the policeman replies, 'but I should think, at a rough calculation, that, between the hours of eight and twelve, there must be five or six hundred at least, from one end of Argyle Street to the other.'

In the closes and wynds off the principal streets, Shadow contemplates the damp cellars and fever nurseries of the poor, falsely called homes. 'The presence of such places in the centre of princely wealth, surrounded by monuments of art, and all the elements of outward civilization, is a libel upon the city, and upon her high professions of Christianity in particular.' If only, Shadow pretends to lament, good Christian people knew how these others were living! But of course he knows very well that these good Christian people are fully aware of the fate of their fellow citizens, for as he also says: 'The social evil that exists in Glasgow to a most sorrowful extent, is only too apparent to the common observer who walks our streets...'

The sector of the city that the number 40 is now approaching was once an essential part of the engine room of Britain. Parkhead is

famous around the world nowadays as the home of Celtic FC, but
once it was no less famous as the home of Parkhead Forge, the
industrial base of the Beardmore company, among the greatest of
the Glasgow autocrat employers. Sir William Beardmore, later
Lord Invernairn, inherited his father's boilermaking business at
Parkhead, to which he added a shipyard at Govan. It became in time
the biggest industrial enterprise in Scotland, with a workforce of
40,000, adding further companies on both sides of the border.
Beardmores did well out of the First World War, building an extensive and profitable armaments business, and expanded further
thereafter into new areas such as motor vehicles, aircraft and even
airships. For a time Sir William flourished on a scale that not only
brought him a barony but a fine house and sporting estate in
Invernesshire. But his companies did less well. By the 1920s,
Parkhead, like the Govan shipyards, belonged to an age which no
longer existed. The business had gone elsewhere. Accountants
brought in to assess the firm's state blamed Sir William's style of
management, that of an autocrat reluctant to take advice. The Bank
of England was called in to rescue the company and remove the
great man. Parkhead Forge closed its doors in 1975 and was demolished. The name lives on in the Parkhead Forge shopping centre.

Parkhead is the prelude to Shettleston: row after row of tenements
– red here, rather than the standard grey closer into the city – with
tower blocks lurking behind. The shops repeat the earlier pattern:
discount outlet, tanning parlour, betting shop and a liquor barn.
This part of Glasgow gives its name to the Shettleston constituency,
which takes in the east and south of the inner city, including the
Gorbals and surrounding territory south of the Clyde, about which
statistics from the 2001 census tell a grim and incontrovertible
story. It's the worst of all the constituencies of Great Britain for the

incidence of life-threatening illness among people of all ages, and the second worst for the same blight among people of working age. Only one other constituency has a higher proportion of people who spend more than twenty hours every week as carers. It has the highest proportion of people who have never attained a qualification (the only UK seats which score higher here are Belfast West and Belfast North). It is fourth worst for unemployment, and the seventh for overcrowded housing. It has the highest percentage anywhere of people who don't own cars, and is seventh among constituencies in which they're dependent on buses.

Life expectancy here is declining. The chances of recovery from a typical cancer are said to be many times worse in Shettleston than places of equivalent deprivation in cities like Sheffield. 'Demoralization' is a word as freely used now as it was by Shadow. One element in Shettleston's state of health appears to be Shettleston's state of mind. In 2004 Dr Carol Craig published a book called *The Scots' Crisis of Confidence*, which went beyond the already familiar theme that the Scots are habitually down on themselves and do not expect to succeed, and began to search for credible remedies. Very well, it asked, we know we have got this problem: so what are we going to do about it? The book awoke a vast academic and media interest: the Scottish first minister, Jack McConnell, endorsed the thesis, and against a background of right-wing complaint about Panglossian do-gooders wasting taxpayers' money, public money was found for a research project, directed by Craig, to explore practical ways of lifting the Scottish spirit, of freeing the Scots from their dependency culture, and breaking that tradition of crushing negativity in which its children grow up. 'We canna do this,' they say, 'we come from a deprived area.' Craig recounts a story told by the Scottish writer Moray McLaren about a couple fresh back from honeymoon who went to visit an uncle and show him their holiday photographs. The old man examined them, one at a time, and then, saying nothing, went through the lot again. Then, 'putting a broad spatulate finger upon one picture', he said, 'That's the worst.' A lot of people in Scotland would recognize this story. 'There's just something about our city', says the ad in the glossy magazines, 'that makes you feel good inside.' Outside the Burrell Collection, perhaps; less so in Shettleston.

Of course there have been brave attempts to rescue Glasgow before. The filthy tenements that Shadow inspected, and a further generation of inadequate housing thereafter, were swept away in ambitious schemes of improvement, creating brave new estates on the city's fringes. One of these, through which the number 40 bus has come on its journey from Clydebank – another near-graveyard of what once must have seemed unstoppable industrial growth – is Drumchapel. Another is the eastern end of this route, Easterhouse.

In the post-war years, the population of Glasgow seemed to be draining away. Within the East End it fell from 151,000 in 1951 to 80,000 by 1971 and 45,000 by 1976. Decline was as swift and as startling as growth had been in the late nineteenth century. One reason was the lure of new towns. The city council thought this decline could be countered by building what in effect were new towns within or close to the city. Easterhouse was one. 'Nowadays,' Carol Craig writes, 'it is easy to look at some of the huge council schemes (or "deserts wae windaes" to use Billy Connolly's phrase) that were created in places like Pilton, Craigmillar, Easterhouse or Drumchapel and ask why on earth they were ever built. But when you read about the scale of Scotland's housing problems over centuries it becomes clear that desperate solutions were needed. The tragedy is that within decades of these brave new council housing projects thousands of new Scottish slums had been created.'

The city chose for its Easterhouse scheme a site in the lee of the hills beyond, on the edge of open country into which decanted Glaswegians might wish to wander. Provan Hall, a late fifteenth-century mansion bought by the National Trust for Scotland in 1938, ornaments the skyline. There are fringes of recently built owner-occupation on the edge of the estate and within it, tracts of land which look to be awaiting development, some of them sectors of the original scheme which for various and depressing reasons have already been cleared. At the heart of Easterhouse, the bus puts you down in front of a new shopping mall, the first decent shopping centre to be established in a development where building began half a century ago. Some of the names in the precinct are the same household names you will find in better-heeled shopping malls around the land: Greggs the bakers, Iceland, Haddows, R. S. McColl, Superdrug. But as ever in outer Glasgow, the rest tell another story: Around a Pound, Poundzone, Cut Price Cards, H and T pawnshop. Little of the 'seriously seductive shopping' extolled in the Glasgow Style ad is going on here.

In December 2004 the Joseph Rowntree Foundation published a report that focused on areas of conspicuous poverty in four conurbations: Tower Hamlets in London, Harpurhey in Manchester, Everton on Merseyside, and Easterhouse in Glasgow. Infant mortality here in Easterhouse, it found, was 4.5 times the national average. More than half of all adults were unemployed. Crime rates were high, with an 8 per cent chance of a break-in each year; around 77 per cent of tenants were dependent on housing benefit. Easterhouse recorded the lowest educational achievement in Scotland. Only in recent years, said the Foundation, had Britain awoken to the huge damage caused by poverty and disadvantage. That the world south of the border knows as much as it does about Easterhouse is partly due to a man called Bob Holman, a former professor of social administration at the university of Bath who, as a Christian socialist, gave up his job and comfortable life to work with and for the people first of the Southdown estate in Bath and then in Easterhouse. You cannot help places like Easterhouse, he argues, without a head-on assault on inequality. This does not mean that he thinks the future of places like these hangs only on government generosity; he also believes in, and has sought to organize, communal self-help through neighbourhood projects. But unless they have adequate money the people can never pull themselves up. There has to be an all-out attack on poverty. 'The question now', Shadow had written in 1858, 'is not so much an equality of social and political privileges, as the more important one of bread, and the wherewithal to keep body and soul together in a land unsurpassed for luxury and wealth.'

One thing that has changed in Glasgow since Shadow's day is the nature of Friday. 'Friday night!' he writes, 'and scarcely a drunkard reels across our path...The streets, despite all, are empty. It is the policeman's Sabbath, his night of rest!' Not any more. On Friday nights, Glasgow is on the town. Great hordes of people, especially young people, converge on the centre, apparently intent on drinking themselves silly before the last bus goes home. There are plenty of them about on Saturday night as well. A noisy, bingey, quite often violent Friday night out was thought of once as a Glasgow speciality, though nowadays everyone's loudly, boozily, doing it. Newcastle is no different, or even smaller towns like Northampton.

At half past ten this Friday night the main bus station on Buchanan Street is as quiet as a cathedral out of hours. There are very few people about. One man, who has finished his bingeing early, is denouncing the staff, the bus companies, indeed every known authority up to the rank of God, for the fact that there isn't a bus running to Prestwick which will get him there in time for his plane. Elsewhere, the passengers are assembling for the night buses to London; even a night bus all the way to Penzance. The only voice raised is that of the newspaper seller: 'Echo, Echo,' he seems to be calling but in fact it's tomorrow's *Daily Record*. The stop from which my bus is due to depart for Balfron, part way to Stirling, is still deserted ten minutes before the bus is due to leave. And then suddenly it's awash with rowdy and jubilant revellers, singing and shouting. The girls pretend to fight off the boys; the boys, who outnumber the girls something like six to one, mill about, staging mock fights and mock copulations. (But when one of the boys treads on my foot he apologizes as penitently as if they had taught him to do it in charm school. This looks like being a bit of a middle-class bus.)

The sweet smell of cannabis is soon in evidence as a spliff is passed from hand to hand: a few, at the risk of being thought pious, refuse. A man who looks like a minder is standing next to the driver, but just as the bus is about to move out, he hops off, to ecstatic cheers. And away we go, to a roof-raising chorus of traditional Friday choral works, few of them ever sung by the great Scottish music-hall singer, Harry Lauder; the only detectable word in most of the verses is 'fuck'. The older people aboard – that's to say, anyone over twenty – sit at the front, doing their best to pretend they're not here. They are texting, or listening to music through headphones, or, like me, purporting to read the paper. Behind me sits Tam, who was checked by the driver when he embarked because he was carrying bottles. I could not hear what was said, but the body language suggested that their exchanges went something like this:

The driver: Excuse me, sir, but I am required to draw your attention to the company's rules which, rightly or wrongly, forbid the consumption of alcoholic liquor by those admitted to the company's vehicular fleet.

Tam: By my troth, you have my assurance as an honest citizen that I would never contemplate any such irresponsible action.

At which point Tam takes his seat, whips the bottle out of his bag, and takes his first swig. Soon he is doing his best to persuade the girl who is sitting next to him to take a swig from it too. 'What is your name?' he inquires. 'Una,' she says. 'And what do you do?' It is something to do with horses. 'You seem like a very nice girl,' Tam tells her kindly. 'Have a drink.' But Una will not have a drink, and when he persists, maintains that she only drinks vodka. A thoughtful silence ensues. Then Tam says: 'You know, I'm sure I've seen you before.' Una thinks this unlikely, but the more she denies it the more certain he seems to become. We are now out of Maryhill and as far as I can see in the dark, into a posher suburb. Three girls of around fourteen or fifteen, only vestigially dressed, descend from the bus. Tam observes them through the window with an air of disapproval, lightly seasoned with lust. 'If I was their dads,' he announces, mainly to Una but to anyone else who can hear him, 'I would never let them go out like that.' But most of what he says is lost to the boys and girls at the back amidst all the singing and shouting and banging and thumping. The driver, meanwhile, makes no effort to quell the cacophony. He simply drives it along.

On we surge through the night. Around midnight, we stop at Milngavie, presumably to meet the last train, though for many of the passengers this is a moment to leap out of the bus and pee against a wall. We have after all been going for half an hour. Tam, to Una's relief, falls asleep for a moment. As he wakes, he catches sight of another comely young woman a row or two in front. 'Have a drink,' he suggests, and holds out his bottle. And she takes it, moving up to the seat in front of him. Una, at this point, has ceased to exist. She doesn't even rate a 'goodnight' when she leaves. There is nobody in the world for Tam now but Kelly. 'And what do you do?'

She's a hairdresser. 'You seem like a very nice girl,' he muses. 'You know,' he tells her after they've each had another swig, 'I'm sure I've seen you somewhere before.' She finds this unlikely. 'Yes,' says Tam, 'but I know that I have.' After a while they establish that her brother went to the same school as he did. Tam now appears disconsolate. 'What's the matter,' asks Kelly. 'That means I can't go out with you,' Tam informs her. Why not? Apparently it's against courtship etiquette. 'If you're at school with someone,' Tam tells her mournfully, 'you can't go out with their brother.' 'Sister,' says Kelly.

We are now well out of the city and rattling through the invisible countryside. At Killearn, three lads get on, struggling to cram some mysterious objects of a sporting nature into their bags. They are clearly not drunk and might not have even been drinking. Perhaps for that reason, Tam takes against them. 'Come on,' he roars as they struggle with their bags while the driver patiently waits. 'Some of us have a home to go to.' He has now taken up a position at the front of the bus alongside the driver. He begins to stare steely-eyed down the gangway as if someone had appointed him monitor. The singing has now abated, since most of the singers have got off the bus and might by now have even rolled home. As the bus pushes on through an all-enveloping darkness, Tam continues to rebuke the Killearn contingent, who reply in accents so broad that even he cannot understand them. He makes a muttered protest to the driver, who takes no notice.

We are now approaching Balfron, the final destination for this early Saturday morning chariot of booze. At this point Tam appeals first to the driver and then to the bus to tell him where we have got to. Almost into Balfron, we tell him. Tam won't believe it. 'That can't BE!' he roars. 'The last place we stopped was Milngavie.' Even the Killearn contingent assure him that this cannot be so. He is still standing at the front of the bus, protesting, as it drops off the rest of its passengers and heads for the depot. The driver's final ordeal of the night, I deduce, will be to decide what to do with Tam. Lock him up for the night in the depot, someone suggests.

When I return from this excursion, my Glaswegian friend Audrey, who had pointed me towards the joys of her city's Friday-night buses, asks a number of questions about my presumed ordeal. Had they sung shaunimaho, shaunimahay, or something like it? No idea, I'm afraid. Had they sung Showmethewaytogohome? Oddly enough I don't think they had. I know the words of that and would possibly have joined in. So, had anyone been sick over my shoes? Not that I was aware of. 'Then, [triumphantly] you haven't been on a Glasgow night bus!'

Ah well, another time, perhaps. For the moment, though, it is time to head back to England, to examine on behalf of the Queen what might possibly be the most prized tract of land in her whole dominions.

21

SLAIDBURN

*Elizabeth II wishes to live in the Forest of Bowland – my search
for a suitable home for her – the attractions of Chipping and
Ribchester and the many merits of Clitheroe – a blissful ride in
a bus full of texting children – to Dunsop Bridge, the heart of the
British Isles, it claims – and Slaidburn, Lancs, which some want
to put back in Yorkshire – I scent a solution in Bolton-by-
Bowland, but fail to reach it by bus.*

The Queen has many homes, almost as many in fact as the late Alan
Clark, but left to herself she might perhaps dispose of the lot of
them. The place she would most like to live, as she once confessed
in an unguarded moment to her biographer Sarah Bradford, is the
Forest of Bowland. This led to fevered speculation across southern
England and even much of the North as to where this forest might
be. Within days intrepid reporters despatched from the metropolis were able to claim they had tracked it down to Lancashire. The
Forest of Bowland, it transpired, was an AONB, a SSSI, and a SPA
under the EBD, which, being translated, meant it was an Area of
Outstanding Natural Beauty, a Site of Special Scientific Interest,
and a Special Protection Area under the European Birds Directive.
In simpler language, the forest might be described as some 400
square miles of moorland, fell, majestic river and bubbling stream
east of Lancaster and north of the Preston–Blackburn–Burnley
industrial belt.

So when it was announced in January 2003 that the Prince of Wales would be visiting the Forest, there were many who wondered if the point of his mission might be to seek out a suitable place for his mum to spend her last years. Officially he was going to launch a new network of buses out of Clitheroe, serving the Forest, run by an organization called Bowland Transit – a pioneer of the kind of demand-responsive, ring us up and we'll stop in your village service which also operates in Lincolnshire. This is also the only bus company I have come across which appoints a Writer in Residence. The prince, it was also announced, would attend an exhibition by Lancashire Rural Futures, a rural regeneration initiative, in the village hall, Chipping. But investigative reporters are not easily fooled by cover stories like that.

The Bowland Transit buses are open to all, not just the royal family. The service from Clitheroe to Chipping runs on Thursdays, on a route through to Garstang, and on Saturdays all the way to Preston. This is one of those jolly buses where the passengers and the driver chat away as if they were part of the same happy family. 'Fares going up next week?' a passenger inquires. 'News to me,' says the driver. 'We're the last to be told.' The bus goes out past a picnic spot by the river at Edisford Bridge which is no doubt where much of Clitheroe disports itself on a summer's day. There is plenty of middle-aged laughter, rising at times to the level of raucous, as we press on through Chaigley to the Gibbon Bridge hotel. The sun streams down on us as the bus makes its way contentedly along the undulating road between parallel hills with now and then a fine house to be glimpsed through the trees.

Chipping is quite astonishingly Prince-of-Walesy. If the stone was more honey-coloured this could be Chipping Campden in the Cotswolds. There's a friendly, wandering village street punctuated by inns – the Sun, the Talbot Arms, the Tillotsons Arms – cottages of 1675, a post office, and Ye Olde Curiosity Shop, 1823. The Anglican church of St Bartholomew, the noticeboard says, is awaiting a new vicar, 'since Arthur left for sunny Italian shores'. A seventeenth-century memorial here commends the two wives of Robert Parkinson of Haresnape, gent, though perhaps not that much of a gent, since the epitaph says that at the end of their 'vertuous lyfe' they rest in peace, 'freed from the bonde of wyfe'.

Down the hill to the south is a school founded by John Brabin, gentleman, in 1684; his name also appears on nearby cottages. This is a very satisfactory street, not least because its new buildings have been so sensitively harmonized with its old ones. Up the hill to the north is another delightful scene: a chairmaking factory, a stream, an irregular assemblage of buildings called Grove Square, and at the top of the hill beyond, a millpond with a lively contingent of ducks, most with heads down in the pool but some sunbathing. One can sit in the sun on a convenient wall and drink in the scene. All in all, this Chipping is such an agreeable spot that one cannot understand why Prince Charles did not counsel his mother to move here immediately.

The bus south from Chipping is a route 104, run by a company called J. and J. Lakeland. The driver is grumpy and taciturn. This bus will take me to Longridge, which one of my books describes as the principal town of the Forest, though to me it is merely the gateway to Ribchester. The scenery does not look at all like genuine signed-up Forest of Bowland. We pass an end-of-the-season cricket ground, though the score which I assume was left over from the last match is less than convincing: one batsman has 3, one 4, and the last man out had hit 40, and yet the innings total is 0. I can't imagine a scoreboard in Yorkshire being left for the winter in this condition.

Longridge was once a stone town, then a mill town, and then a town which grew with the railway; now the mills have all gone, as has the railway. What is left I write down in my notebook as 'decent though boring' but it seems less decent after a traipse from pub to pub looking for a lunch which offers a pie as well as a pint. A Blackburn Transport route 3 takes me to Ribchester, a very different experience. This was the Roman Bremetenacum Veteranorum – a place where veterans came to settle. As he pondered his mother's relocation, Prince Charles might have found that appropriate. Streets of weavers' cottages lead to the river Ribble. There are two bold pubs, the White Bull and the Black Bull. But best of all, on such a glorious day, is to sit as I did on a seat by the great crescent sweep of the river, with the excited sounds of the school playground behind, among a small congregation of contented elderly people, or as they say around here 'veterani'. How the Queen (I muse) would enjoy coming here on a day such as this to mingle quietly with some of her older subjects out of the media's eye. Perhaps she could wear a headscarf as a kind of disguise, as she did as a girl among the wartime crowds in London. Unhappily, scrutiny of my authorized Forest of Bowland map reveals that although this is the lovely Ribble Valley, it is quite a few miles short of being authentic Forest of Bowland. The same is true of Longridge. So it does not quite fit with the royal specifications. But I bet she wouldn't say no to Ribchester.

It is time to take a deeply enjoyable road through to Clitheroe, on Lakeland route 210. The tourist authorities describe this as Tolkien country. Much of the epic *Lord of the Rings* is set, they say, in this territory, and especially in and around Stonyhurst, previously famous for its Catholic boarding school, where Tolkien used to come to visit his sons. This countryside is also said to have inspired Conan Doyle's *Hound of the Baskervilles*: Doyle was an old boy of Stonyhurst. Such claims rarely go undisputed, and a rival Tolkien industry is at work in the West Midlands, where the former Millstream Project in Birmingham has been renamed the Shire Country Park. None of this will carry much weight with the rising generation, all of whom have been to the cinema and know that the Tolkien stories are set in New Zealand.

Pleasant villages and alluring pubs are stationed along this road, which dips down now and then through green dells of sun and shadow to a voluptuous river. At Hurst Green, a middle-aged woman clambers aboard, followed, at tortoise pace, by a very old man. 'I'll let my dad get the tickets,' she tells the driver, and then, addressing the bus, 'He's ninety-two.' Having paid, he settles himself in a seat across the aisle from his daughter and gives us all a huge benign smile which makes me think of the Aged Parent in Dickens's *Great Expectations*. The shopping streets of Clitheroe, the end of our route, are full of a pleasing sense that local endeavour has not yet been swept away by big names from big cities. Cowman's, with its glorious array of local sausages, must be a particular treat. An encouraging number of other shop names also suggest long-established family businesses, though perhaps a shop called Holistic Therapeia does not quite fall into this category.

The town is set on a hill with higher hills ranged about it; the two main streets climb up to a junction in the shadow of little Clitheroe Castle. Do not miss Church Street, just out of the centre, which is really distinguished. There are markets here three days a week and a flea market on Fridays. If you've got Clitheroe, the town seems to be saying, do you really need anything more? If that is indeed what it's saying, I rather agree with it. 'Thai jail inmate's living hell' says a billboard: it all seems a world away. The Clitheroe interchange, where the buses park close to the station, is a place of welcome diversity. This is not one of those bus stations where everything is dominated by the big battalions, Arriva, Stagecoach,

First. Here, beside Lakeland and Bowland Transit, are Tyrer, Northern Blue, and a company called Lancashire United which, oddly, is based in Harrogate, Yorkshire. It is teatime, and the B10 Bowland Transit to Settle is full of cheerful young people straight out of school. And comparing notes before they get down to serious business, like texting. 'Miss Peat's a good teacher,' says one, 'but she is a bit *stressy*.' 'I notice Vicky and all her mates come and sit on *his* table,' another girl says bitterly to her neighbour about some boy. But mostly they tease the driver, who seems to enjoy it.

This must be as blissful a summer day, in September, as we have had all this year, and perhaps, because the summer, such as it was, is dying, the most cherishable of all. It's another ride that reminds me what a beautiful country Britain can be. The road beyond Bashall is captivating. Nearby is Browsholme Hall, home of the Parker family – another place the Prince of Wales should perhaps have inspected, though the Parkers have lived here for 400 years and might be reluctant to move. Simon Jenkins, in his *England's Thousand Best Houses*, calls it 'magical', exulting especially in its library, where 'on either sides of the fire are giant tusks, as if the fireplace were a walrus spoiling for an argument'. As we pass through high hills, a shriek goes up from the mobile phonesters behind me: 'Omigod, I've lost my signal.' The boys are joshing the girls. 'Jimmy,' a girl asks the driver, 'would you mind if I slapped him?' 'I know what you're doing,' a girl says balefully to a boy. 'You've gone on to template.' (Not what the girls used to complain about when they said 'I know what you're doing' when I were a lad.) Before Whitewell we emerge from dark woods to discover a river below sparkling in the evening sun. One by one, the school contingent departs, barely seeming to notice the gorgeousness of a journey they do every day. Ideally, this ride would have lasted for ever; but half an hour out of Clitheroe we reach Dunsop Bridge.

This used to be Yorkshire. For centuries this part of the forest belonged to the West Riding, but a local government boundary review snatched it away and gave it to Lancashire. There are people here who still yearn for the restoration of Yorkshire, much as some yearned through the Commonwealth years for the restoration of kingship. There's a continuing campaign around Slaidburn, a village which we shall come to soon, which asserts that the boundaries should be redrawn to put the old Bowland rural district unequivocally back in Yorkshire. 'The area', says a Slaidburn website, 'is currently administered by Lancashire county council as opposed to the old West Riding Council abolished in 1974.' Note that *currently*.

Whichever county it belongs to, Dunsop Bridge, apart from its lack of a pub, is a very endearing place. The Post Office, country store and tearoom where the bus stops is called Puddleduck's, and you don't need to be Sherlock Holmes to see why: on the green between the road and the river, more than a hundred ducks are pecking away and clucking genteelly. This place has a kind of strategic significance: a road leaves the highway to Slaidburn and runs north-west into the Trough of Bowland, to which Dunsop Bridge, I see, claims that it is the gateway. There are buses along this road on a Sunday that take you into this territory where the duke of Westminster, the richest man in the land after Roman Abramovich, according to some assessments, lives in style in Abbeysteads. Since the Trough is said to be the essence of the Forest, a mansion along this road might appeal to Her Majesty too. There are huge empty spaces here into which you could smuggle a marvellous twenty-first century palace. But the countryside is very remote, and a promiscuous building would spoil it. And the bit that isn't remote is wedded, no doubt indissolubly, to the duke of Westminster.

The start of the road, however, must not be missed, since up here is the church of St Hubert: a Catholic church in a heavily Catholic part of England. Beside it is a distinguished house, the home of the Towneleys, a great Lancashire Catholic family. St Hubert's is the work of Edward Pugin, one of the sons of the celebrated architect Augustus Welby Northmore Pugin. It was built as a private chapel for the family: some of the money is thought to have come from a Towneley success in the Derby. St Hubert, not I think a saint who gets many church dedications, was a keen hunter who saw a vision of the Cross while pursuing a stag.

According to a leaflet at St Hubert's, before this church was built the Towneleys used to say Mass in the domestic chapel of Thorneyholme Hall. Thorneyholme Hall, eh? That sounds the kind of address at which the Queen might happily settle. The hall is just east of the green and the ducks, and a right of way takes you close enough to get a fair look at it. It would need some extension to house all the necessary retainers, and the right of way would no doubt require a diversion, but otherwise this seems quite a promising spot. Better still, a notice fixed to the phone box on the green says it has been ascertained by scientists that Dunsop Bridge is the village nearest to the very centre of the British Isles. What could be more appropriate than for the Queen to make her home at the scientifically ascertained centre of the country? But one obvious problem is the Anglican church, a modest affair, one wall of which looks more like part of the next-door garage than a place for the head of the Church to worship in. Time, then, to look further afield.

The Bowland Transit bus pushes on through Newton and up the hill into Slaidburn, a simple, sturdy, stone village the heart of which is the meeting point of two roads outside the Hark to Bounty. This is where I shall stay tonight: a sizeable pub, once called The Dog, but specifically renamed after the favourite dog of the parson, who was also the squire. Bounty was loudest of all, it was said, in its barks of protest when the pack of hounds was parked outside while their masters drank within. It's a rather smarter village than it seems to be at first sight, with one or two serious houses and an eighteenth-century grammar school, erected by John Brennard, gentleman. A clumsy modern extension has been tacked on at the back, and it's still a school, Brennard's Endowed Primary. St Andrew's church, on a mound near the school, is a very fine sight. Open from 9 a.m. till dusk, says a notice, but dusk must have fallen early tonight, for it's locked, denying me the sight of an interior good enough to earn it a place in Simon Jenkins's book of England's thousand best churches. The pub is pleasantly busy and boisterous, but the village itself is far enough off the beaten track to feel like a secret place, as if a notice had been hung over it saying 'do not disturb'. Amazingly, a squadron of bikers on their way past the church is doing no more than twenty miles an hour.

Roads full of promise radiate from the village. One leads back through Dunsop and up through the Trough on the route that buses take on Sundays and bank holidays. The Yorkshire dales, the Lake District (minus the lakes), the Highlands of Scotland, wild Wales – there are echoes of all in the Trough of Bowland, and it's wonderfully unravaged by time. Or you can travel north-east into what is still unconditionally Yorkshire; or north-east then north, to Stocks Reservoir, in which the villages of Stocks and Dalehead were drowned when the reservoir was created in the 1930s. I'm not sure, even so, that this place is right for the Queen. The church is a plus, good enough for a royal worshipper, but no house that I spotted looked ripe for a place on Prince Charles's shortlist, and perhaps the perpetual presence of petitioners at her gate, begging her to put them back into Yorkshire, might be a trial.

There is one further solution – in every way but one, I think, the best of the lot – a few miles east of Slaidburn on the farthest edge of the Forest. In the very desirable village of Bolton-by-Bowland, just south of the church, there's a gate with a long and dignified avenue stretching into the distance. Follow the track and you come to a huddle of buildings which clearly used to belong to something statelier. This is the site of Bolton Hall, now demolished, but once the home of the Pudsay family. A monument in the church celebrates Sir Ralph Pudsay, his three wives and twenty-five children sleeping beside him: 'the faithful adherent' says a plaque 'of King Henry VI whom he sheltered at Bolton Hall after the battle of Hexham'. This is a near-perfect site for the Queen's new home. There is ample room to exercise corgis. For Prince Philip, there are regular trotting races just up the road at Hellifield. Communications, it has to be said, are imperfect. But visiting heads of state could travel by rail to Hellifield on the breathtaking line between Leeds and Carlisle, and then on by state coach through delightful lanes (which might need a bit of widening) down to Bolton. For more mundane occasions, a station could be added to the rarely used line between Hellifield and Clitheroe, linking with the Virgin mainline service at Preston. There would still be times when the Queen had to travel to London, for instance to open Parliament. But if Parliament were moved to Harrogate, as recommended long ago by *The Economist*, Her Majesty would be able to swap the trip down the boring old Mall for a glorious coach ride through Yorkshire.

There is, however, one drawback. Since I first went to Bolton in the late 1990s, the bus service has been withdrawn. There is a community bus, but when I rang the operators they said I would not be able to travel on it since I did not belong to their community. The Queen, on the other hand, if installed at Bolton, would, as I understand it, automatically qualify. If she fancied popping into

Clitheroe for the afternoon, perhaps to top up the larder with some of Cowman's homemade sausages, the community bus would be ready and waiting to take her. So what is she waiting for? Were she an autocrat in the tradition of the duke and duchess of Sutherland, she would order the immediate acquisition of the property and summon the finest architects, building contractors, goldsmiths, silversmiths, carpenters, carvers, gardeners landscape, jobbing and otherwise, versatile artisans and reliable plumbers from every distant part of her mighty Commonwealth to knock the place into shape. But she's not, so she won't. You do not need to be an ardent monarchist, or indeed any kind of monarchist, to conclude that this is a pity.

But now, south again, into Staffordshire, where we shall meet a man whose reputation transcends that of most mere monarchs.

22

LICHFIELD

*Dr Samuel Johnson's inadvertent incitement to market
researchers – Stafford, a model county town – the mysterious
allure of Uttoxeter – its town hall in jeopardy – a messy affair at
Ingestre – Abbots Bromley, home of the (sanitized) horn dance
– in advancing to Lichfield, I only just miss out on Rugeley –
bloody events in Lichfield market place, and a visit by Jeffrey
Archer – Lichfield as cultural treat: even the names of its dogs
come out of Jane Austen.*

'Let observation, with extensive view,' wrote Dr Samuel Johnson,
'survey mankind from China to Peru.' His instruction has been
obeyed, even though it was contained in a work called *The Vanity
of Human Wishes*. Hardly a day passes without somebody, somewhere, publishing a new survey. Many are quite ridiculous – one,
for instance, identified Clacton as the English town most disposed
to like Brussels sprouts – but that does not stop newspapers print-
ing them. In March 2003 *Country Life* magazine published a league
table of English counties, based, it was claimed, on ' clear, cold-cut,
and ruthlessly scientific criteria'. Devon, it concluded, was best,
Gloucester and Cornwall came next, and Dorset was fourth. Down
at the very bottom was Staffordshire, jointly with Hertfordshire,
but only because Hertfordshire's housing was pricey and
Staffordshire's cheap. When examined for more than 9.7 seconds,
the criteria on which this farrago was based turned out to be about

as clear, cold-cut and ruthlessly scientific as the average teddy bear. As Staffordshire promptly pointed out, the rating awarded to its countryside, which was 1 out of 10, appeared to ignore the fact that much of the glorious Peak District falls within its boundaries.

The criteria used were woefully arbitrary. One of the tests of a county ought to be whether or not it has a good county town. There Staffordshire would have scored very well. A county town needs a good central square, and Stafford has one, in the market square halfway along its entertaining main street. It changes its name at this point from Greengate to Gaolgate before running into Gaol Square. You have to admire a town which has never called in consultants to help it change the names of Gaolgate and Gaol Square to something more soft and yielding.

The market square has a real county town shire hall, built in 1795 and a very fine sight indeed. Some of the old Staffordshire names have gone – the old established Stevenson Salt and Co. bank long ago succumbed to the power of Lloyds, while Mummery and Son, jewellers and opticians, and the ladies' fashion emporium next door were swept away in the 1960s by a building society with little feel for architecture. But the Staffordshire Railway Building Society encouragingly survives, alongside Pizza Express. In the streets behind the square you will find the borough hall of 1876, plainly the work of men who were really proud of Stafford. It is now a theatre, offering when I was there *Mahler, Song and Dance Man*, and *Girls' Night* ('difficult not to join in' – *The Stage*). The old county buildings in Martin Street are confident and robust. Greengate Street fields the four-storey High House of 1555, alongside which is the old-fashioned Swan Hotel, for many years the epitome of the kind of eating and drinking place which could make a real occasion out of a day spent for business or pleasure in town. Behind is the parish church, which you can reach by Church Street, some of which is impertinently pretty. There are several odd little byways, and some street names to match (Crabbery Street, Tipping Street, Tenter Bank). A lot has been saved that might have been lost, and some older buildings that have started new lives have lost little or none of their dignity. The town is built on a river, the Sow, which joins just outside town with the Penk (they are economical with the names of their rivers around here). When you follow the Sow, you come to a park with a bandstand – ideal for local brass and silver bands from nearby villages to perform in while the populace sits in its deckchairs, tapping its toes, fanning its brows and applauding.

The second great urban justification for Staffordshire is the city of Lichfield, which is reachable by an Arriva bus from the railway station on the edge of the park. This goes by way of Shugborough, one of the county's great houses, and then through Rugeley, a town which reminds me of something the Paris newspaper *Le Figaro* said of the manufacturing town of Lens: 'its charms do not necessarily explode in one's face'. But I shall take a much more circumnavigatory route. I cannot resist the lure of Uttoxeter. What is it about Uttoxeter that so often causes its name to fall from the lips of people who may never have been there? A friend of mine sat many hours at the bedside of his mother, who was dying. At times he did the crossword. 'Can you think of a town whose name has nine letters with an X in the middle?' he asked, and his mother, who never did crosswords, replied without hesitation, 'Uttoxeter.' Uttoxeter, I suggest, lingers deep in the consciousness of many without them ever suspecting that is there. At any rate, the Arriva 404 is about to go there, and so am I.

It is raining hard now – tipping down in Tipping Street – and the bus has a doleful air. 'One journey nearer the grave,' an old man says to his wife as they clamber on board. He cheers up a bit when he sees the driver. 'Bet you didn't get 7 across,' he says. The driver admits that he didn't. 'It was "introit",' the old man tells him triumphantly. As the bus heads out of Stafford, a conversation begins about accents. Within ten minutes or so, the following have been condemned. Gateshead (interestingly enough, not Newcastle, or even Geordie, but specifically Gateshead): can't understand a word of it. Carlisle: worse. Dumfries: completely incomprehensible. Cambridge University: couldn't understand a word, you had to ask for an English translation. Wiltshire: a slovenly drawl. Inverness folk, it's suggested, are supposed to speak perfect English, but someone disagrees: Inverness folk cannot possibly speak perfect English, because they are Scottish. As we reach the campus of Staffordshire University the conversation shifts to what's wrong with TV. The unanimous answer: everything. The attitude of the old couple is a sort of cheerful defeatedness. We're old, we're useless, the rest of the world despises us. Bit of a laugh, eh?

We pass the Beacon Business Park, which looks as though it might have been designed for military occupation, and the county showground. All, like the conversation aboard, is drizzle and mist. The countryside, as far as one can still make it out through the murky windows, is flat. The road bends and twists. The afternoon is wasting away. At one point we leave the main road and turn down a road called Back Lane, always a sign that a bus is taking its time. Stowe-by-Chartley gives a bit of a lift: it has one very good-looking house, but I see that Henry Thorold's *Shell Guide* says Victorian restorers have made a mess of the church, as so often. And then, with a sudden squawk and judder, we are over the district boundary, into East Staffordshire and the first dreary stretch of what promises to be Uttoxeter. Here the elderly couple get off, still as cheerfully dismal as when they got on. 'I have to get out of my seat!' the wife warns, struggling out of it, as the husband makes for the door. 'That is your problem, not mine,' he tells her. I guess deep down they are really quite fond of each other.

The bus deposits us at the top of the town, in the very unlovely Smithfield bus station, where our 404 changes itself into a 4 to run around Uttoxeter's outer circle. Uttoxeter is probably best known nowadays for its racecourse, and then as the birthplace of the JCB digger. The racecourse has not just survived, when in larger and better known towns such as Lichfield racing has perished, but has come to be recognized as a model of competent and intelligent management. 'The racecourse,' *The Times*'s expert Alan Lee wrote in 2004, 'announces itself with a boldness that tells of success, its showy entrance gates and colourful new signage giving an unmistakeable sense that you have arrived at somewhere special... Everywhere you look, Uttoxeter hums with vigour...' If only that could be said of the town.

Nevertheless it is an attractive place. In the centre of the market place is the kiosk where Samuel Johnson came, in his seventies, to stand in the rain all day as atonement for having as a lad disobeyed his father, who had told him to go and sell books there. Johnson's father stored his books in what is now the Old Talbot Inn, survivor of two great fires. A shiny device was installed near the kiosk to mark the millennium. It commemorates Uttoxeter's high achievers, some well known, like Joseph Cyril Bamford who started in a small lock-up in 1945 and gave his name to the JCB; others, people little known outside Staffordshire, such as Mary Howitt, author and poetess. The main shopping street is enlivened by Uttoxeter town hall, not a building of great distinction, but one which still reflects a Uttoxeter that directed its own affairs, before its independence was lost to East Staffordshire. Two lads sit on the steps, reading *The Sun*. When Uttoxeter was really Uttoxeter, some official, a beadle perhaps, would have come importantly out of the building and sent them packing.

There's a problem here common to many old market towns now struggling to hold on to their shoppers. A shopping survey in 2001 ranked Uttoxeter 650th in a field of 650. Much the busiest store is Tesco, down on the bypass. The shopping mall in the centre is a meagre affair. There are still traditional markets three days a week, but on the afternoon when I was there the shops looked ready to shut up and go home by half past four. In the hope of saving the town, and staving off a death-dealing shopping drift to Burton and Derby, East Staffordshire council devised a redevelopment plan based on the old cattle market, and incorporating the old town hall. Local newspapers ran stories suggesting that the building might be demolished, and that even if it was spared that fate, its dignity might be blown by some vulgarizing change of use. Once, Uttoxeter decided what happened in Uttoxeter. Now its fate is decided in Burton, by East Staffordshire council. The loss of local independence in the reforms of the middle 1970s was inevitable, since the old authorities were simply too small, but the consequences in public disjunction and the sense that a community's fortunes are now at the mercy of alien forces has been far more damaging than was predicted. There were those who foresaw, and welcomed, this loss of local pride and identity. Writing in 1972, John Boynton, clerk to Cheshire county council, argued that old loyalties needed to be deliberately extinguished, a process which he foresaw might lead to the sale of £80 million worth of redundant town halls.

Uttoxeter is on the very edge of the county. Cross the river Dove at the northern edge and you are in Derbyshire. The next part of my journey goes into the heart of Staffordshire; but not, tonight, to Lichfield, since the only bus left at this late hour (5 p.m.) goes no further than Abbots Bromley. This route, which used to be run by

Arriva, has been taken over by a small operator, D and G. The bus that comes in has no number and a blank destination board: indeed, the writing on the side proclaims it to be running on a wholly different route out of Newcastle-under-Lyme. Either D or G, I mutter, ought to do something about it. We go out of town through modern estates with the usual gently bucolic countryside names (Kingfisher, Chaffinch, Sandpiper, Swallow, Avocet) and are soon on the open road, past the Red Cow public house and into Kingstone, headquarters, I notice, of D and G, and nowadays home to the earls of Shrewsbury, the latest of whom is otherwise known as Charles Henry John Benedict Crofton Chetwynd Chetwynd-Talbot.

I cannot, as Gerald of Wales would say, resist telling you that this family was involved in the 1950s in a spectacular Staffordshire scandal. Nadine, countess of Shrewsbury, had survived his family's opposition and married the 21st earl. A young man called Anthony Lowther, twenty-one and just out of Cambridge, arrived at the family home at Ingestre near Stafford in 1954 to tutor the couple's four daughters. He was gradually promoted to become a kind of administrative factotum and organizer of opera festivals. But when in 1958 the countess had a miscarriage the earl was told by her gynaecologist's secretary that Lowther was the child's father. The subsequent divorce case, which lasted eighteen days, made lurid headlines, shedding light on various quirks of life at Ingestre. Young Lowther, it was testified, used to address the earl as John, while John would call Lowther Tonykins. A temporary butler called van der Plaats said he had witnessed the countess and Lowther kissing on the Blue Landing in a manner he described as 'rather passionate', while a housekeeper testified that she had seen a letter from the countess to Lowther which ended: 'At this late hour, are you afraid of being found out?' Lowther was further alleged to have been overheard telling the countess: 'Nanny knows too much, she must go.' The earl for his part admitted a wartime affair with a woman called Nina Mortlock, but said this was partly due to the fact that his countess had said she could never love him as much as she'd loved a previous boyfriend, a steeplechase jockey; also, that she had had an affair with a Frenchman. The earl's petition for divorce was denied, and so was the countess's counter-claim. Although the earl had walked out in the previous September, the countess, so she told the *Daily Mail*, had never given up hope of winning him back. A place was laid for him every night at the dinner table at Ingestre, and no one else was ever allowed to sit in his chair. The earl later put Ingestre on the market and moved to Madeira to grow bananas, an enterprise in which he was assisted by Nina. Eventually the countess divorced the earl; he married Nina, and the countess developed her career as an opera singer. The earl died in 1980, the countess in 2003, aged ninety.

While I've been pondering these events, D and G have been transporting me towards Abbots Bromley. Most people I know have never been to, or even heard of, this place. That is their loss. The black and white Goats Head Inn, on the triangular green by the butter cross, used to be the town hall and courtroom. Now it's one of five inns that survive, along with the Crown, the Bagot Arms, the Royal Oak and the Coach and Horses. Every September, on a date that is determined by a formula designed to tax the mathematical skills of the townspeople, a horn dance takes place. Like so many pagan festivities designed to celebrate sex, this one was later superintended, and its rules of procedure rewritten, by the church. These days the day starts with holy communion at St Nicholas church and ends there with the ancient service of compline. Horns are collected only after the first church service and put back before the late one. All five pubs, you may not be surprised to hear, are visited during the day.

The village is strung along a main road, with a 1619 church house and almshouses just west of the centre, a very elegant house called The Crofts between the church and the green, and a Woodard girls' school, claimed to be one of the oldest girls' schools in England, on the rambling road at the east end. The only disfigurement here is the traffic. But even this has an air of nostalgia about it: a notice on the wall near the school reminds you of the rules about parking your motor.

Either D or G must have sorted things out overnight, for the morning bus to Lichfield has both a number and a destination blind. It is drizzling. 'See you've been singing again,' says a passenger to the driver. The ride is brisk but rattly. At Blithbury there's a pub called the Bull and Spectacles; no time to get off and ask why. The landscape is uneventful. The main theme of the run seems to be the avoidance of Rugeley. Often the bus takes roads signposted to Rugeley, but it always shies off again. Rugeley went through difficult times in the late nineteenth century when its reputation became intertwined with that of Dr Palmer the poisoner. 'The Rugeley poisoner' people invariably called him. This so upset the townspeople that they petitioned the prime minister to be allowed to change the name of the town. Certainly, said the prime minister, but on one condition: that you change its name to mine. His name was Palmerston.

Having tacked through various preliminary estates, the bus enters Lichfield by a route which gives a fine foretaste of one of the best towns in England. The road comes in by the medieval church of St Chad, with Stowe House beside it, at the eastern end of a lake called Stowe Pool. Now I can see the cathedral – the tops of its spires this morning lost in the mist. No matter, the mist will clear. From the bus station there are lanes that lead to the centre of town.

When I came here in 1990 for the Mid Staffordshire by-election, I heard a woman exclaim to her friend 'He is here!' with such joy that I followed them as they ran to see what manner of man 'He' might be. In fact, it was Jeffrey Archer. This is the only detrimental thing I know about Lichfield.

Let us start in the market, which is where Jeffrey Archer was speaking. It's a site that recalls some other terrible days. Martyrs were burned at the stake here in the reign of Mary Tudor: Thomas Hayward and John Goreway in 1555, Joyce Lewis in 1557. Edward Wightman of Burton-on-Trent 'was burned at the stake in this market place for heresy, 11 April 1612, being the last person in England so to die'. There is also a plaque that recalls how George Fox, released from Derby prison in 1651, stood without shoes in this market place and denounced the city of Lichfield. This is how Fox described it: 'I walked on about a mile till I came into the town, and as soon as I was got within the town the word of the Lord came to me again, to cry, "Woe unto the bloody city of Lichfield!" So I went up and down the streets, crying with a loud voice, 'Woe to the bloody city of Lichfield!" It being market day, I went into the market place, and to and fro in the several parts of it, and made stands, crying as before, "Woe to the bloody city of Lichfield!"' At first he thought he had been moved to do this by the bloodshed in the city during the Civil War, but as he meditated further, he came to understand that in the Emperor Diocletian's time a thousand Christians were martyred in Lichfield.

There is more, thankfully much less blood-curdling, to the market place, which I shall save for later. Meanwhile there are good subsidiary streets to explore. Bore Street has the Guildhall of 1846–8, though when I was there banners for clearance bargains you'd be mad to miss were demeaningly draped across it. The problem here is the same as that with Uttoxeter town hall. Many once dominant buildings, religious and secular, will never return to their former use. They're too good to pull down, so other purposes need to be found for them. Yet that frequently serves to humiliate them. A church becomes a lurid and raucous nightclub; an old courthouse is festooned with signs inviting the populace to drink itself silly during 'Happy Hour'.

There is no particular virtue, however, in mere catalogues: best just to wander the streets and let them delight and surprise you. Then go back to the market place and take the short walk along the Dam, a causeway flanked by elegant Georgian houses. Beyond is a pond, called the Minster Pool; behind that a stately house; and beyond and above, the red sandstone cathedral. The cathedral close is a kind of unpremeditated triumph: a hugely successful conjunction of contrasting dimensions and styles, from the slightly domineering old palace through the delicious deanery to the cottagey square of Vicars' Close through an arch to the west. The front of the cathedral is decorated with a vast collection of statues: Old Testament prophets and just a few Old Testament women, apostles and early disciples, celebrated missionaries, Norman kings, early bishops. And amidst them all, Queen Victoria; a reminder that, although a cathedral has stood on this site since 700, and the original west front was created around 1300, much of what we now see was put there by the Victorians. Nearly all the original statues were removed in the eighteenth century and replaced by the present collection in the 1880s, with Jesus squeezed in, in place of King Charles I.

Across the shimmering water of Stowe Pool to the east of the cathedral, there's the irresistible vision of Stowe House and the church of St Chad. Once, as I walked beside Stowe Pool, I heard a woman berating her dog with the words 'You must not do that, Darcy.' How can *Country Life* still claim that Staffordshire is lacking in culture? Walk, alternatively, westwards from the cathedral, by the water, and you come to the foot of Beacon Street, which sweeps up the hill past Erasmus Darwin's house on the road out towards Rugeley. In the park just beyond is a gesture of conspicuous generosity: a statue to the captain of the *Titanic*, Edward John Smith, whose home town, Stoke, denied him one. Arms folded, he gazes so searchingly out to sea that instinctively one looks around for icebergs. 'A great heart, a brave life and a heroic death', says the plaque, 'Be British'. The sculptor was Kathleen, widow of Scott of the Antarctic.

But a pilgrimage to Lichfield must end as it began, in the market place. This was the town of Samuel Johnson and David Garrick. How extraordinary that two figures of such undisputed genius should have emerged at much the same time from this town. Garrick was born in Hereford, but to a Lichfield household, and Lichfield was where he grew up. Johnson was twelve years older than Garrick, and had been his teacher. In 1737 they walked together to London to seek their fortunes. Garrick is commemorated in Lichfield's new theatre, which opened in 2003. The market place belongs to the doctor. Here, outside the house where he grew up, now a museum to him, is Samuel, seated, brooding, surrounded by scenes from his life, including the Uttoxeter penance.

A little way off is his biographer James Boswell, on a smaller scale, foppish, sporting a sword and a rather ridiculous hat. It is right that Boswell too should be honoured here, since, as Lord Macaulay said, without Boswell we would not have Johnson. 'That he was a coxcomb and a bore,' the great historian says of the Scotsman, 'weak, vain, pushing, curious, garrulous, was obvious to all those who were acquainted with him. That he could not reason, that he had no wit, no humour, no eloquence, is apparent from his writings. And yet his writings are read beyond the Mississippi, and under the Southern Cross, and are likely to be read as long as the English exists, either as a living or as a dead language.'

But the deeper reverence must always be for the master. At the close of his noble and moving essay on Johnson, written in December 1856, three years before his own death, Macaulay wrote: 'The old philosopher is still among us in the brown coat with the metal buttons and the shirt which ought to be at wash, blinking, puffing, rolling his head, drumming with his fingers, tearing his meat like a tiger, and swallowing his tea in oceans. No human being who has been more than seventy years in the grave is so well known to us. And it is but just to say that our intimate acquaintance with what he himself would have called the anfractuosities of his intellect and of his temper serves only to strengthen our conviction that he was both a great and a good man.'

23

Northampton — Earls Barton — Rushden
Higham Ferrers — Raunds

IRTHLINGBOROUGH

*A county of boots and shoes – Northampton, its radical history,
its taste for knocking things down, its foul-mouthed schoolboys
– Earls Barton, its Saxon tower and its kinky boots – Rushden,
which grew too fast, and its antidote, Higham Ferrers – when
Raunds marched on London, and a government surrendered –
Irthlingborough: a possible British Hollywood, had the Kaiser
not intervened.*

'Anfractuous', the word Lord Macaulay used about Dr Johnson,
means winding, involved, circuitous – much like my route for these
journeys, which takes me now, anfractuously, into
Northamptonshire, a county where assistant commissioner
H. W. Lord, on a fact-finding tour in the year 1864, could not understand why so many people he met had only one eye. At first he
thought it must be pure coincidence; but then he met Mr Bostock.
Mr Bostock was a bootmaker, and explained that Wellington and
Blucher boots made locally by children were still stabbed by hand.
The stabbing, he said, was laborious and often dangerous, since the
children who were given this work often sat so close that when they
drew the thread with both hands, the awl, which was always held
point outwards, not infrequently struck the next-door child in the
face, which not infrequently cost them an eye.

Lancashire, one was taught in primary school, meant cotton and
Yorkshire meant wool, and Staffordshire, in so far as anyone talked

of Staffordshire, meant the potteries. But no county in England could have been as uniquely devoted to a single industry as Northamptonshire was to the production of boots and shoes. I pulled at random from the shelves of the county local studies library a dissertation submitted to Nottingham University by Peter Reginald Mounfield in 1962. The figures it contained were staggering. In 1841, 13.4 per thousand of the population of England and Wales worked in this industry. The figure for Northamptonshire was 35.2. In 1871 the national figure was down to 9.8 but the Northamptonshire figure had gone up to 78.9. By 1901 the figure for England and Wales was 6.7, the figure for Northamptonshire, 125.1.

And so the pattern continued. In 1951 the figure for England and Wales was down to 2.8, but the figure for Northampton-shire was 97.4. This meant that the average Northamptonshire person was thirty-four times more likely than the average English or Welsh person to be busy at any given moment making boots and shoes. Even though Northampton was the biggest and most productive centre, this obsessive involvement with footwear had gripped some of the smaller towns, particularly those in the valleys of the rivers Nene and Ise, even more fiercely. The 1951 census showed more than half of workpeople in Rushden, Higham Ferrers and Raunds making their livings this way.

Individual towns had their own specialities. Northampton was originally the fount of high-class shoes for men. Kettering served the medium reaches of the trade, while Rushden and Welling-borough concentrated on cheapness, and on slippers. Rushden was deep into the making of military boots, as was Raunds. At one time Earls Barton concentrated on the needs of firemen, but later it became very upmarket indeed. The museum in Guildhall Street, Northampton, has a boot and shoe section, where you may find displayed not just Wellingtons and Bluchers but postilion boots, leather snow boots, football boots of all codes, red suede walking boots (though these are as late as 1995), fencing shoes, red, white and blue Union Jack shoes issued to mark the 1953 coronation, Hungarian theatrical thigh boots, and even a small fetish subsection, together with a smattering of the more modest kinds of shoe which Northamptonshire wore for going to work.

Precisely why this explosion occurred in Northamptonshire is, needless to say, a matter of academic dispute. Some credit King Alfred, who, it is said, having gained some ascendancy over the Danes, stationed numbers of them in this area, and ordered them to make coverings for his soldiers' feet. What is clear is that the trade got a great boost from the Civil War – as from most wars thereafter. Huge orders poured in from 1642 which suppliers were pushed to fulfil. In 1648, Oliver Cromwell sent to Northamptonshire for 4,000 pairs of shoes (before Cromwell, soldiers had to provide their own), while William III also ordered 4,000 pairs, plus 600 pairs of boots, to boost his campaign in Ireland. Thomas Fuller, in his *Worthies of England*, published in 1662, said you could tell when you were getting close to Northampton because of the sound of the shoemakers' lapstones (stones they held on their knees to hammer against). A good run of wars through the late eighteenth and early nineteenth centuries had the industry roaring away.

With the help of a guide that is sold in the county library, *A Guide to the Industrial Heritage of Northamptonshire*, the work of Peter Perkins, Geoffrey Starmer and Roy Sheffield of the Northamptonshire Industrial Archaeology Group, you can still find the architectural evidence of the town's most prolific bootmaking days scattered around the streets. The great names of the mid-twentieth-century high street were here in profusion – Trueform, Manfield, Barratts – as well as also some which catered more for specialist tastes, like the Northampton Legging, Gaiter and Spat Co.

Originally most of the work was done in the workers' homes, but gradually, as mechanization advanced, factories were built in the town, some of which still survive, though usually turned to new uses. Some, like Church's in Duke Street, were austerely functional, as if to drive any notions of hilarity out of the workers' heads as they trudged in of a morning; others like the headquarters of Barratts in Kingsthorpe Road, with the words 'Footshape Boot Works' lettered across the top, glow with exuberant confidence.

Not, of course, that Northamptonshire's history turned entirely on shoes. All Saints church, in the centre of town, was one of the most grievous casualties of a monstrous fire in 1675 which destroyed much of the old Northampton. The church was rebuilt in a much altered form with help from Charles II, which is why he appears on the portico. The Gothic Guildhall is a delight – a tale in three episodes, the first from the 1860s, the second from the 1880s, the harmonious third from 1992 – with its stately effigies of the rich and famous of Northampton festooned across the frontage. On the other hand, Northampton is a town where buildings that ought to be cherished too often get knocked down. Charles I destroyed most of the castle to punish Northampton for backing Parliament, as well no doubt for having made Parliament's shoes. Two centuries later, the rest of the castle was knocked down as well, to make room for the station. A chunk of the famous market place was similarly obliterated in 1972 to allow for a shopping centre. Another casualty was the 1901 Emporium Arcade, which seems to have been regarded as an obtrusive relic. I remember the great topographer Ian Nairn defending this threatened arcade on television one night against its municipal would-be assassins. He was almost in tears by the time he had finished. But the programme was a repeat, and as he reached his last sentence a caption came up on the screen to announce that the deed had already been done.

The former headquarters of the British United Shoe Machinery company is now the Charles Bradlaugh pub – a reminder that Northampton was once a radical town. Radicalism and boots and shoes seem to go together. Working at home may have had something to do with that. 'The boot and shoe makers', wrote Henry Mayhew in around 1850, 'are certainly far from being an unintellectual body of men. They appear to be stern, uncompromising, and a reflecting race. This, perhaps, is to be accounted for by the solitude of their employment.' When in that year one of the town's most progressive shoe manufacturers introduced a factory full of modern machinery, it set off a bitter strike which ended in victory for the employers. And then, a further fomenter of radical passion, no doubt, there were all those lost eyes...

Certainly Northampton was radical enough to vote for the flaming radical politician Charles Bradlaugh, and when he was disqualified for refusing to take the oath – it was against his conscience to do so, he said, as an atheist – to re-elect him three times and send him back to Westminster. His fellow Liberal MP from 1880 until 1891 was the maverick and famously undisciplined Henry Labouchere, whose conduct so unsettled Queen Victoria that she ordered Gladstone not to give him a seat in the Cabinet. Not one of nature's conformists, either.

On its way out of town the number 46 Stagecoach bus into this boot-making county passes Charles Bradlaugh on his plinth, traffic whirling around him. On his right are the Penny Whistle bar and Guy Salmon Motors; on his left are Woodlows, your local family furnishers, and a sturdy Victorian building bearing the legend Abington Square Mission, complete with a replica of the foundation stone laid in 1878 by the Rev. E. T. Prust. Today, it's the Urban Tiger gentlemen's club. This bus is a double-decker and three boys have bagged the front seat upstairs. They are perhaps twelve or thirteen. What subjects inspire their childish prattle today? 'I'm going to give it to her good and hard – doggy style,' one, whose voice has not yet broken, promises his companions. Past Abington Park – Northampton is a good town for parks – which is said to have a lake, a tower and a bandstand, and by way of somewhere called Lumbertubs, we come to Earls Barton, upmarket home of upmarket shoes (though with such a useful sideline in kinky boots that a film about them packed cinemas in 2005). Charles Barker, who built its best-known business, is buried in the churchyard close to the south door. Aside from shoes, the village is even more famous for the extraordinary and majestic Saxon tower of its church – perhaps, says the *Shell Guide*, the best known in England. The shops and pubs and houses of Earls Barton square are gathered reverentially below and alongside the church. Some of the stone in the village has a warm orange tone which makes the place seem all the more welcoming.

The long and monotonous descent into Wellingborough is enlivened by new estates with streets named not just after poets – that is commonplace nowadays – but after the works of those poets. Clusters of houses set around greens on Longfellow Road have been given their own Longfellow names: Hiawatha, Excelsior, Hesperus. How many people living in Longfellow Road, I wonder, have ever read any Longfellow? How many who live in Hiawatha have worked their way through that huge rhythmic epic? How many in Hesperus know that in the end it gets wrecked? The bus takes a curious route through the centre of Wellingborough, visiting some parts twice, but giving only a tempting glimpse of the best bit, which includes the church, All Hallows, and the grammar school of 1682, with an inscription partly in Greek and partly in Latin, a practice which turns the stomach of pedants.

The next leg, as it were, for this boot and shoe pilgrimage is Rushden, home town of the earthy novelist H. E. Bates, who wrote about the trade in a book called *The Vanished World*. Bates's boot and shoe workers sound rather less reflective and intellectual than those Mayhew met. Their tradition, according to Bates, was to get roaring drunk on Saturday and Sunday nights and recover on Mondays – 'Saint Monday' as it used to be called by workers in many trades whose Victorian values did not include reporting for work on a Monday. The three boys with their strenuous aspirations have left the bus and two casually snazzy princesses of fifteen or sixteen are now installed in their place. What is it about Northamptonshire? Their language is about the filthiest I have ever heard on a bus, not just for words but for content, which mostly concerns the imperfections of the louder one's mother and to a lesser extent the louder one's mother's lover. A weakness for double standards appears to be the principal fault of this inadequate parent. 'Does she think her daughters are fucking angels?' her child snarls through rosebud lips. The rest of us try to pretend we are taking no notice. Fortunately they soon get off, but this is because they have seen a girl they do not like leaving the bus ('Just look at her. What a slag!') and fancy a spell of taunting. The outskirts of Irchester bring the mind restoratively back to boots and shoes, since here there's a boarded-up factory, formerly the domain of R. Griggs, abandoned perhaps when Griggs moved, as we shall see when we get to Irthlingborough, on to more ambitious enterprises. Through blank unimaginative side roads that could belong anywhere, we come in to Rushden.

Rushden is one of those places that simply grew up too fast. Standing by the church in the original village you can speculate on what might have happened had Rushden developed gradually, or even if those who created the town to serve the burgeoning shoe industry has stopped now and then and said: let us, just here and there, put up something a little memorable. Apart perhaps from the old railway station with its self-conscious parade of nostalgic tin signs advertising such products as Bovril, there is not a lot to remember in Rushden. At the far end of the narrow and charmless shopping street, on the old A6 to the north, there's what looks as if it was once an art deco cinema. In fact, in a rare Rushden surprise, it's an old art deco coach station. Just beyond is an art deco shoe factory, the work of Sir Albert Richardson, an architect vilified by expert opinion when he was practising but now enjoying a modest rehabilitation. My industrial heritage guide lists half a dozen more dead shoe factories in this small town. The great Kettering schoolmaster, historian, writer and publisher of very small books, J. L. Carr, once listed the brass bands of Rushden as one of the six world-famed treasures of his adopted county, but unfortunately none of them is playing today.

But go a little way north out of Rushden and you come into Higham Ferrers, which is a treat. There is still, despite the bypass, the tyrannical traffic of the A6 to contend with, but even that cannot destroy the charm of the long main street, with plenty of trees and Cotswold-cosy stone cottages, some seasoned pubs and a market square with a fine town hall displaying the seal of the old municipality. Just off the street is the very fine church of St Mary the Virgin (locked) with a separate chantry chapel grouped in a happy harmonious scene. This was a boot and shoe town too, but it evolved from a larger and older core than Rushden, and enough survives from before the great boot and shoe rush to make it still distinctive and pleasing, a place to be contentedly wandered and lingered in.

The bus, however, is off to Raunds. There used to be a tale of a man immune to classical music who, hearing a mention of Brahms, inquired, 'What's a Brahm?' Raunds being more obscure than Brahms, people have no doubt sometimes asked 'What's a Raund?' Oddly enough, this is a perfectly sensible question. *The Oxford Dictionary of Place-Names* says the name derives from the Old English word 'rand', which meant a border. Raunds establishes its provenance as a boot and shoe village on the way in from Higham Ferrers when the 46 takes you past the once important gates of Wellington Works. Given its modest size, this perhaps was the most besottedly boot-and-shoe oriented community in all Northamptonshire. All gone now, of course. The last two factories closed in the late 1990s. The industry here was built by shrewd, hardworking and thrifty men; so thrifty that the managing director of one Raunds factory used to catch the bus in to work every morning using a workman's ticket. If anyone offered to give him a lift at the end of the day he would sell his return ticket to an employee.

Raunds specifically shod the army; boots for the War Department were the core of its being. And the meanness, as Raunds saw it, of the rates of return that the War Office offered led the village to march on London in 1905. The campaign began with a strike by 300 workers in twelve Raunds firms in March. After a few weeks a drift back to work began. The union organizer supervising the strike, a man called James Gribble, hit on a notion which would put the fight back into Raunds. The shoemakers of Raunds and its neighbour Ringstead would march on London to demand fair treatment from the War Office. From among 300 men who had volunteered for the march, he picked 115, whom he organized into six companies, the sixth of which was the band. Gribble – whom the men called the General – was their commander, aided by three subordinate officers: a paymaster, a billetmaster and an official to whom he awarded the very grand title Commissariate-general.

They set out on their great adventure in their stout Northamptonshire shoes on 8 May. They stayed the first night at Bedford, and then soldiered on to St Albans, with a one-legged man on crutches called Pearson at their head. The man from the *Manchester Guardian* joined them along the road. He was greatly impressed by their calibre. 'Army bootmaking,' he wrote, 'seems to have an effect even on their physique, for many of them have the clean, well-controlled face of the good soldier, and this appearance is heightened by their bronzed skins.' When a funeral passed, he noted, they all raised their hats. 'They cherish the perhaps pathetic hope that when once they stand before Mr Arnold-Forster [the War Office minister] and speak to him face to face, the irresistible right-eousness of their cause will sweep away all the official cobwebs and send them home triumphant.' By the time they reached Watford next day, there was hardly a man, the reporter revealed, with a whole skin on his feet. More beds were being offered for the night than they could use, and some benefactor had taken Pearson's crutches and soled them with rubber. At Cricklewood they were greeted by a crowd of around 2,000, and the Crown Inn put on a free meal for them; at St John's Wood they were offered a further meal and copious supplies of drink. They were so much held up by these kindly proceedings that by the time they reached Hyde Park on Friday, only 2,000 were left of the crowd of 10,000 that had gathered to welcome them. Gribble and some others, meanwhile, had headed for Westminster, where a friendly MP had arranged for them to have seats in the Strangers' Gallery. The House was dis-cussing women's suffrage, and though the friendly MP had hoped to raise the issue of Raunds, he could not get in to the debate. Eventually the General stood up in his place in the gallery and shouted, 'Mr Speaker, is the Honourable Member talking the House out? I want to call your attention to my presence and that of 115 men who have walked here to ventilate their grievances.' Gribble and his friends were ejected. In the process he wrenched his ankle, which must have made for an awkward march home.

On the Sunday, a rally was held in Trafalgar Square, at which Keir Hardie spoke and the suffragette leader Mrs Despard. There's a picture in a book in Raunds library showing Gribble addressing his forces. He has a big black hat and a dramatic moustache. His supporters are wearing flat caps. By now it seemed clear that his march had been a success. The government announced that inquiries were to be made into the wages and conditions paid to the workforce in Raunds, and improvements were ordered. The Raunds and District Historical Society commemorated the centenary of the marchers' achievement in May 2005, although the celebratory march lasted only one mile, where the real one had stretched to 160.

The decline in the boot and shoe trade began, at first quite gently, after the First World War and accelerated after the Second. Except in some specialist areas, it could not compete with cheap imports. The British Shoe Corporation bought up many Northamptonshire companies, kept the high street outlets, but closed the factories. While much of the county's industry looked doomed, one company at least had hit upon a strategy for keeping itself in business. Griggs and Co. were the makers of Doc Marten's boots, which married the appeals of strength and solidity, a romantic nostalgia for working-class values, and celebrity endorsement. Madonna teamed hers with a corset and fishnet stockings. Disappointingly, it seems that these boots had not been designed in Northamptonshire: their inventor was a young Bavarian doctor called Klaus Maertens. Max Griggs, the new power in the boardroom, set up a fine new factory on an industrial park at Chowns Mill near Irthlingborough, where he also established a football stadium for a local team called

Rushden and Diamonds – a merger of two former rivals, Rushden and Irthlingborough Diamonds, in 1991. Under Griggs's benevolent direction, Rushden and Diamonds played their way into the Football League the season after the merger. In October 2002, however, he announced that he would be transferring the shoe-manufacturing business to China, and he subsequently agreed to sell the football club to its supporters.

Irthlingborough, oddly enough, had known this kind of disappointment – the charismatic figure, the miracle worker even, who arrives in a cloud of excitement, only to find that his venture is unsustainable – at least once before. The duke of Wellington, victor of Waterloo, who used to come to these parts to visit one of his mistresses, said it reminded him of the countryside south of Brussels. One day in 1912 an American called Charles Weston, impressed by Wellington's comparison, arrived in Irthlingborough to make an epic film called *The Battle of Waterloo*. He set up camp in the little town and started recruiting his cast. Because much of the action was taken up with battle, he needed hundreds of extras, and by offering 7s 6d a day, as well as the prospect of possible fame, he soon found plenty in Irthlingborough. So many went absent from some of the local factories that employers had to shut down until Weston had finished work. He further bumped up the numbers by recruiting unemployed men from Northampton labour exchange. 'Never before in the annals of Irthlingborough', said the *Northamptonshire Evening Telegraph*, 'have there been scenes so exciting and magnetic as those enacted this week in the making of this historic film. For three days the battle raged, and whether in the town itself or on the stretch of land lying behind the Three Chimneys, or on the sloping surface of the Feast Field, or in the large meadow lying off Finedon Road, a crowd of immense proportions gathered to see the spectacle being presented before the camera.' Since not a lot of Irthlingborough extras could ride, Weston borrowed additional horsemen from Weedon barracks. Even that wasn't enough; if you watch his film closely you see that one of the officers riding across a ford is in fact a dummy. The dead horses, of which there were quite a lot too, came from a knacker's yard. Napoleon's fine coach was brought into town on a railway train.

By the time filming was finished, Weston had become attached to the place – all the more so because having given the landlord of the Horseshoe Inn a starring role in his battlefield epic, he had married his daughter. He went on to use the town in subsequent movies too, notably one called *The Poacher's Sweetheart*, for which an Irthlingborough man wrote the screenplay. Local historians believe that nine films were made there in all. Had conditions been right, Irthlingborough might have become a modest British answer to Hollywood. What killed such ambitions was the outbreak of war just a year after *Waterloo* was completed. Weston gave up his film-making, and Irthlingborough, its cinematic excitements over, reluctantly went back to the manufacture of boots and shoes. But Weston is still warmly remembered in Irthlingborough, since the local history society has a copy of that part of the film which survives and puts it on from time to time in a hall behind the Methodist church. The film, of course, is silent, so, as in the old days, an appropriate musical accompaniment is hammered out on the piano. However many times they stage it, the hall is always full, and the evening is punctuated by cries of pleasure as people recognize familiar Irthlingborough locations, and sometimes even familiar faces ('that's my Grandad!' someone exults). There are other favourite moments, too, that are usually worth a cheer: the arrival, for instance, of Blucher, at the head of reinforcements.

Quite a chunk of the film has been lost, but the history society has accumulated evidence of some of the material that is missing, including one of those ballroom scenes on the eve of battle much favoured in films like this, not least for the poignant reminder they give the audience that so many of these gallant soldiers waltzing their starry-eyed ladies around the floor under huge chandeliers will be dead within twenty-four hours. Much of what survives consists of soldiers milling about, charging through fords, stamping about waving guns and swords, reeling in agony and falling down dead – although it's sometimes a little difficult in *The Battle of Waterloo* to tell who is dead and who isn't, since the apparently dead will suddenly lift their heads and gaze around distractedly as if looking for further instructions from the director. The fog of war is liberally administered to cover up other confusions. It is pretty clear at all times, even so, which side is winning, since the actor playing Napoleon is frequently pictured observing the action through a spyglass and reacting with expressions which proceed from apprehension through alarm to total hopelessness. You can tell he has lost when his glittering coach explodes, a disaster to which he responds with a look of utter despair. 'What will France think?' says a caption. The final sequence shows Napoleon exiled to St Helena, brooding on what might have been, cursing destiny and the military genius of Wellington, or possibly even the imperfections of his director, who at one point blunders into a scene with the megaphone which he uses for haranguing his actors. Charles Weston, on this evidence, was no Eisenstein or D. W. Griffith, but a light must have gone out in Irthlingborough when he departed.

There is one thing, though, on which you can bet your boots: the boots in this movie, whether Wellingtons, Napoleons, Bluchers or mere standard issue, would all have been made around here. Just like those of the Cromwells; to whose territory I shall now move anfractuously on.

Huntingdon — Cambridge
Royston — Ware
CHESHUNT

*Huntingdon, home of the Cromwells – Richard's 'unfortunate
greatness' – through Cambridge to Royston, where James I
knocked down pubs, and asked not to be disturbed – on a bus
with a whistling driver into undervalued Hertfordshire –
Orwell's days at Wallington and his unsettling experience on a
bus – some useful guidance for people visiting Ware – Cromwell's
exile and quiet obscurity in the town that gave us Cliff Richard.*

One day late in the seventeenth century, or perhaps early in the
eighteenth, an old man stood on the roadside in the Hertfordshire
village of Cheshunt to watch the king pass by in procession. He was
simply one of the crowd, a person of no special importance. Few
around him would have known that, long before, the old man had
been as eminent as the king was today, had ridden himself in procession past cheering crowds, had been celebrated as the greatest
name in the land. The old man knew the road well. It had in a sense
been a theme of his life, since his birthplace was Huntingdon. Most
people thought his name was John Clarke; in fact, he was Richard
Cromwell.

It is recorded that, two centuries earlier, King Henry VII, having
overcome the challenge to his legitimacy by the pretender Lambert
Simnel, chose not to execute him, but employed him as a scullion
in the royal kitchens, smilingly pointing out to visitors the contrast
between his past aspirations and his present condition. The fall of

Richard Cromwell, successor to his mighty father Oliver, was neither so precipitate or complete. He too had cause to be grateful for the clemency which had spared his life, even while the body of his father was being taken from Westminster Abbey to be hanged at Tyburn, with his head exhibited on a pole in Westminster Hall. But then Richard's had always been – in the words that a friend would one day use of him – 'an unfortunate greatness'. He had never really aspired to rule the country; he had even acquired some reputation as a secret royalist sympathizer.

The house in which Richard Cromwell grew up no longer exists. Its place in the Old North Road on the northern side of the centre of Huntingdon is now occupied by a clinic – the Cromwell Clinic. The town was once the capital of tiny Huntingdonshire, merged into Cambridgeshire in 1965. In the centre of Huntingdon, on the edge of the square, close to the church of All Saints (locked) and the old town hall, is the former free hospital of St John, later a school which Oliver Cromwell attended (as in time did Samuel Pepys). It now contains a small museum of Cromwell memorabilia. There's a picture of Richard Cromwell, looking a bit of a fop; not Lord Protector material at all. His father had property in Huntingdon and was MP for the town in 1628–9. Richard, born in 1626, was his third son, and would never have been considered as his father's successor had not his two older brothers, Robert and Oliver, died young. Even then, there were doubts until hours before the death of the Lord Protector, at the height of a terrible storm on the anniversary of his decisive victories at Dunbar and Worcester, about who would succeed him. Richard had served as an MP for Hampshire and later for Cambridge University, and his father had picked him out to be chancellor of Oxford University; but he had also often berated Richard for his idleness, lack of seriousness, and debts. Although he was given a place on the Council of State in 1657, his succession was still not assured. It was thought that Cromwell might choose instead his son-in-law, Charles Fleetwood, a man far better equipped by temperament and experience for ruling than Richard. But Cromwell's chaplain and two of his most senior lieutenants, who had been at the deathbed, swore on oath that the father preferred the son. Those who oppose royal dynasties are not always hostile to founding dynasties of their own, as the case of Rupert Murdoch reminds us.

On the shelves of Huntingdon library I found a book called *The History of Richard Cromwell and the Restoration of Charles II*, by François Guizot. In the 1830s Guizot entered French politics, becoming France's minister for the interior and then for education, but he grew so unpopular that he fled to London, as did his master Louis-Philippe, during the revolution of 1848. His prose is wonderfully florid, but he knew far more of the nature of plots and coups and political manipulations than any academic practitioner. Richard, he says, had little desire to hold the supreme rank, but did not stint from accepting it when it was offered. He had until then lived happily as a country gentleman at Hursley in Hampshire: 'an idle, jovial and somewhat licentious country squire, very fond of horses and hunting, on intimate terms with the gentlemen of the neighbourhood, nearly all of whom were Cavaliers, disposed to adopt their opinions as freely as he shared their pleasures, and sometimes drinking with them to the health of their "landlord", as they termed the king, whom they did not venture to name openly.' It was even said that Richard had pleaded with his father in 1649 to spare Charles I. Richard's accession was greeted with the customary messages of warmth and loyalty, which he stored in a tin box and insisted on keeping when he was deposed. But some of those who welcomed his arrival did so simply because they thought him too weak to last. Many thought that his own forecast of the likely character of his administration – 'a golden mediocrity'– erred on the side of optimism. Attempts to get rid of him began from the moment he was installed, and before very long it was clear that his days were numbered.

To get from Huntingdon down the Old North Road to Cheshunt, a journey when made direct of some sixty miles, is, if your rules require you to do it by service bus, more complicated than you might have expected. But the first stage of it is appropriate, since it takes you to Cambridge, where Oliver was once a student (though he pulled out after only a year) and which both he and Richard represented in Parliament. The journey can be accomplished either on the cream and blue buses of Huntingdon and District, which runs three buses an hour on slightly varying routes, or the cream, black and light blue liveried fleet of Go Whippet. Mine is a Huntingdon bus, which is soon rambling gently around an estate suburb called Oxmoor, which looks to have been picked off the same shelf as developer suburbs everywhere except for a pub called the Lord Protector, with a sign that shows the great man slumped in an armchair, looking dyspeptic. It's a flat journey. They don't go in for hills much around here. Apart from a marina at Hartford, the main event is a tour of historic St Ives, where the road to the bus station goes in by Cromwell Place and out by Oliver Road. The view of the river and the long medieval bridge and boat haven on the way out of town is very agreeable. On the main road beyond Fenstanton, near Bar Hill Village, are two conjoined signs, one for a hotel and golf complex and the other for an immigration reception centre, an unintentionally cruel conjunction. Later there is another: 'Airport' and 'Crematorium'. 'Fight the Cambridgeshire wind farm' notices here advise. (They did, and in the spring of 2005, they won.) The route into Cambridge runs past the wall of Sidney

Sussex, Oliver's college, where, after many adventures and mis-adventures, his severed head at last found a permanent home. You are not, though, allowed to inspect it. The route into the bus station, Dummer Street, is a work of great intricacy which might almost have been created to give the visitor a view of many colleges great and small, as well as Parkers Piece, where many great cricketers have turned out down the years to play the university cricket team. The crowded, chaotic bus station will shortly serve up a 26 Stagecoach bus for the next stage of this journey, to Royston.

It is the fate of bus drivers in university towns, especially this one, to weave among cyclists, almost as if this were Holland. But grad-ually they abate and soon we are in Trumpington, which in 1980 gave its name to the redoubtable Tory peer, Baroness Trumpington. In her youth she had been a Land Girl on the Surrey estate of David Lloyd George, a statesman who perhaps not unjustly attracted the sobriquet the Goat, and from whom, it was said, few Land Girls could consider themelves entirely safe. Even more excitingly, a sign points down a lane to Grantchester, which used to mean Rupert Brooke, but now additionally, if not indeed primarily, means Jeffrey Archer. Grantchester should think itself lucky that he didn't, on the model of Baroness Trumpington, style himself Lord Grantchester. Communities have no appeal and no right of redress when their place names are appropriated by peers. At Harston, a pub called the Old English Gentleman is now, I see, running an Indian take-away. Foxton has its moments of interest and Melbourn, quite apart from boasting a science park, is distinctly attractive, a jumble of red brick and black and white and clapboard, in no particular order and punctuated by pubs.

Communities are often said to be 'at the crossroads' and Royston is more at the crossroads than most, since the crossroads is why it is there. It's the point at which one ancient road, Ermine Street, intersects with another, the Icknield Way. It used also to be the border, or raund, between Hertfordshire and Cambridgeshire, but today it is all in Hertfordshire. The solemnity of all this is marked by a stone called Roysia's Stone at the crossroads. Roysia may or may not have been a countess of Norfolk. This spot would be rather more numinous were it not so cluttered with unlovely street furniture.

There are plenty of echoes of the Cromwells here too, though not on the scale of Huntingdon. James VI of Scotland, displaying the usual royal preference for the Old North over the Great North road, chose this route to London when he came to collect the English Crown in 1603, and took such a fancy to Royston that he built what was called a palace (though it was really not much more than a hunting lodge), knocking down at least two pubs in the process. An excellent history of Royston, published in 1906 by Alfred Kingston, editor of the town's local paper, *The Crow*, quotes an account of the king's devotion to Royston: 'King James finds such felicity in the hunting life that he hath written to the council that it is the only means to maintain his health, which being the health and welfare of us all, he desires them to take the charge and burden of affairs, and see that he be not interrupted or troubled with too much business.' This must be one of the grandest sicknotes in history. But not everyone wanted him there. In 1604 a petition was prepared by people 'adjacent to the town of Royston' telling him, in effect, to behave himself better. The king sent the petitioners away, but he allowed them to present their address to his council. Later the king's favourite dog disappeared, and when it returned a message was found attached to its collar. 'Good Mr Jowler,' it said (that was the name of the dog), 'we pray you speak to the King (for he hears you every day, and so doth he not us) that it will please His Majesty to go back to London, for else the country will be undone; all our provision is spent, and we are not able to entertain him any longer.' Charles I also came to Royston, but less often.

In June 1647 Parliamentary forces headed by Oliver Cromwell arrived here and occupied the palace. From there, they addressed a letter to the aldermen and council of the City of London, signed by Cromwell and such other top brass as Fairfax, Ireton, Desborough and Rainborough, warning them to co-operate when the Parliamentarians reached London. They intended no evil, they said, 'although you may suppose that a rich city may seem an enticing bait to poor hungry soldiers'. But should any considerable part of the City be seduced into taking up arms 'in opposition to, or hindrance of, our just undertakings' then here was a 'brotherly' warning that Cromwell and friends would not accept responsibility for what might follow. 'We rest, your affectionate friends to serve you,' they said in a farewell line of which the Mafia might have been proud.

What baffles me about Royston today is that it does not make more of its cave, a place of great mystery, ten metres underground, not far from the crossroads. Found by chance in 1742, it is said to be full of mysterious carvings, possibly the work of Knights Templar. Amazingly it is open only part-time and not at all between October and Easter. Have these people, I ask myself, never heard of Dan Brown and his world bestseller, *The Da Vinci Code*? Were they not aware of the lust of the reading public for anything touching on grails and templars? Why had they passed up this chance to turn Royston into a boom town?

Musing on this omission, I leave this agreeable, slightly disconsolate place and catch a bus on to Ware. This is a much more entertaining and eventful ride from the moment when, within minutes of leaving the bus stop, we go up quite a serious hill. Soon we encounter Barley, two of whose rectors, my *Shell Guide* says, went on to become archbishops of Canterbury; it also produced the first mayor of New York. Barkway has a fine main street, although the bus frustratingly turns away before you've had more than a glimpse of it. Reed is a hilltop village with a complicated pattern of streets and a cricket ground. Buntingford's unremarkable church is upstaged by a dishy parade of almshouses at its door. It's perhaps because he's caught sight of the almshouses, making him think of retirement, that our driver begins to whistle. An inanely indirect road takes us on through Hare Street and then through Dassels (an experience which lasts rather less than a minute) to Braughing, a village which tempts me to stop and explore. It still has a proper grocer and butcher.

The whistling which has emanated from our driver ever since Buntingford is reaching a feverish pitch. There are even hints here and there that the tune which is lodged in his head might be 'The British Grenadiers', but alternatively it might be something by Dallapiccola. Perhaps it is the strain of driving this highly erratic route. As we close in on Ware it seems that my Arriva bus 331 will do everything in its power to put off the awful moment when we arrive there. Yet infuriatingly, having earlier in this journey taken us tantalizingly close to the village of Nasty, it now declines a possible detour to Wallington, which is where for some time in the late 1930s George Orwell and his wife Eileen (whom he married at the church just down the road) ran a village shop. Here, Orwell worked on *Homage to Catalonia*, *The Road to Wigan Pier*, and *Coming Up For Air*.

Orwell had a nasty moment on a bus ride from here, chronicled in a characteristic outburst in *Wigan Pier*. 'One day this summer,' he writes (it was the summer of 1936), 'I was riding through Letchworth when the bus stopped and two dreadful-looking old men got on to it. They were both about sixty, both very short, pink and chubby, and both hatless. One of them was obscenely bald, the other had long grey hair bobbed in the Lloyd George style. They were dressed in pistachio-coloured shirts and khaki shorts into which their huge bottoms were crammed so tightly that you could study every dimple. Their appearance created a mild stir of horror on the top of the bus. The man next to me, a commercial traveller I should say, glanced at me, at them, and back again to me, and murmured, "Socialists", as who should say, "Red Indians". He was probably right – the ILP [Independent Labour Party] were holding their summer school at Letchworth. But the point is that to him, as an ordinary man, a crank meant a Socialist and a Socialist meant a crank.'

What you need to remember, if you do not wish to upset the people of Ware, is that Ware is not Hertford, nor is it a suburb or any other kind of dependency of Hertford, nor, although they are linked by road and river, is it some mere continuation of Hertford under another name. Indeed, Ware has long liked to see itself as more important than Hertford, even though Hertford is the county town – big in growing and manufacturing corn and malt and sending barges along the Lea and New River. And more strategically placed than Hertford, since it's bang on the Old North Road. John Gilpin's horse from Cheapside, a knowing creature, carried him not to backwater Hertford but to far more mainstream Ware. I went once to an inquiry into plans to redraw electoral boundaries in such a way that Hertford would be joined with Ware. This was resisted on various grounds, one of them being that these towns had fought each other in the twelfth century. This unlikely allegation turned out to be true. The encounter followed the untoward action of the bailiff of Hertford, who said he was acting in the name of the king, in attempting to block passage over the bridge at Ware, and then, when that right was denied him, trying to claim the tolls which were paid on the bridge. According to a rather patchy history of the town in the library, the men of Hertford descended on Ware and broke down the bridge in a bid to ensure that all the traffic had to cross the river at Hertford. That was little more than 800 years ago. No wonder the grievance still rankles.

The town used also to be able to boast the Great Bed of Ware, which slept twelve and is mentioned in Shakespeare, and used to be housed in the Saracen's Head inn, although it is now at the V & A. Was there a Great Bed of Hertford? Of course not. The old Saracen's Head has gone too, replaced by a new Saracen's Head which is not the same thing at all, but it's still a pleasant spot at which to dispose of a pint while watching flotillas of swans on the river. For the purposes of my inquiries, though, Ware has little to offer except for the stop where you catch the bus to Cheshunt. Oliver Cromwell came here in 1647 and crushed a mutiny, but for all that I managed to find about him in Ware, poor Richard Cromwell might never have existed.

The final stage of this journey is executed by another Arriva bus, the 310, which is heading for Enfield, in London. And the imminence of London is very much the theme of this journey: every mile takes you deeper into the grip of what Cobbett called (when it was only a fraction of what it is now) 'the Great Wen'. Ware is still recognizably a country town, and the way out along the New River with little bridges spanning it even has echoes of Holland. But the nearer you get to Cheshunt the more boring the road becomes. At first there are fields between houses, but soon the build-up is all but continuous. For a very long time we seem to be going through the borough of Broxbourne. The monotony of this suburbscape is like a kind of illness. The high street at Hoddesdon would be a pleasant relief except that most of it is now closed to traffic, which is good for Hoddesdon but less good for travellers on the 310 bus. Near Sunny's News and Booze, a sign to Rye House recalls a plot laid in 1683 to ambush and slay the restored Charles II and his brother, the even more patently Catholic James, on their way to Newmarket. The plot was foiled when the royal party changed its plans, and several plotters were caught and executed. Then, though not a lot in the view out of the window seems to have changed, we are passing through Wormley. And Wormley – one might credibly say in a world where as I've discovered over the months so many places advertise themselves as the gateway to somewhere else – is the gateway to Cheshunt.

The road that Richard Cromwell stood beside is a mere B road now: the A10 London to Cambridge is a tearaway bypass close to a mighty junction with the M25. The entry of the 310 bus into Cheshunt is a dispiriting affair. The old high street, at the north end of the place, is sadly diminished. These shops must once have been real independent grocers and greengrocers and butchers and bakers and the kind of hardware store where you could still buy a single picture hook rather than a packet of fifty. There was certainly a fish-monger here. You can still just about make out his advertisement on the wall: Fish dinners and suppers. Home cured haddocks and bloaters. Phone Waltham Cross 49. But like the rest of the high street, the legend is fading away, and the shop is now a hairdressers. The main shopping centre is at the southern end of the town around Cheshunt Pond with its fountain, its Tesco Metro, its Harry Ramsden's, and, glorious to relate, a real butcher's shop. This part of the town has little to do with Richard Cromwell's Cheshunt. On his return to England, after the time in exile which followed his ejection from office, he lived in a pleasant tucked-away precinct close to the church, in a house that belonged to a Sergeant Pengelly.

Guizot, in Huntingdon library, describes in the gloriously orotund periods which help explain why some of his works ran to thirty volumes, how the vultures closed in on Richard. 'Republicans and Cavaliers, generals, officers, soldiers, mystical sectaries and free-thinkers, parliamentary and regimental orators, all the parties that Cromwell had held in check; the malcontents who trembled before him, and the ambitious men who bowed beneath his irresistible superiority, the high-minded patriots and the chimerical visionar-ies whom he had offended – indeed all those various classes whom, by consent or force, by persuasion or constraint, he had reduced to silence and inaction – began again, after an interval of a few days, to hope and to act, at first with some reserve and little noise, but ere long with presumption and almost with publicity.'

General Monk, who would in time emerge as the architect of the Restoration, initially stayed aloof, but Desborough was involved and also Fleetwood, the husband of Oliver's daughter Bridget. It was Fleetwood who led the group of officers which demanded that the Lord Protector should no longer be head of the army. Richard resisted, though characteristically conceding that it might have pleased God, and the nation too, to have chosen a person more fit and due for his work than he was. But the lavish funeral given to his father, at a time, it was noted, when the army was distressed and the government in penury, offended Puritan consciences. The army attacked him for filling the upper chamber with his friends instead of with honest soldiers. He was warned of grave disaffec-tion welling up in the army. Friends urged him to stand and fight. But Richard was reluctant. In a sentence that could have served as his political epitaph, he said: 'I have never done anybody any harm and never will. I will not have a drop of blood shed for the preser-vation of my greatness, which is a burden to me.'

It would not be a burden for very much longer. When he ordered the dissolution of Parliament, Parliament would not budge. He was turned out of Whitehall Palace, then told to leave Hampton Court. By now a deal was being constructed, in which Richard would give up office in return for a financial settlement to sustain himself and his family, with a guarantee of safe conduct. On that basis, he retired first to his Hampshire estates and then in 1660 to France, thus escaping both political persecution and his clamorous creditors. Later, still using his sobriquet John Clarke, he moved to Switzerland, where he lived until 1680.

At which point, twenty years after the Restoration, he ended his exile and came to Cheshunt. A man called John Ashton, who used to encounter him at the home of Richard's daughter in Hampshire, said of him: 'He was of a very genial, kindly disposition, and even in his old age he was full of innocent pleasantry. He made himself believed by all with whom he came into contact and had it not been for the unfortunate greatness which was almost thrust upon him, he would only have been remembered for a generation or so as a good old country gentleman.' The hymnodist Issac Watts, who knew him well, said he only once heard his friend so much as glance at his former eminence, and then in a distant manner. But that cannot have been quite true. During the reign of Queen Anne, Richard Cromwell came up to London to attend a court which was trying to settle a family dispute. Afterwards, it was said, he took a stroll through Westminster Hall and on to the House of Lords, where someone asked if he had ever been in the chamber before. 'Never,' he replied, 'since I sat in that chair'; and he indicated the throne.

Cromwell lived on through torrid times. First plague and then fire devastated London. Charles II died, and James II, who succeeded him, was deposed in favour of a monarch brought in from Holland, in a 'glorious revolution' which made the future power of the monarch conditional – an arrangement for which Parliament might well have been ready to settle forty years earlier had Charles I not insisted on his divine right to rule. He lived on through the years of the Act of Union and Marlborough's victories over the French. He was eighty-six when he died, in 1712, still at the home of the faithful Pengellys, in the arms of one of the family's servants. A later memorialist wrote: 'He enjoyed a good state of health to the last, and was so hale and hearty that at four score years he would gallop his horse for several miles together; in his last illness and just before his departure, he said to his daughters: "Live to love; I am going to the God of love."' Everyone seems to have found him, at the end of this extraordinary life, a sweet and kindly old man.

There's a Cromwell Road not far from Parsonage House, where he lived in Cheshunt. But for most of the people who live there now, the only famous Richard from Cheshunt they are likely to name is the singer Cliff Richard, who, though born in Lucknow, India, grew up on a Cheshunt council estate, where they knew him as Harry Webb. And he made his name in a movie called *Summer Holiday*, in which he co-starred with a London bus.

25

Acton — Shepherd's Bush
Marble Arch — Piccadilly

TRAFALGAR SQUARE

*Acton, London: the epitome of an unfamous place – Bedford
Park, inspirational home to artists and intellectuals –
Shepherd's Bush, a boisterous suburb not famous for either –
via Marble Arch and Oxford Street to the hub of the nation
– though modified by Ken Livingstone, Orwell's red buses
continue to run through Trafalgar Square.*

So to the last of these journeys; and where better to start than
Acton, west London. Why Acton? Because Acton is one of those not
very special places that do not often get written about. Few thrill
at the thought of visiting Acton. Not everyone who lives there, in
my experience, boasts about living there. Often they point you
gently away from the concept of Acton, hinting at something more
glamorous, possibly more exotic: Chiswick perhaps, or Shepherd's
Bush. Yet Acton is an ancient place with its own individual history
and geography, culture and institutions, all of them lovingly
charted in a book called *Acton A to Z* by Gwilym Rowlands, who died
in 1994. It's published by Ealing borough council, which may not
have been entirely to Rowlands's taste, since he ends his book with
a cry of 'Floreat Actona!' and at one point refers to Ealing's pretensions as a *soi-disant* 'queen of the suburbs'. No one would ever
call Acton a queen of the suburbs, but Rowlands makes it sound a
far richer experience than people passing accidentally through
Acton would ever suspect.

For a start, it has a cathedral. If you've never heard of Acton cathedral, that's because it's a Ukrainian Autocephalic cathedral, converted from the former South Acton baptist Church. Acton was once a spa town, and people took the waters at Old Oak Well. It had an aerodrome too, of sorts, where in 1909 a Lieutenant Colonel Noel was experimenting with a plane of his own design. Acton was rich in industry, enabling the local chamber of commerce to claim at one point that it ranked as the biggest industrial town south of Coventry. One particular speciality was laundering. In one area of South Acton in 1899 there were 178 laundries in 19 roads. 'The washtub of London', this sector was called, and 'Soapsuds Island'. Also, 'the Klondike'. Gwilym Rowlands, as ever, knows why: '"Klondike" is a river in the Yukon Territory, made famous in the 1896 gold rush. Its use here referred to the supposedly enormous profits to be made out of laundering.' There's an individual entry for Zion House laundry here, but only, Rowlands endearingly confesses, to get a Z into his index. (This device has also, please note, got a Z into mine.)

Then there's Acton Green, close to an underground station which calls itself Chiswick Park, although there isn't any immediately obvious reason, apart from the local preference for wanting to believe you live somewhere other than Acton, why the earlier name of Acton Green was abandoned. How many who wait here at the start of the 94 bus route know this was part of the ground on which the battle of Brentford was fought in 1642?

All around the country, some bus routes are talked of, and even occasionally loved, more than others. The number 11 London bus – one of the routes which passes the Houses of Parliament and the government buildings along Whitehall – is a staple of political conversation, since it's long been the Westminster practice when speculating on a possible change in the leadership of a party to ask what might happen if the present leader got knocked down by a number 11 bus. In Margaret Thatcher's day, the obvious answer was that no bus could ever survive such a collision. The 94 Acton Green to Piccadilly Circus has never enjoyed quite such eminence, but it has its aficionados. Perhaps there is something about number 94s. My friend Bryan, who has travelled from time to time on the 94 bus from Bath to Limpley Stoke, Somerset, said that one day a woman came aboard with a cup of tea for the driver.

The controller of Radio 4, Helen Boaden, was riding on one of these London 94 buses in 2000 when she suddenly solved the problem of how she could transmit a long recording that Stephen Fry had made for her of J. K. Rowling's *Harry Potter and the Philosopher's Stone*. She could run the whole thing, she suddenly realized, in one continuous dollop on Boxing Day. Reports of this moment of inspiration led me to imagine the 94, on which I had never travelled, as a kind of mobile Actonian Left Bank, a haunt of intellectuals, writers and artists, each one with a pen poised to write down some enlightening thought halfway up the Goldhawk Road. And sure enough, a remarkably impressive collection of eminent people emerged to issue a public denunciation of Transport for London when it announced its plans to take the much-loved Routemaster buses off this route, and replace them with modern conductorless buses. One possible reason why this kind of congregation of thinkers might occur on the 94 will emerge as soon as the bus leaves its starting point on the green, by a French restaurant called Le Vacherin and a pub called The Duke. For immediately on our left there appears a parade of fine late-Victorian villas – the outer edge of Bedford Park, developed in 1875 by Jonathan Carr, which, according to those who live there, was the capital's first garden suburb. Sure enough, Gwilym Rowlands has a list of names establishing its exceptional cultural credentials. Arthur Wing

Pinero, dramatist, was a resident here, as were Lucien Pissarro, painter, and William Terriss, the actor who often appeared with Irving and Ellen Terry, and grandest of all, W. B. Yeats.

A suitable territory, then, and a suitable moment, as I wait for the last of my buses to unlock its doors and let its would-be passengers in, to reflect on these twenty-four journeys spread over a year or more, down implacable city streets and cosseted suburban avenues and wandering country lanes and windblown coastlands, in a kind of random anthology of early twenty-first-century Britain. What has struck me most on my meandering way is how much is lost when a place neglects or erases its history. The most successful communities I came across on these journeys seemed to be those that balanced change with continuity. Places that do not change, atrophy; but those that abandon or crush their past seem uneasy, unsettled places. You can also see how places suffer that have too little history, that lack that feeling of rootedness which most of us crave. I used, in the days when football hooligans terrorized the streets, to check the addresses they had when they came to court, and note how many seemed to come from rootless new towns. Places, like people, are incomplete if they have no memory. Some sense of the past should always be with us, whether in substantial buildings erected, like my beloved Leeds town hall, at the high point of civic pride, or in quiet, contemplative graveyards like those at Slough, St Dogmaels, Tynemouth and St Andrews, where tombstones, some of them barely decipherable, evoke, as vividly as any historical novel, what life and death in these places used to be like.

The communities that seem to work best are those where despite all the pressures of change, the past has been respected and not – as in Basingstoke – brutally trampled down; where the bulldozers, sweeping away the slums, have been kept out of streets which Victorian and Edwardian Britain built well, and which, lovingly refurbished by a new generation, will last for many years more if given their chance. Built to the plans of local architects, or more often to the designs of unscholarly local builders, sometimes using local brick or stone, these sturdy survivors have about them a sense of place that is missing from their successors, which for all the individual character they display might have been bought in bulk from Ikea. In that process, the parish of everywhere comes more and more to resemble the parish of everywhere else; and the shopping mall of the parish of everywhere, to offer exactly the same range of names over doors as the shopping mall of everywhere else.

This deep human need for a sense of continuity is richly demonstrated, and recognized, elsewhere in twenty-first-century Britain. You can see it in the explosive growth of interest and activity in tracing family history; also in the eagerness of many quite small communities, especially at the time of the millennium, to chart their particular history, often as a communal undertaking, with older inhabitants wheedled and pestered to download their memories before it became too late. The history of Hemsworth I found by chance in its local library is one of hundreds, perhaps even thousands. Such memories can be melancholy, recording prouder, more settled, times in places now in decline; of which, inevitably, as new patterns of life evolve, there are many. To keep alive the appeal of old market towns like Uttoxeter, or little Corwen in Wales, in the face of cheaper prices and greater choice only half an hour's car ride – or even an hour's digressive bus ride – away, may be beyond the ingenuity and financial resources of any agency, national or local. They're not doomed to fade out of existence like the lost villages whose remains one comes across here and there in the country, but everyone knows they can never again be what they used to be. Any more than Acton will ever regain that sense of local pride and separate identity it had when Gwilym Rowlands was young, when Acton had yet to bow its knee to neighbouring Ealing, when Floreat Actona was a sentiment to be uttered without any sense of irony.

Some of the buses that carried me around the country will not survive. Indeed, one of the routes I rode on during my travels (that journey is not in this book) was scrapped the following week. Bus travel can hope to expand in a great city like London, though even then it will only do so if alternative means of travel, and especially of private travel, are made too expensive or too inconvenient. But that cannot be done in the shires. Most services there are kept alive by a level of local government subsidy which leaves them hopelessly vulnerable to cost-cutting plans. Here and there such economies have left villagers more cut off from their neighbouring towns than at any time since the nineteenth century. Except for the buses which carried children chatting and bantering and texting to school, the passengers on my journeys were mostly elderly, with elderly women outnumbering men. Some people prefer not to travel by car; many do not have the chance. Market day buses, especially, have a value which transcends mere travel and shopping. Their journeys to town in the morning, back home in time for tea, are social occasions – even, sometimes, therapeutic occasions. The same cheerful elderly passengers clamber aboard every week, until illness or death removes them. One senses how much this means for widows in particular, and I noted how, gently and unobtrusively, established widows counselled the newer ones. 'How long,' they would ask, 'have you been on your own, dear?' Never, 'When did your husband die?' (Though it isn't, even now, so often 'husband', as 'hubby'.) The best of the drivers, cheerful, helpful, climbing out of their seats to help with shopping baskets, are an essential part of

the market day ritual too: they are the genial masters of cere-
monies, there to ensure the party goes with a swing. When these
buses are lost, as many will be, all that will be lost as well.

The not conspicuously genial driver of our London 94 bus unlocks
his doors and lets us in. Even beyond Bedford Park, the 94 picks its
way through salubrious streets, with houses still as substantial as
Bedford Park's. It cannot be said, however, that the top deck of this
bus is quite the powerhouse of intellectual ferment that my brood-
ings on Helen Boaden's Eureka moment had made me expect. One
passenger is reading *Metro*, and another, *Hello!* The rest are looking
out of the windows, or sleeping. But once on the Goldhawk Road,
the whole atmosphere changes. This is cosmopolitan London. We
are into a world of Texas fried chicken and Afro and European
unisex hair styling, tropical foods wholesale and retail, Cash City,
Cheque Cashiers, and cheap flights to Damascus, Dakar and Abu
Dhabi. Around half the people in the gatherings at some bus stops
(we used to call them queues, but nobody queues today) are black,
which certainly wasn't the case at Acton Green, and there seem to
be conversations in progress in at least five languages. Someone is
reading the *Guardian*, and someone else has a novel by
V. S. Naipaul, and no doubt if one could only decipher the Japanese,
one would quickly discover that mould-breaking ideas are being
promulgated in the back seats.

By the time we reach Shepherd's Bush, progress is slower. We
ease around the green, past the old Shepherd's Bush Empire,
where maybe William Terriss once trod the boards, though the
place was long ago turned over to the making of TV spectaculars.
Chicken Cottage, Pound Crazy, William Hill, Fun City adorn the
north side of the green along with Age Concern and a Slug and
Lettuce. At the end of the green there's a roundabout now occupied

by an unimpressive object that calls itself the Thames Water Tower. Beyond the Hilton hotel we enter a seriously expensive terrain, on and around Holland Park Avenue, which takes its name from a famous Whig family which owned the Jacobean mansion in Holland Park. And here one begins to get that increasing sense of real London which used to excite provincial visitors so acutely when they came this way on the old road from Bath. Explaining the contrast between his respectable life in the country and his louche life in London, the poet John Wilmot, Earl of Rochester, explained: 'The devil enters into me as I pass through Brentford.' The same thing no doubt happened to others, round about Shepherd's Bush.

Here and there the 94's route evokes memories of those I'd travelled before. An unexpected statue on the south side of Holland Park Avenue commemorates St Volodymyr, tenth-century ruler of the Ukraine, who, having once been a pagan, converted to Christianity and ordered the whole of Kiev to do the same. He fathered eleven sons by five wives, but none I think emulated the children of Brychan by following him into sainthood. Beyond this is Notting Hill Gate, with affluent streets to the north and the south and a glimpse of the opulent enclave of Campden Hill. There's a deluge of buses now with every kind of destination advertised on the front. One just has time passing the top of Queensway to pick out the domed tower of the old Whiteley's store. The 94 surges on past the successive gates of Hyde Park, with long mansion terraces, now mostly hotels, on the northern side of the road, built to give their earlier individual purchasers views to admire and show off to their friends. Near Marble Arch there's an inscription on a wall to commemorate an earlier landmark here – Tyburn tree. This was the spot where crowds used to gather to enjoy public executions. At one stage a gallows stood at this site on which eight people could be hanged simultaneously. In his *London Compendium*, a street by street guide to the capital, which I've brought with me today, Ed Glinert says the biggest crowd-pulling attraction at Tyburn was the execution of Dr William Dodd, hanged in 1777 for forging the Earl of Chesterfield's signature on a bond, which seems odd, since that could hardly have qualified as the crime of the century.

The 94 pushes on down Oxford Street, passing the great post-Whiteley department stores: Selfridges (Gordon Selfridge eventually took over Whiteley's), D. H. Evans (now House of Fraser), John Lewis and Debenhams, which is where Marshall and Snelgrove used to be when Lady Florence Paget absconded with the disreputable lover she preferred to poor Henry Chaplin. Oxford Street must be a trial for drivers. Although private cars were long ago banned, there are always some infiltrators, and today is no exception. Some drivers are compounding the offence by chattering into their mobile phones. Yet the 94 bus is on time. These journeys are scheduled to take just twenty-nine minutes in the early and late hours, but one minute under an hour for the busier parts of the day. And exactly fifty-nine minutes after we left Acton Green, the 94 has circumnavigated Piccadilly Circus, where I notice that the electronic newscaster is making the unlikely claim that the temperature in London is minus 48 degrees Centigrade, and turning into the Haymarket. Here, down a side street just past the stage door of Her Majesty's Theatre, is the end of the 94's journey.

But not quite the end of my journey. A minute or so down the hill past Her Majesty's you can see the beginnings of Trafalgar Square. The fountains are playing, there are people clambering over the paws of the Landseer lions, and the pigeons are strutting about just as they did in Orwell's day, happily unaware that the mayor of London has promised to banish them. Here is the traditional procession of red London buses, just as Orwell, whom I recollected in

Leeds at the start of this book, twenty-four journeys ago, remembered them when he got back from Spain. But now they're interspersed with buses of other hues: the brown tourist buses of the Big Bus Company, a black number 3 London bus advertising a musical called *The Woman in White*, and another in black dedicated to the English National Opera's *Barber of Seville*, and a blue one for *Mary Poppins*. There are no buses now on the northern side of the square, since that is reserved for pedestrians, so it's not quite the circus it was; and yet it's a scene which Orwell would still immediately recognize. 'It was a bright cold day in April,' he wrote at the start of *Nineteen Eighty-four* in one of the best opening sentences ever, 'and the clocks were striking thirteen.' As I leave the square on this brisk morning in April 2005, the clock of the church of St Martin's is striking twelve. Whatever else may be wrong with this country today, whatever the daunting headlines on the newspaper stands about terrorist threats and draconian government responses in this strange, dogged, unpredictable, sometimes gorgeously beautiful, sometimes foully unjust, and still, thank goodness, wildly various country of ours, at least we can feel assured that it won't, an hour from now, be striking thirteen.

FURTHER READING

Books consulted throughout include: *Dictionary of National Biography* and *Oxford Dictionary of National Biography*; Pevsner's *Buildings of England* series; *Shell Guides*; Post Office and Kelly's directories; Simon Jenkins, *England's Thousand Best Churches*, (Penguin/Allen Lane, 1999) and *England's Thousand Best Houses* (Penguin/Allen Lane, 2003); E. S. Turner, *Amazing Grace: the great days of dukes* (Michael Joseph, 1975; Sutton Publishing, 2003).

Books relevant to individual journeys include:

Chapter 1
George Orwell, *Homage to Catalonia* (Secker & Warburg, 1938; Penguin, 1962)

Chapter 2
George Gissing, *A Life's Morning* (Smith, Elder, 1888; Home & Van Thal, 1947); John Halperin, *Gissing: a life in books* (OUP, 1982); Leo McKinstry, *Geoffrey Boycott: a Cricketing Hero* (Harper Collins, 2005); Steve Truelove (ed.), *We're All Immigrants Round Here* (Hemsworth & District Community Initiatives/Yorkshire Art Circus, 2000); Dickie Bird, *My Autobiography* (Hodder & Stoughton, 1997).

Chapter 3
Henry Thorold, *Lincolnshire* (Pimlico, 1996); Marchioness of Londonderry, *Henry Chaplin: a Memoir* (Macmillan, 1926).

Chapter 4

Kimberley Cornish, *The Jew of Linz* (Century, 1998); E. A. Thompson, *A History of Attila and the Huns* (Clarendon Press, 1948); James Woodforde, *The Diary of a Country Parson 1758–1802*, passages selected and edited by John Beresford (OUP, 1935).

Chapter 5

Dennis Hardy and Colin Ward, *Arcadia for All: the legacy of a makeshift landscape* (Mansell, 1984); Francis Wheen, *The Soul of Indiscretion: Tom Driberg, poet, philanderer, legislator and outlaw* (Fourth Estate, 1990); Tom Driberg, *Ruling Passions* (Jonathan Cape, 1977).

Chapter 6

David Hodgkins, *The Second Railway King: the life and times of Sir Edward Watkin, 1819–1901* (Merton Priory Press, 2002); E. F. Benson, *As We Were: a Victorian peepshow* (Longmans, Green, 1930; Penguin, 2001).

Chapter 7

Linda Stratmann, *Whiteley's Folly: the life and death of a salesman* (Sutton Publishing, 2004); Kit Bartlett, *Paul Gibb; his record, innings-by-innings* (Association of Cricket Statisticians and Historians, 1995).

Chapter 8

John Betjeman, *Collected Poems* (John Murray, 1958), see 'The Planster's Vision', as well as 'Slough'.

Chapter 9

Thomas Hardy, *The Well-Beloved* (Macmillan, 1897); Michael Millgate, T*homas Hardy: a biography revisited* (OUP, 2004); Stuart Morris, *Portland: an illustrated history* (Dovecote Press, 1985); Jabez Spencer Balfour, *My Prison Life* (Chapman & Hall, 1907).

Chapter 10

Joshua Schwieso, *Deluded Inmates, Frantic Ravers and Communists: a sociological study of the Agapemone, a sect of Victorian Apocalyptic Millenarians* (University of Reading, 1994); Ronald Matthews, *English Messiahs* (Methuen, 1936); Aldous Huxley, *The Olive Tree* (Chatto & Windus, 1937).

Chapter 11

Nicholas Orme (ed.), *Nicholas Roscarrock's Lives of the Saints: Cornwall and Devon* (Devon and Cornwall Record Society, 1992) ; Edwin Stark, *St Endellion* (Dyllansow Truran, 1983).

Chapter 12

Gerald of Wales, *The Journey Through Wales; the Description of Wales*, translated by Lewis Thorpe (Penguin, 1978).

Chapter 13

W. J. Crosland-Taylor, *Crosville: the Sowing and the Harvest; State Owned Without Tears: the story of Crosville 1948–53* (Littlebury Bros, 1948, 1954); Edward Gibbon, *Decline and Fall of the Roman Empire* (Dent/Dutton, 1910); George Borrow, *Wild Wales* (Dent/Dutton, 1906).

Chapter 14

Robert Waller, *The Dukeries Transformed* (Clarendon Press, 1983);
John Timbs and Alexander Gunn, *Abbeys, Castles and Ancient
Halls of England and Wales* (Frederick Warne, 1872).

Chapter 15

Joanna Richardson, *Verlaine* (Weidenfeld & Nicolson, 1971).

Chapter 16

Eden Camp – The People's War 1939–45 (Eden Camp Museum,
2004); Dave Colledge, *Labour Camps: the British Experience*
(Sheffield Popular Press, 1989).

Chapter 17

Tom Faulkner and Andrew Greg, *John Dobson, Newcastle
Architect, 1787–1865* (Tyne and Wear Museums Service, 1987).

Chapter 18

Adam Smith, *The Wealth of Nations* (Everyman's Library, 1991);
Glen L. Pride, *The Kingdom of Fife: an illustrated architectural
guide* (Rutland Press, 1990, 1999); Billy Kay (ed.), *The Dundee
Book* (Mainstream Publishing, 1990, 1995).

Chapter 19

John Prebble, *The Highland Clearances* (Secker & Warburg, 1963;
Penguin, 1969); Donald MacLeod, *Gloomy Memories: the Highland
Clearances of Strathnaver* (Strathnaver Museum, Bettyhill,
Sutherland, 1996); Eric Richards, *Highland Clearances: People,
Landlords and Rural Turmoil* (Birlinn, 2000).

Chapter 20

Shadow (Alexander Brown), *Shadow's Midnight Scenes and Social Photographs – Glasgow 1858* (University of Glasgow Press, 1976); Carol Craig, *The Scots' Crisis of Confidence* (Big Thinking, 2003).

Chapter 22

Lord Macaulay, *Literary and Historical Essays contributed to the Edinburgh Review* (OUP, 1913).

Chapter 23

E. Royston Pike, *Human Documents of the Victorian Golden Age, 1850–1875* (Allen & Unwin, 1967); Peter Reginald Mounfield, 'The Location of Footwear Manufacture in England and Wales', unpublished dissertation in Northampton Library; Peter Perkins, Geoffrey Starmer and Roy Sheffield, *A Guide to the Industrial Heritage of Northamptonshire* (Northamptonshire County Council, 2001); David Hall, Ruth Harding and Cyril Putt, *Raunds: Picturing the Past* (F. W. March and Co. and Biscott Publications, 1998); Tony Ireson, *Northamptonshire* (Robert Hale, 1954).

Chapter 24

François Guizot, *The History of Richard Cromwell and the Restoration of Charles II*, translated by A. R. Scobie (Richard Bentley, 1856); Alfred Kingston, *A History of Royston, Hertfordshire* (Elliot Stock/Warren Bros, 1906); Bernard Crick, *George Orwell, a Life* (Secker & Warburg, 1980); George Orwell, *The Road to Wigan Pier* (Victor Gollancz, 1937; Penguin, 1962); Percy Charles Archer, *Historic Cheshunt* (Cheshunt Press, 1923).

Chapter 25

Gwilym Rowlands, *Acton A to Z* (London Borough of Ealing, 1997);
Ed Glinert, *The London Compendium* (Penguin/Allen Lane, 2003).

INDEX

Bus companies are indexed under the heading 'Bus companies' and not under individual company names.